JAMES KOUZES | BARRY POSNER

THE STUDENT LEADERSHIP CHALLENGE

FIVE PRACTICES FOR BECOMING AN EXEMPLARY LEADER

THIRD EDITION

THE LEADERSHIP CHALLENGE®
A Wiley Brand

Published by The Leadership Challenge™
A Wiley Brand
One Montgomery Street, Suite 1000, San Francisco, CA 94104-4594
www.leadershipchallenge.com

Cover design by Wiley

For additional copies or bulk purchases of this book please contact our Customer Care Department within the U.S. at 800-762-2974, outside the U.S. at (317) 572-3993, or fax (317) 572-4002. To learn more about the Student Leadership Challenge or the Student LPI please contact us at leadership@wiley.com.

Wiley publishes in a variety of print and electronic formats and by print-on-demand. Some material included with standard print versions of this book may not be included in e-books or in print-on-demand. If this book refers to media such as a CD or DVD that is not included in the version you purchased, you may download this material at http://booksupport.wiley.com. For more information about Wiley products, visit www.wiley.com.

Library of Congress Cataloging-in-Publication Data are available
ISBN 978-1-119-42191-7 (paper); ISBN 978-1-119-42224-2 (ebk.); ISBN 978-1-119-42225-9 (ebk.)

Cover design by Wiley

Printed in the United States of America

THIRD EDITION

PB Printing   SKY10036974_101922

PRAISE FOR *THE STUDENT LEADERSHIP CHALLENGE, THIRD EDITION*

"In the ten years that separated the first edition of *The Student Leadership Challenge* and this one, a lot has changed in our world. Numerous world leaders have also changed. Some for the better. What haven't changed are the fundamentals of leadership. Neither has the dream of young leaders around the world to make a difference. In fact today more than ever, we need young leaders to step up. *The Student Leadership Challenge, Third Edition* draws on the inspirational stories of young leaders who have made an impact in their communities in recent times and lays out very practical leadership lessons and commitments that will help any youth in their own journey of leadership. If there is ever a guide that young people can have in their leadership journey of making this world a better place, this book would be it! Read it, Live it, and Lead."

—**Martin Tan**, executive director, Institute for Societal Leadership, Singapore Management University

* * *

"Reading this book will inspire students to be their best selves as leaders and empower students with the knowledge of The Five Practices of Exemplary Leadership. For educators, *The Student Leadership Challenge* has superb resources for teaching leadership through assessments, case studies, experiential learning activities, and reflective assignments that are based upon research and tailored for a student audience."

—**Lynn Perry Wooten**, PhD, dean, Dyson School of Applied Economics & Management, Cornell University

* * *

"At HKUST we have been using *The Student Leadership Challenge* framework in our leadership development programs since 2011. With the personal-best narratives of students from all over the globe, our students easily grasp and apply The Five Practices of Exemplary Leadership in their individual contexts. The reflective exercises at the end of each chapter are exceptionally helpful guides for deeper learning, and the Student Leadership Practices Inventory (SLPI) allows students to get 360 feedbacks to plan their development path. *The Student Leadership Challenge* is a highly versatile resource for students to use in their leadership journeys and for practitioners to integrate into their educational programs."

—**Helen HF Wong,** associate director of student affairs (Co-Curricular Programs), The Hong Kong University of Science and Technology

* * *

"*The Student Leadership Challenge* is by far the book of choice for students and for teachers educating the next generation of leaders. In my leadership course at UC Berkeley I refer to Kouzes and Posner's book as 'our bible,' as it lays out both a philosophy of leadership and the steps to implement it. Reading it while utilizing the Student Leadership Practices Inventory (the book weaves them together) will help you gauge how you lead and how you can take practical steps to improve your leadership."

—**Dan Mulhern**, lecturer at the schools of Business, Law, and Public Policy, UC Berkeley, and author, *Everyday Leadership: Getting Results in Business, Politics, and Life*

* * *

"At a time when young people are bombarded with inconsistent and confusing messages about what constitutes effective, committed leadership, along comes the third edition of *The Student Leadership Challenge*. As in their previous works, Jim Kouzes and Barry Posner present young people with the crucial elements of exemplary leadership. Young people want to shape their world right now. What they need to move from commitment to action are proven methods to uncover the leader within and tools to put their leadership into practice. This book will offer an important first step in that journey."

—**Cathy Tisdale**, president and CEO, Camp Fire

* * *

"We utilize *The Student Leadership Challenge* as a foundation for our campus leadership platform, and it continues to provide guidance and support for leaders with all levels of experience. It is easy enough for new leaders to engage with, and yet sophisticated enough to take experienced leaders to the next level. The third edition has new examples for the practices and commitments. We find that all students can connect with The Five Practices, the Ten Commitments, and the new cases that provide real-life leadership examples. As we continue to implement our collaborative leadership model on our campus, this edition is a good refresher for those who are trained facilitators."

—**Matt Baker** EdD, vice president of student affairs,
   Northwest Missouri State University

* * *

"The third edition of *The Student Leadership Challenge* has it all. Leadership stories from students who've implemented the practices. Workbook elements that allow reflection of the material and action planning. The Student Leadership Practices Inventory that offers students a reliable assessment of how they are currently performing as leaders. Tried and true leadership practices backed by thirty years of research. This is the one book to have in your library to develop and sustain student leadership."

—**Kevin W. Bailey**, PhD, vice chancellor for student affairs, UNC Charlotte

* * *

"With a conversational tone and an interactive approach, Jim Kouzes and Barry Posner convey The Five Practices of Exemplary Leadership to students in a way that is both relatable and inspiring. *The Student Leadership Challenge* retains all the sophistication and credibility of their original text and brings the material alive with examples of college-aged leaders from around the world. Even after more than ten years working with this material, I found this new edition to be full of new insights, examples, and applications."

—**Miles Ashlock**, assistant dean and director, Office of Student Life,
   University of California, Santa Barbara

* * *

"I use *The Student Leadership Challenge* as the foundation of the Blue Hen Leadership Program because it ties leadership directly to values-based action. This new edition reaffirms that The Five Exemplary Practices of Exemplary Leadership are hugely applicable to the student experience. Through new case studies and tools for practical application, students will see themselves in the stories shared, and easily understand that leadership is an option to anyone who uses these five practices to create positive change."

—**Susan Luchey,** associate director for student leadership development, University
   of Delaware, and board of directors, Association of Leadership Educators

* * *

"*The Student Leadership Challenge* is the best leadership guidebook for college students available today. The third edition is especially relevant and applicable to helping college students overcome leadership challenges they face in the ever-changing landscape of higher education. This book is a comprehensive manual for students on how to practice the leadership behaviors needed to get extraordinary things done with others and for others. Employers will want every college graduate they hire to have read *The Student Leadership Challenge*."

—**Shannon Cleverley-Thompson,** EdD, visiting assistant professor
of executive leadership, St. John Fisher College

* * *

"The evidence-based leadership practices empirically identified and expertly described by Jim Kouzes and Barry Posner advance and elevate the field of leadership education towards deliberate practices. *The Student Leadership Challenge* gives emerging leaders a detailed roadmap for feedback, self-reflection, and application of leadership practices that contribute to human flourishing and performance. The five leadership practices are empirically supported, replicable, and integral to all academic disciplines preparing students for careers."

—**Adrian Popa,** PhD, chair, Department of Organizational Leadership,
Gonzaga University

* * *

"The University of Tennessee at Martin is striving to develop a student leadership development model that is integrated into the policies, practices, and culture of student life. *The Student Leadership Challenge* is a key component of this effort. The research behind The Five Practices of Exemplary Leadership and their related behaviors sells the curriculum to students, administrators, and faculty. Most significantly the 360 Leadership Practices Inventory is the unique component that opens students' eyes to where they can improve the frequency of their leadership behaviors. Furthermore, the very thorough 360 LPI Feedback Report becomes their guide for developing a specific action plan to increase the frequency of those behaviors outside their comfort or awareness zone."

—**Phil Dane,** coordinator of student leadership development,
The University of Tennessee at Martin

* * *

"The third edition of *The Student Leadership Challenge* is replete with intense and action-oriented stories and examples of how young leaders around the world are making a difference. This book is about 'doing leadership,' not just learning about leadership. It is a call to action, and I guarantee if you apply The Five Practices described in this book, you will make a difference in your world on a daily basis."

—**Gary M. Morgan**, founder/CEO, Student Leadership Excellence Academy

* * *

"If students were to ask me for the one book that clearly and inspiringly demonstrates how to maximize their leadership potential, *The Student Leadership Challenge* is the first book I would recommend. It is the 'Bible' of leadership for all aspiring leaders. Students reading this book will quickly understand that following The Five Practices of Exemplary Leadership described in vivid detail in this book will help them maximize their leadership effectiveness. Most importantly, students reading this book will realize they already have the power to lead, and they have an obligation to lead. That's what makes *The Student Leadership Challenge* so powerful and definitely a book worthy of being the first leadership book in your library."

—**Jody Rogers**, PhD, FACHE, visiting professor, Department
of Healthcare Administration, Trinity University

* * *

"With so much going on in our world, this guide is ever-important in helping us to create the much-needed leaders that are required on campuses and in our communities. Practical, filled with rich examples, and an important call to action, Kouzes and Posner unlock the daily practices to liberate the exemplary leader within us all."

—**Victor K. Wilson**, vice president for student affairs, The University of Georgia

* * *

"In working over the years with first-generation students pursuing a career in medicine, I have come to rely on the leadership principles found in *The Student Leadership Challenge*. Based on solid research, this book is an essential guide to students in discovering the leader within. Jim Kouzes and Barry Posner's leadership insights truly inspire the hearts of those seeking to lead others in making a meaningful and positive change in their organizations, communities, and world. I highly recommend this book to all emerging leaders!"

—**Mark Gutierrez**, assistant director, Center of Excellence in Diversity
  in Medical Education, Stanford School of Medicine

* * *

"The Student Leadership Challenge will enable you to make a difference in the world. On a daily basis, we all have opportunities to work within our circles of influence. The Five Practices make the prospect of leadership within these circles more concrete and tangible. The Ten Commitments equip you to direct your energy and take positive action. These are behaviors you can develop and practices you can foster in yourself and others. Regardless of your future career path, this book will show you how to build your leadership skills and fulfill your calling to contribute to the greater good."

—**Kristin Kari Janke**, PhD, professor, University of Minnesota College
  of Pharmacy, and director, Wulling Center for Innovation & Scholarship
  in Pharmacy Education

* * *

"The third edition of *The Student Leadership Challenge* provides a practical, tangible, real-life leadership development read for young leaders. This new work is inspiring and real. The stories included in this edition will enable the reader to see themselves as leaders who have utilized The Five Practices of Exemplary Leadership in their everyday lives. The 'Reflect and Act' component added to every chapter is excellent and provides specific action steps for student leaders to enhance their leadership practice. Acknowledging the role of reflection throughout enables self-awareness and meaning making, which are critical to the leadership development process."

—**Katie G. Burke**, assistant dean, Weppner Center for LEAD
  & Service-Learning, Florida Atlantic University

* * *

"Practical, inspiring, down to earth. The stories of everyday student leaders make the concept of leadership accessible to everyone, especially those who think they are not leaders. Jim Kouzes and Barry Posner's research on the impact of leadership behaviors gives profound yet practical insight on how students can become better leaders. *The Student Leadership Challenge* will cause young readers to deeply reflect about what they want their student life to count for and how they will do something about issues that matter to them. This book is a must-read for every student or adult who works with students."

—**Sean Kong**, chief training officer, Halogen Foundation, Singapore

Contents

PRACTICE 4: ENABLE OTHERS TO ACT

Reflections from the *Student Leadership Practices Inventory*

PRACTICE 5: ENCOURAGE THE HEART

Reflections from the *Student Leadership Practices Inventory*

THE STUDENT LEADERSHIP PRACTICES INVENTORY

If you purchased a new copy of this book, you will find a unique single-use access code for the *Student Leadership Practices Inventory Self Online* assessment in the back of it. Go to slpiself.studentleadershipchallenge.com and enter your code to take the inventory. If you purchased a used copy, or rented or borrowed a copy of this book, the code may already have been used, in which case you can purchase a new code at www.studentlpi.com/assess.

The *Student Leadership Practices Inventory®* (*Student LPI®*) is the cornerstone of The Five Practices of Exemplary Leadership® model. Created by leadership educators James M. Kouzes and Barry Z. Posner, this powerful leadership development model approaches leadership as a measurable, learnable, and teachable set of behaviors, because everyone can be a leader—whether in a designated leadership role or not. The *Student LPI* offers you a method for accurately assessing your leadership skills based on The Five Practices of Exemplary Leadership®, by measuring the frequency with which you engage in thirty behaviors that research shows lead to the best leadership outcomes.

Preface: Making Extraordinary Things Happen with Others

The Student Leadership Challenge is about how young leaders—people just like you—mobilize others to make extraordinary things happen anywhere, from a classroom, residence hall, Greek chapter, club, community service project, and student government, to the entire campus, neighboring community, and even the state and nation. It's about the practices student leaders use every day to get people moving toward a better future. They use these practices to transform values into actions, visions into realities, obstacles into innovations, separateness into solidarity, and risks into rewards. Leadership is what turns challenging opportunities into remarkable successes.

This third edition of *The Student Leadership Challenge* comes out ten years after the publication of the first. Since then, we have continued to research, consult, teach, and learn about what young leaders do and how anyone, regardless of age, can become a better leader. We're honored by the reception we've received in the education marketplace and by hearing that students, educators, and practitioners continue to find that *The Student Leadership Challenge* is conceptually and practically useful.

The foundation for *The Student Leadership Challenge* has stood the test of time. We continue to ask the same question that started our inquiry into exemplary leadership: *What did you do when you were at your personal best as a leader?*

One of the most common yet profound realizations from the answers to this question is that leadership is an identifiable set of skills and abilities that are available to anyone, no matter their age or position. As one student explained: "Growing up, I assumed leaders had certain traits and qualities that I didn't seem to have. I thought there were 'natural' leaders who were born to lead. I thought leadership was the description of what these people did. When you asked me to describe my personal-best leadership experience, I found to my surprise that I had those leadership abilities myself." Another student said that she learned "that anybody can be a leader. I had never considered myself a leader, but when I was needed to step up and deal with a difficult situation, I was able to find the leader within me and do so."

We've talked to thousands of young men and women, representing many educational institutions and youth organizations around the world. Their stories, and the behaviors and actions they've described, combined with examples from thousands of other leaders, validate The Five Practices of Exemplary Leadership framework. When students do their best as a leader, they Model the Way, Inspire a Shared Vision, Challenge the Process, Enable Others to Act, and Encourage the Heart. These are the practices that you can use to become a more effective leader and that we describe in detail in this book.

The Student Leadership Challenge is evidence based. We derived The Five Practices from research, and we illustrate them with examples from actual student leaders doing real things. In this third edition, we provide new stories, cases, examples, and illustrations of exactly what young people like you do when they are at their leadership best. The concepts are presented in a way that allows you to focus on applying what works. Also, with this latest edition, you have the opportunity to more closely link how you see yourself behaving as a leader, through completing the *Student Leadership Practices Inventory*, and reflecting on practical ideas for how you can take action. Our intention is to help you discover new ways to be the best leader you can be.

The more we research and write about leadership, the more confident we become that leadership is within the grasp of everyone and that opportunities for leadership are everywhere. No matter what your experience is as a leader, we know that you have the capacity to lead if you choose to. Leadership is not about a position or title, as many young people presume. It is about the choices you make throughout your life—with the goal of making the situations and places you find better because you were there. Great leadership is not about making the leader look good but about how individuals use leadership in service to others to make the people and groups around them better.

In reading this book, you will get a deep understanding of The Five Practices and what they look like in action. By using The Five Practices in your life, you will continue to grow, develop yourself as an exemplary leader, and make a positive difference. You are in a stage of life where the opportunities to make a difference are all around you: in your classes, youth groups, clubs, organizations, athletics, schools, and community. As you take advantage of these opportunities to learn and lead, others will begin to take note and look to you to help them figure out how they can develop their own leadership skills.

You don't just owe it to yourself to become the best leader you can be. You have a responsibility to others as well. You may not yet know it, but people all around you need you to do your best and be your best.

A GUIDE FOR YOUNG LEADERS

How do you get other people to want to follow you? How do you get other people, by free will and free choice, to move forward together in a common purpose? How do you get people energized to work hard together to get something done that everyone can feel proud of? These are the important questions we address in *The Student Leadership Challenge*. Think of this book as a guide to take along on your leadership journey. Think of it as a manual you can consult when you want advice and guidance on how to get extraordinary things done with others. Think of it as a place to go when you're not sure what to do as a leader.

In the Introduction we describe our leadership framework by sharing a personal-best leadership experience case study about how one leader acted on her values and pursued a path of commitment and action to make a difference in gender equality education. We provide an overview of The Five Practices of Exemplary Leadership, summarizing the findings about what student leaders do when they are at their best, and show how these actions make a difference. A major benefit of accepting and adopting this framework of leadership is that it isn't difficult to understand, and it doesn't cost any money or require anybody else's permission. It just requires a commitment from you and ongoing practice to make these leadership behaviors habits in your life.

The ten chapters that follow describe the Ten Commitments of Leadership—the essential behaviors—that leaders use to get extraordinary things done. Here we explain the fundamental principles that support each of The Five Practices and offer interactive worksheets for you to reflect on the state of your skills and behaviors in each leadership practice and identify abilities that you can strengthen and improve. Each of these chapters ends with an invitation to reflect on what you learned from reading it and to decide how you will put your learning into action.

In the final chapter, we offer a call to action to accept personal responsibility for being a role model for exemplary leadership and making these leadership practices part of your daily routines, in all aspects of your life. The first place to look for leadership is within you. Accepting the leadership challenge requires practice, reflection, humility, and making the most of every opportunity to make a difference. We'll assert that leadership is not an affair of the head. Leadership is an affair of the heart. In this Afterword you'll see what we mean by this claim and how it applies to you.

We recommend that you first read Chapter 1, but after that there is no prescribed order to proceeding through the rest of this book. Go wherever your interests are. We wrote *The Student Leadership Challenge* to support you in your leadership development. Just remember that each practice is essential. Although you might bounce around in the book, you can't skip understanding and practicing any of these fundamentals of leadership.

This book will contribute to the success you have working with others, to the creation of new ideas and enterprises, to the renewal of healthy schools and prosperous communities, and to greater respect and understanding in the world. We also fervently hope that it enriches your life.

Meeting the leadership challenge is a personal—and daily—challenge for everyone. We know that if you have the will and the way to lead, you can. You must supply the will. We'll do our best to keep supplying the way.

James Kouzes
Orinda, California

Barry Posner
Berkeley, California

Leadership is the art of mobilizing others to want to struggle for shared aspirations.

Leadership as defined by Jim Kouzes and Barry Posner

When People Are at Their Best as Leaders

Madeline Price grew up on a beef cattle farm in rural Queensland, Australia. After high school graduation, she joined fifteen other recent graduates on a trip to see the world and do volunteer work along the way in Cambodia and Thailand. While visiting a school in Cambodia, Madeline noticed that all twenty-three students in the first-grade classroom were male. When she asked the teacher where the girls were, she was shocked by his answer: "Boys are more valuable to educate," he told Madeline.[1]

As soon as she got back to Australia, it clicked that the teacher's answer represented a problem that occurred everywhere. "I just hadn't perceived it yet," Madeline said. "But those simple words, 'Boys are more valuable,' opened my eyes to the gender disparities faced both abroad and in Australia." Madeline's growing sensitivity to the gender inequality she saw back home in Australia clarified for her the need to speak out about it. However, she didn't find a receptive audience among her friend groups—at least, not at first.

"I talked about it with my friends, and very few people felt what I was feeling," she told us. "My friends all truly believed that women were as equal as we could get. It wasn't that my friends didn't care; it was just that they didn't know." To Madeline, however, it was obvious that just because not everyone agreed with her, gender inequality was still a global issue. She didn't put it out of her mind, and she didn't stop trying to speak to others about it.

A few years later, while at university, Madeline enrolled in a community development and leadership seminar. "I knew, going into the class, that I had to do something related to gender inequality," Madeline said. She came up with the idea of conducting educational seminars for high school students and community organizations to open their eyes to the ways that gender inequality still played a role in their lives and how they might combat it.

"I couldn't stop talking and thinking about it, even when other people I knew didn't seem to think it was as big a problem in Australia as I did," Madeline said. She created an organization called the One Woman Project (OWP) and began recruiting volunteers to help her develop and lead the seminars. "The name comes from the idea that if we educated just one woman to empower herself, the world is already a better place," Madeline said.

OWP works with schools and community organizations through invitation. Schools call OWP in to conduct an educational seminar when an incident of gender bias has occurred on campus or just because they believe in the importance of gender inequality education.

Framing the information in ways that students could identify with was an early challenge for OWP. "It's not enough to say, 'Gender inequality is a problem,' especially for the girls in the high schools. They think it's a 'me thing' and not a culture thing." One of the best ways of engaging students, Madeline found, was to enable them to find their voices. She explained:

> They're students, and they're not given very many platforms to say, "This is what I think about sexuality or gender."

> Student voices aren't often listened to when it comes to curriculum or educational issues. We want to hear what their answer is regarding those questions, and I think it's really important to let them know you want to hear them. That seems to make such a difference in getting them to share their opinions and feelings.

OWP also works to show that gender inequality is not an issue that affects women alone. The curriculum covers all the ways a patriarchal culture reinforces beliefs and behaviors that are harmful to men as well as women. For example, in cultures where masculinity is measured by "toughness" and the expectation that men not show emotion, men have higher rates of suicide and accidental death, as well as an increased chance of mental health concerns during their lifetime. Madeline also recruited male volunteers to OWP, which helps give male students a visual connection to the idea that gender inequality is not an issue that affects only women. "I wanted to find ways to make sure that students see that both men and women are affected by these issues. Making certain that we have men going into schools to give these seminars along with our female volunteers is extremely helpful in that respect," Madeline told us.

Starting the first gender inequality education program in the country was not without its challenges. "There was no one else in Australia running an educational program like this," Madeline said. "That meant there was both a huge vacancy in the space and that there was no template for us to work from." As a young woman in the midst of her collegiate career tackling a sensitive issue head-on in local schools and communities, Madeline enabled others in her community to believe that their ideas for making the world a better place can be achieved. Within OWP itself, Madeline supports that principle by cultivating an atmosphere of sharing ideas and developing leadership skills with her volunteers.

Today, the One Woman Project works in an average of forty-five schools each year. Outposts in China, Tanzania, and India grew organically from volunteers who were so engaged in Australia that they wanted to stay connected and spread the message in their home countries. By 2020, OWP aims to be in every state in Australia and to be registered with the National Curriculum of Australia so that students or community members can earn academic credit for taking the seminars. OWP also aims to be fully funded so that its volunteers can become full-time employees.

> There is no set formula for creating change and making it happen. Anyone can do it! You just have to make a decision to do something, to make a difference, and then do it. If you want to make the pledge for achieving gender equality, all you really need is passion and the drive to take the first step.

Madeline's story speaks to a fundamental question: When does leadership begin? The answer is that leaders seize the moment. Madeline saw an opportunity and took it, first when she returned from Cambodia and started talking with her friends about gender issues, and then at university where she hatched her plan to launch the One Woman Project. Those fairly small opportunities transformed into something much greater. Madeline didn't wait for someone to appoint her as "the" leader. She recognized an issue, had a passion for it, found others with a similar vision, and just got started. Then she kept going. Leadership, just like any other skill in life, can be learned and strengthened through coaching and practice, but you don't have to wait until that support and preparation are lined up before you start to lead. In fact, no amount of coaching or practice can make much of a difference if you don't care about making something better than it currently is.

Everyone can lead, whether or not they are in a formal position of authority or even part of an organized group.[2] That's what we mean when we say *leadership is everyone's business.* It is not about being a student government officer; team, chapter, or club captain; program director; editor; supervisor; president; CEO; military officer; or government official. Nor is leadership about fame, wealth, or even age. It's not about your family status, the neighborhood you come from, or your gender, ethnic, or racial background. It's about knowing your values and those of the people around you and taking the steps, however small, to make what you do every day demonstrate that you live by those values.

Also, as Madeline's experience illustrates, leadership is about transforming values and goals into action. When members of her community and students at her university heard of OWP, enthusiastic volunteers showed up looking to become a part of her project because they shared the vision of eradicating gender inequality through education. "People wanted to get on board almost immediately because it was a cause they believed in," Madeline said. "Like me, they'd experienced friends telling them things they knew were false: that misogyny was no longer an issue, that things were okay as they were. The One Woman Project gave them a place to say, 'That's not true; let's change things.'"

From that outpouring of support from volunteers, Madeline learned a valuable lesson in leadership. "I'm here to facilitate the passion of other people as well as my own, and from that, OWP has grown into monthly events, conferences, International Women's Day events—all because of the passion of the people I work with," Madeline said. Within the OWP, Madeline has cultivated an atmosphere that encourages people to share their ideas and aspirations. During weekly meetings, for example, volunteers pitch ideas for potential projects for the OWP to implement. In one case, a volunteer proposed the idea of a monthly calendar, with art from local artists, to be sold to help fund some of the OWP initiatives, and it turned out to be a huge success.

Madeline makes it a point to provide encouragement to every-body involved in OWP and its various projects, because she realizes how important it is in helping everyone keep going as they work toward making their hopes and dreams come true. What's more, she told us, how much she appreciates that there isn't a single leader in their organization; rather everyone takes the lead in different ways, and this makes leadership development of its volunteers an integral part of OWP's growth plan. "These are exactly the kind of team members I want, people who are willing to take an idea and grow it and find new opportunities for us," Madeline said. "I want them to take an idea or existing endeavor and ask, 'How can I make this better?'"

Because OWP's success depends on the support of volunteers, Madeline works hard to ensure an atmosphere of fun for everyone involved, and emphasizes the importance of mental health and taking care of yourself. To that end, she arranges seminars for the volunteers to learn to recognize the symptoms of burnout in themselves and other team members. "Everyone who works with us comes to us in their spare time," she explained.

> Most of them are students, but some have full-time jobs. In other words, it's easy to get burned out, just from the sheer volume of work. We have a no-fault policy where anyone can back away from their work at any time, no questions asked—maybe it's the middle of finals, maybe it's a problem at home, maybe someone just needs a break. The only way to keep passion and commitment high is to let people know they need to take care of themselves first, and I try very hard to encourage that.

For example, Madeline makes sure that at every meeting, every volunteer team member completes a self-care survey on which they rank their well-being on a scale from 1 to 10. Anyone who self-reports being under heavy stress receives ideas on how to relieve it from Madeline and other team members. "Self-care has to be a priority," Madeline said.

Madeline also makes sure to host social events for her community of volunteers, such as dinners or events out in the town where the focus is on having fun and promoting teamwork. These celebrations foster a sense of community and friendship, and they also help keep the passion high among the OWP team. "I have a lot of people say, 'I've never had feminist friends before, and now I get to go out and do fun projects with them.' Everyone is so excited to see each other and work with each other," Madeline said.

Madeline knows that it's important to acknowledge the contributions of everyone on the team, because her volunteers are taking on responsibility outside of their daily student lives. At their social events, Madeline takes the time to recognize volunteers who have put together proposals outside of their usual work or who have done an exceptional job in recent projects. By attending these dinners and social gatherings, Madeline reinforces the idea that she's still one of them and just as much a part of the team as the volunteers.

Madeline's experience shows something we have seen over and over: leadership begins when you find something you care about. It doesn't necessarily require an organization, a budget, a hierarchy, a position, or a title. Of course there are challenges, but leaders like Madeline face them one at a time and make progress in their unique manner. Leadership potential is lost when people are convinced that there is just one straight path and one certain type of person who is destined for success. You don't need to be perfect to start anything; you simply need passion, initiative, and the desire to make a difference.

THE FIVE PRACTICES OF EXEMPLARY LEADERSHIP

In undertaking her leadership challenge, Madeline seized an opportunity to make a difference. And although her story is unique, it is not unlike countless others. We've been conducting original global research for more than thirty years, and when we ask young leaders to tell us about their personal-best leadership experiences—experiences that they believe are their individual standards of excellence—there are countless stories just like Madeline's.[3] We've found them everywhere, and it proves that leadership knows no ethnic, cultural, or geographical borders; no racial or religious bounds; no differences between young and old. Leaders reside in every city and every country, in every function and every organization. We find exemplary leadership everywhere we look.

After analyzing these leadership experiences, we discovered, and continue to find, that regardless of the times or settings, individuals who guide others along pioneering journeys follow surprisingly similar paths. Although each experience was distinctive in its individual expression, there were clearly identifiable behaviors and actions that made a difference. When getting extraordinary things done with others, leaders engage in what we call The Five Practices of Exemplary Leadership:

- Model the Way
- Inspire a Shared Vision
- Challenge the Process
- Enable Others to Act
- Encourage the Heart

These practices are not restricted to the people we studied. Nor do they belong to a few select shining stars. Leadership is not about personality, power, or privilege; it's about behavior. The Five Practices are available to anyone who accepts the leadership challenge—the chal-lenge of taking people and organizations to places they have never been before. It is the challenge of moving beyond the ordinary to the extraordinary.

The Five Practices framework is not an accident of a special mo-ment in history. It has passed the test of time. Although the *context* of leadership has changed dramatically over the years, the *content* of leadership has not changed much at all; and this is similarly true as we peer into the future. The fundamental behaviors and actions of lead-ers have remained essentially the same, and they are as relevant today as they were when we began our study of exemplary leadership. The truth of each individual personal-best leadership experience, multi-plied thousands of times, and substantiated empirically by hundreds of thousands of students and scores of scholars, establishes The Five Practices of Exemplary Leadership as an "operating system" for leaders everywhere.

Let's begin in this chapter with a brief overview of each of The Five Practices of Exemplary Leadership. When you explore The Five Practices of Exemplary Leadership in depth in Chapters 1 through 10, you'll find many examples from the real-life experiences of students like Madeline who have accepted the leadership challenge and, be-cause of their leadership, enabled others and their teams and organiza-tions to achieve the extraordinary.

Model the Way

Titles are granted, but it's your behavior that earns you respect. This sentiment reverberated across all the cases we collected. Exemplary lead-ers know that if they want to gain commitment and achieve the highest standards, they must be models of the behavior they expect of others. To effectively Model the Way, you must first be clear about your guid-ing principles. You must *clarify values by finding your voice*. When you understand who you are and what your values are, then you can give voice to those values. Finding your voice encourages others to do the same, paving the way for mutual understanding. But *your* values aren't the only values that matter. In every team, organization, and community, there are others who also feel strongly about matters of principle. As a leader, you also must help identify and *affirm the shared values* of the group. Leaders' actions are far more important than their words when others want to determine how serious leaders are about what they say. Words and actions must be consistent. Exemplary leaders *set the example by aligning actions with shared values*. Through their daily actions, they demonstrate their deep commitment to their beliefs and to the groups they are part of. One of the best ways to prove that something is important is by doing it yourself and setting an example, by "walking the talk."

Inspire a Shared Vision

Students describe their personal-best leadership experiences as times when they imagined an exciting, highly attractive future for themselves and others. They had visions and dreams of what *could* be. They had absolute and total personal faith in those dreams, and they were confident in their abilities to make those extraordinary things happen. Every organization, every social movement, every big event begins with a vision. It is the force that propels the creation of the future.

Leaders *envision the future by imagining exciting and ennobling possibilities*. Before starting any project, you need to have an appreciation of the past and a clear vision of what the results should look like, much as an architect draws a blueprint or an engineer builds a model. But you can't command commitment to a new future; you have to inspire it. You have to *enlist others in a common vision by appealing to shared aspirations*. You do this by talking to others and, even more important, listening to them to understand what motivates them. You enlist others by helping them feel they are part of something that matters, something that will make a difference, and something that everyone believes is important to accomplish together. When you express your enthusiasm and excitement for the vision, you ignite a similar passion in others.

Challenge the Process

Challenge is the crucible for greatness. Every single personal-best leadership case involved a change from the status quo. Not one student achieved a personal best by keeping things the same. The challenge might have been launching an innovative new event, tackling a problem in a different way, rethinking a service their group provides, creating a successful campaign to get students to join an environmental program, starting up a brand-new student group or team, achieving a revolutionary turnaround of a school or university policy, or getting a new event under way with the intent that it become a new institutional tradition. It could also be dealing with daily obstacles and challenges, such as finding ways to resolve a group conflict or to design and deliver a major class or school project. Regardless of the specifics, all the personal-best experiences involved overcoming adversity and embracing opportunities to grow, innovate, and improve.

Leaders are pioneers willing to step out into the unknown. However, leaders aren't the only creators or originators of new ideas, projects, services, or processes. Innovation comes more from listening than from telling, and from continuously looking outside yourself and your group for new and innovative ways to do things. You need to *search for opportunities by seizing the initiative and by looking outward for innovative ways to improve.*

Because innovation and change involve *experimenting and taking risks,* one way of dealing with the potential risks and failures of experimentation is *by consistently generating small wins and learning from experience.* There's a strong correlation between the process of learning and the approach leaders take to make extraordinary things happen: the best leaders are simply the best learners.[4] Leaders are always learning from their errors and failures. Life is the leader's laboratory, and exemplary leaders use it to conduct as many experiments as possible. School is a great incubator environment for learning how to become the best leader you can be.

Enable Others to Act

Grand dreams don't become meaningful realities through the actions of a single student. Achieving greatness requires a team effort. It requires solid trust and enduring relationships. It requires group collaboration and individual accountability.[5] No leader ever got anything extraordinary done by working solo. True leadership is a team effort.

Leaders *foster collaboration by building trust and facilitating relationships.* You have to engage all those who must make the project work—and in some way involve all who must live with the results. Leaders appreciate that people don't perform at their best or stick around for very long if they feel weak, dependent, or alienated. When you *strengthen others by increasing self-determination and developing competence,* they are more likely to give it their all and exceed expectations. Focusing on serving the needs of others rather than self-interests builds trust in a leader. The more that people trust their leaders, and each other, the more they take risks, make changes, and keep moving ahead. When students are trusted, have choices in how they do their work, feel in control, and have ample information, they're much more likely to use their energies to produce extraordinary results. Through that relationship, leaders turn others into leaders themselves.

Encourage the Heart

The climb to the top is arduous and steep. People can become exhausted, frustrated, and disenchanted, and are often tempted to give up. Genuine acts of caring keep people in the game and draw them forward.

Leaders *recognize contributions by showing appreciation for individual excellence.* Appreciation can be expressed one to one or with many people. It can come from dramatic gestures or simple actions. Being a leader requires showing appreciation for people's contributions and creating a culture of *celebrating the values and victories by creating a spirit of community.* Recognitions and celebrations need to be personal and personalized. They aren't necessarily about fun and games, though there is a lot of fun and there are a lot of games when students acknowledge people's accomplishments. Neither are they necessarily about formal awards. Ceremonies designed to create "official" recognition can be effective, but only if participants perceive them as sincere. Encouragement is valuable and important because it connects what people have done with the successes the group gathers to celebrate. Make sure that people appreciate how their actions connect with their personal values and the values of the group. Celebrations and rituals, when done sincerely and from the heart, give a group a strong sense of identity and team spirit that can carry them through tough times.

The Ten Commitments of Exemplary Leadership

The Five Practices of Exemplary Leadership are the core leadership competencies that emerged from analyzing thousands of personal-best leadership cases. When student leaders are doing their best, they Model the Way, Inspire a Shared Vision, Challenge the Process, Enable Others to Act, and Encourage the Heart.

Embedded in The Five Practices are behaviors that can serve as the basis for your learning to lead. We call these the Ten Commitments of Exemplary Leadership. They focus on actions you need to both apply to yourself and that you need to take with others.

The Five Practices and Ten Commitments of Exemplary Leadership

 MODEL THE WAY	1. Clarify values by finding your voice and affirming shared values. 2. Set the example by aligning actions with shared values.
INSPIRE A SHARED VISION	3. Envision the future by imagining exciting and ennobling possibilities. 4. Enlist others in a common vision by appealing to shared aspirations.
CHALLENGE THE PROCESS	5. Search for opportunities by seizing the initiative and by looking outward for innovative ways to improve. 6. Experiment and take risks by consistently generating small wins and learning from experience.
ENABLE OTHERS TO ACT	7. Foster collaboration by building trust and facilitating relationships. 8. Strengthen others by increasing self-determination and developing competence.
ENCOURAGE THE HEART	9. Recognize contributions by showing appreciation for individual excellence. 10. Celebrate the values and victories by creating a spirit of community.

The Ten Commitments serve as the guide for explaining, understanding, appreciating, and learning how leaders get extraordinary things done with others, and we discuss each of them in depth in Chapters 1 through 10. But what's the evidence that these practices, commitments, and behaviors really matter? Do they truly make a difference in how we lead others to create change? The research we've conducted makes the case that they do.

The Five Practices Make a Difference

Exemplary student leader behavior makes a profoundly positive difference in the level of commitment, motivation, and work performance in the students with whom they work. In generating a high level of commitment and performance, student leaders who most frequently use The Five Practices of Exemplary Leadership are considerably more effective than those who seldom use them.[6]

In other words, the way student leaders behave is what explains how hard their colleagues work and how engaged they feel in the work, projects, and programs they are doing. Our research tells us that the more you use The Five Practices of Exemplary Leadership, the more likely it is that you'll have a positive influence on others and on their efforts and commitment to their group, team, campus, or cause. That's what all the data adds up to. If you want to have a significant impact on people, on organizations, and on communities, you need to invest in learning the behaviors that enable you to become the very best leader you can be.

Here's something else we found from the colleagues and constituents of student leaders: the more frequently they reported that their student leader was engaging in The Five Practices, the more they reported being satisfied with that person's leadership and proud to tell others that they were working with this student leader. In addition, they were more likely to feel appreciated and valued, to agree that their efforts were making a difference, and to feel that they were highly productive.

Student leaders were viewed by their constituents (typically their peers) as more effective as a direct function of their using The Five Practices. We found a dramatic relationship between how students assessed the leadership skill level of their leaders and how frequently these leaders were seen engaging in The Five Practices. Those reported as having the best leadership ability by their peers were viewed as using

The Five Practices nearly 20 percent more often than those reported as having "average" leadership skills levels and a whopping 35 percent more frequently than those leaders who are seen as having weak leadership skills compared with their peers.

In addition, student leaders who self-reported that their leadership skills were well developed compared with their peers indicated that they used The Five Practices nearly 30 percent more often than students who felt that their leadership skills were not as well developed as their peers'. Our research also revealed something else that's extremely important to appreciate, and that's how individual characteristics of student leaders, such as their gender, age, ethnicity, and year in school, are not the reason why student leaders are reported as effective or not.[7]

To sum it all up: what matters as a leader is how you behave.

You Make a Difference

It's very clear that engaging in The Five Practices of Exemplary Leadership makes a significant difference—no matter who you are or what you are leading. How you behave as a leader matters, and it matters a lot. It makes a difference. You make a difference. We believe it is the right, and even the responsibility, of all students to look into their hearts, determine what they believe in, and, by acting on that belief, make the world a better place. In the chapters that follow, we'll provide ideas, tool, and techniques that will serve you well on any leadership journey.

MODEL
THE WAY

The first step you must take along the path to becoming an exemplary student leader is inward. It's a step toward discovering who you are and what you believe in. Leaders stand up for their beliefs. They practice what they preach. They also ensure that others stand by the values that they agree on. It is consistency between words and actions that builds credibility.

In the next two chapters, we take a look at how you as a student leader must:

➤ **Clarify Values** by finding your voice and affirming shared values.
➤ **Set the Example** by aligning actions with shared values.

MODEL THE WAY

Reflections from the Student Leadership
Practices Inventory

1. Record your overall score from the *Student Leadership Practices Inventory* for MODEL THE WAY here: _____

2. Of the six leadership behaviors that are part of Model the Way, write down the statement for the one you indicated engaging in most frequently:

3. Write down the leadership behavior statement that you felt you engaged in least often:

4. On the basis of your self-assessment, complete this statement: When it comes to Model the Way, my areas of leadership competency are:

5. What Model the Way behaviors do you see as opportunities for improving and strengthening your leadership capability? Make note of these below so that you can keep them in mind as you read this chapter and the next.

Commitment #1: Clarify Values

"Who are you?" This is the first question people want you to answer if they are going to follow you. Your leadership journey begins when you set out to know "this is who I am" and are able and willing to express it. John Banghoff, for example, knew that he wanted to be in his university's marching band since he was nine years old, when he attended his first college football game with his father. Making the band his freshman year felt like a dream come true. "I was on cloud nine," John said. "It was the coolest experience to hear my name called."

Shortly after that, the band's student leaders took John and his new bandmates under the bleachers, where they passed around a flask; afterwards, the leaders took new members to a party where they introduced them to a band tradition of hazing freshmen recruits. "This turned out to be the worst night of my life," John said. "Seeing all of these people that I looked up to drinking and harassing me and the other new band members left me seriously questioning whether I wanted to be part of this organization."

John's struggle about whether to stay in the band or leave pushed him to think deeply about what mattered to him. Did his personal values align with the band's culture? Being part of a team, having an opportunity to put his passion for music into practice, and expressing his gratitude for being involved in the marching band were important values he discovered in the process of asking himself, "Who am I, and what do I care about?" John told us.

> I realized that the marching band was something that I still wanted to be a part of because it gave me the opportunity to play the trumpet and that I should work on my own feelings of gratitude for the experience rather than focusing on parts that weren't what I wanted.

With this clarity, John soon found other band members who shared his beliefs and his concerns. "Once I talked about values, I realized that there were other people who felt the way that I did. Together we could focus on what was right about marching band and figure out what we might do about the negative aspects," John said. However, before they could do much, the band's tradition of hazing became public news and eventually resulted in the college firing the band director.

It was a time of intense challenge for everyone in the band, as John explained: "It felt like we had no direction and were being punished for the mistakes of a few. We weren't sure who we could trust, and the leaders we'd come to know and respect within the band were just trying to keep the ship afloat." The band felt directionless and unmoored, not at all like the prestigious group that John had once yearned to join.

In the midst of this crisis, John and a few of his peers were selected as squad leaders for the following season of marching band. Under the leadership of the newly appointed band director, John and the other squad leaders helped design a cultural blueprint for the band, which articulated new values to help guide it: a tradition of excellence, extraordinary respect, and an attitude of gratitude. "These values gave us signposts to move to when we noticed things that didn't align with them," John said. The group's ability to relate to each other and feel gratitude even through difficult times helped sustain the marching band's excellence and return it to national prominence.

Implementing the new values and practices began during John's fifth year. During that time, he helped facilitate workshops on the new cultural blueprint, including exercises to show how the band's values could be lived in real life. John recalls, "Although the process of redefining the band's culture was not an easy one, it was extremely rewarding to see everyone rally around the new set of cultural values." At the end of the season, at the annual concert where the band plays for the community and presents awards to its members, John received the Most Inspirational Bandperson Award for his work in helping to bring the band back together after its crisis. "That night, as I drove home, I was in tears," John said. "I was in tears the first night of my band experience and my last night, but in two very different circumstances and for very different reasons. It was the journey between point A and point B that made me the leader I am."

The personal-best leadership cases we've collected are, at their core, the stories of people like John who were clear about their personal values and used this clarity as a bedrock to give them the courage to make tough choices and navigate difficult terrain. Leaders are expected to be able to speak out on matters of values and conscience, and to be clear about what matters to them. But to speak out you have to know what to speak about. To stand up for your beliefs, you have to know the beliefs you stand for. To walk the talk, you have to have a talk to walk. To do what you say, you have to know what you want to say. To earn and sustain personal credibility, you must first be able to clearly articulate deeply held beliefs.

Model the Way is the first of The Five Practices of Exemplary Leadership we discuss in this book, and one of the commitments you must make to effectively Model the Way is to Clarify Values. In beginning your leadership journey, it's essential that you:

- **Find your voice**
- **Affirm shared values**

Becoming an exemplary student leader requires you to fully comprehend the deeply held values—the beliefs, standards, ethics, and ideals—that drive you. You must freely and honestly choose the principles you will use to guide your decisions and actions. Then you must express your authentic self, genuinely communicating your beliefs in ways that clearly represent who you are.

What's more, you must realize that leaders aren't just speaking for themselves when they talk about the values that should guide their decisions and actions. When leaders passionately express a commitment to learning or innovation or service or some other value, those leaders aren't just saying, "I believe in this." They're also making a commitment on behalf of an entire group. They're saying, *"We all* believe in this." Therefore, leaders must not only be clear about their personal guiding principles but also make sure that there's agreement on a set of shared values among everyone they lead. Furthermore, they must hold others accountable to those values and standards.

FIND YOUR VOICE

What would you say if someone were to ask you, "What is your leadership philosophy?" Are you prepared right now to say what it is? If you aren't, you should be. If you are, you need to reaffirm it on a daily basis.

Before you can become a credible leader—one who connects "what you say" with "what you do"—you first need to find your authentic voice, the most genuine expression of who you are. If you don't find your voice, you'll end up with a vocabulary that belongs to someone else, sounding as though you are mouthing words written by some speechwriter or mimicking the language of some other leader who is nothing like you at all. If the words you speak are not your words but someone else's, you will not, in the long term, be able to be consistent in word and deed. You will not have the integrity to lead.

To find your voice, you need to discover what you care about, what defines you, and what makes you who you are. You need to explore your inner self. You can only be authentic when you lead according to the principles that matter most to you. Otherwise, you're just putting on an act. Consider Christian Ghorbani's experience.

Christian returned from a three-week trip to India, where he worked on a construction site building a new village school, spent time playing with and interacting with children and families who live in extreme poverty, and learned about the social issues that people in rural India face. This experience fueled his passion for philanthropy, and when he returned to school he founded an organization called Pledge to Humanity. Christian attributed this action to "the inner reflection where I clarified my values, took action based on these values, and expressed my vision to those I came in contact with. The more I talked, the more I began to see my voice strengthening and my passion deepening."

Leading others begins with leading yourself, and you can't do that until you're able to answer that fundamental question about who you are. When you have clarified your values and found your voice, you will also find the inner confidence necessary to take charge of your life. Take it from Tommy Baldacci.

Throughout college, Tommy had many leadership experiences, and as a result felt that people who don't take the time to engage in personal reflection will lack an understanding of personal values and philosophy. "To know how to lead, you need to know where you are going," he told us.

> To know where you are going, you have to know who you are. Knowing yourself truly means that you have to be honest with yourself. By understanding myself, I was able to figure out professionally where my passions were aimed. Without knowing myself, I would have had no baseline to refer to.

Our research backs up Tommy's observations. There was a dramatic relationship between how leaders assessed their leadership skills relative to their peers and how frequently they reported "talking about their values and the principles that guided their actions." The increase in leadership skills between those leaders who indicated that at most they "sometimes" talked about values and principles and those who often did so was nearly 35 percent. There was still *another* 40 percent increase in people's assessment of their leadership skills between those who indicated they often talked about values and principles and those who maintained they very frequently did so.

Let Your Values Guide You

Values constitute your personal "bottom line." They influence every aspect of your life—for example, your moral judgments, commitments, and personal and group goals—and the way you respond to others. They serve as guides to action and set the parameters for the decisions you make, consciously and subconsciously. They tell you when to say yes and when to say no. They also help you explain the choices you make and why you make them. You seldom consider or act on options that run counter to your value system. If you do, it's generally with a sense of compliance rather than commitment.

Alan Yap was hitting a wall trying to balance all his interests—and not making the most of any of them—until he took some time to think deeply about his values. Doing so helped clarify his priorities, leading him to eliminate some activities and commit more fully to others. For example, he decided to run for a leadership position in the business fraternity Alpha Kappa Psi. Upon being elected, Alan said that he struggled with finding an approach to leading the organization. He had to find his voice and figure out "How do I want to be known as a leader?" He decided "that the best way to lead was through what I valued." All the critical decisions a leader makes involve values.

Alan's experience illustrates how values are the signposts in your leadership journey. They supply you with a compass by which to navigate the course of your daily life. Clarity of values is essential to knowing which way is north, south, east, and west. The clearer you are about your values, the easier it is for you and for everyone else in your group to stay on the chosen path and commit to it. This kind of guidance is especially needed in difficult and uncertain times. When there are daily challenges that can throw you off course, it's crucial that you have some signs that tell you where you are.

Personal values drive commitment. Clear personal values drive motivation and productivity. People who are very clear about their values are more likely to stick around and work harder than those who don't have an internal compass to guide them through uncertainty. It's how you determine if the work you are doing, the group or organization you are in, fits you.

There comes a point when you recognize that what you are doing is or is not a good fit with your values and beliefs. Even if you didn't know the specific values of the organization, you see how the group behaves and performs. You won't stick around a place (or a project, or a team) when you feel in your heart and in your soul that you don't belong. This is a major reason why some people don't stay very long in groups they've joined. Commitment is based on alignment with personal values, who you are, and what you are about. People who are clearest about personal values are better prepared to make choices based on principle—including deciding whether the principles of the organization fit with their own.

Say It in Your Own Words

People can only speak the truth when speaking in their own true voice. If you only mimic what others are saying, no one can make a commitment to you because they don't know who you are and what you believe in.

The techniques and tools that fill the pages of leadership books— including this one—are not substitutes for knowing what matters to you. Once you have the words you want to say, you must also give voice to those words. You must be able to express yourself so that everyone knows that you are the one who's speaking and not someone else.

You'll find a lot of science and empirical data to support the importance of each of The Five Practices of Exemplary Leadership. Keep in mind, however, that leadership is also an art, and just as with any other art form—whether it's painting, music, dancing, acting, or writing—leadership is a means of personal expression. To become a credible leader, you have to learn to express yourself in ways that are uniquely your own. Jacob Philpott provides a useful example.

After his freshman year in college, Jacob applied for a residential advisor (RA) position for the Upward Bound Program (UB). UB is a federally funded educational program created for high school students who come from diverse, low-income families and are the first generation to go to college. Jacob had participated in the program as a high school student, and he told us, "My experience was so enriching I knew I wanted to come back and serve as an RA." During the interview process when he was asked why he wanted to work in the program, he simply answered from his own experience: "I wanted to help prepare the participants for college and provide them with an even better experience than my own while working on a great team."

> My motivation for taking on the role was heavily tied to my core values. The core values that I wanted to share encouraged advancement via individual determination and included management of time and money, work ethic, study skills, and responsibility with freedom. The core values that I wanted to share with the team of RAs, which were imparted to the participants as well, were giving back, being a role model, tutoring with the Socratic method, and creating a connection with the participants.

Jacob's reflections underscore how being clear about your values helps you find your voice and be able to express yourself in your own unique way. There's a genuineness that comes through when you can hear yourself using language and words that are your own rather than someone else's. For example, Jacob told us, on the very first day of the program, "I was given another opportunity to find my voice."

> We got everyone together for an introduction and to discuss our goals for the summer. I took that opportunity to share a story about my experience in the program, values I learned, and the skills that were reinforced which helped me get through college.

All the participants and other RAs had a chance to share their stories. Although each of these stories was unique to its teller, they carried common themes around building connections with people, growing, learning, and stepping outside of one's comfort zone. "I had clarified my values and found my voice," said Jacob, and "this enabled me to share my story and gave others the courage to share their own stories.

The shared values that came from this experience guided us through the rest of the summer."

Like Jacob, you cannot lead out of someone else's values or words. You cannot lead out of someone else's experience. You can only lead out of your own. Unless it's your style, your manner, your words, it's not you—it's just an act. People don't follow your title or your technique. They follow *you*. If you're not the genuine article, can you honestly expect others to want to follow? To be a leader, you've got to awaken to the fact that you don't have to copy someone else, you don't have to read a script written by someone else, and you don't have to imitate someone else's style. Instead, you are free to choose what you want to express and the way you want to express it. In fact, you have a responsibility to others to express yourself in an authentic manner, in a way they would immediately recognize as yours.

AFFIRM SHARED VALUES

Leadership is not solely about *your* values. It's also about the values of those you lead. Just as your values drive your commitment to the organization, club, or team, their personal values drive their commitment. They will be significantly more engaged when they believe they can stay faithful to their beliefs. Although clarifying your values is essential, understanding the values of others and building alignment around values that everyone can share are equally critical. Our research shows that the frequency with which their leader "makes sure that people support the values we have agreed upon" influences the extent that students are proud to tell others they are working with this leader, as shown in Figure 1.1. Only about one in five strongly agrees with this sentiment when they indicate that their leader rarely engages in this behavior, and neither this percentage nor sentiment increases very substantially for student leaders who only once in a while

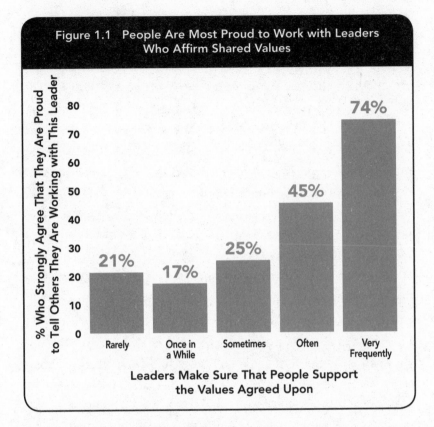

Figure 1.1   People Are Most Proud to Work with Leaders Who Affirm Shared Values

or sometimes use this leadership behavior. Almost twice as many students feel proud to tell people they work with their leader when they observe this individual often affirming shared values, and this percentage goes up to about three in four people when leaders are reported as engaging very frequently in this essential leadership behavior.

Bethany Fristad was a college freshman when she first felt there was something important inside her pushing to come out. In high school, she hadn't been very involved, didn't feel much sense of purpose, and didn't think she had much direction in life. Halfway through her first year in college, something began to change. As she made friends at her new school and around the local small-town community, she started to recognize that she could serve a greater purpose. She brought together a small group of people who helped her establish a nonprofit organization focused on helping underprivileged children. They called it Firefleyes to symbolize its ability to ignite a fire in people's hearts and eyes. Bethany then set out to recruit an even larger group of students at her college who had an interest in helping disadvantaged children.

Firefleyes members believe that underserved children can flourish if they have an environment where they can find their own voices through music, sports, arts, books, and crafts. The group promoted this belief by collecting enough resources to travel to Sierra Leone and start the first of what Bethany calls Creation Nations, which are essentially playrooms where children explore their creative side with all sorts of arts, crafts, and music.

By giving voice to her convictions, Bethany found many supportive and willing participants who shared her beliefs about how to help children do well and who saw the value in what she wanted to do. Had she not been clear on what she was trying to accomplish and why, particularly in such a new and large endeavor, others could have easily cast aside her ideas as impractical. Bethany persisted, and appealed to the ideas she believed others shared about the need to help those less fortunate. She knew that the people she spoke with understood the value of creativity in helping children discover their dreams. Ultimately, she said, it was relatively easy to help fellow students see how they could transform their values into specific actions that would benefit others.

Shared values are the foundation for building productive and genuine working relationships. Exemplary student leaders, like Bethany, honor the uniqueness and individuality of all the members of the group, but they also stress common values. They don't try to get everyone to be in accord on everything. That goal is unrealistic, perhaps even impossible. Moreover, to achieve it would negate the real advantages of diversity. Nevertheless, leaders build on agreement. To take the first step, and then a second, and then a third, people must have some common core of understanding. After all, if there's no agreement about values, then what exactly are the leader and everyone else going to model? If disagreements over fundamental values continue, the result is intense conflict, false expectations, and diminished capacity.[1] Leaders ensure that through the process of affirming shared values, everyone is aligned—uncovering, reinforcing, and holding one another accountable to what "we" value. Once people are clear about the leader's values, about their own values, and about shared values, they know what's expected of them and that they can count on others.

Give People Reasons to Care

Although it's important that leaders forthrightly articulate the principles for which they stand, the values leaders espouse must be consistent with the aspirations of those who follow them. Leaders who advocate values that aren't representative of the group won't be able to get people to act as one. There must be a shared understanding of mutual expectations. Leaders must be able to gain consensus on a common cause and a common set of principles. They must be able to maintain a community of shared values. In this way, a leader's promise is also an organization's promise, regardless of whether the organization is a project team of two, an intramural slow-pitch softball team of ten, a fraternity of one hundred, a campus of seven thousand, a company of twenty thousand, or a town of two hundred thousand. Unless there's agreement about which promises to keep, the organization, its members, and its leaders risk losing credibility.

Recognition of shared values provides people with a common language. When individual, group, and organizational values are in sync, that unity generates tremendous energy. Commitment, enthusiasm, and drive intensify. People have reasons for caring about what they are doing. When individuals care deeply about what they are doing, they are more effective and satisfied. They stay committed to the group, are more engaged in what's going on, and are more likely to participate actively. They experience less frustration with the task or the group.

The quality and accuracy of communication within the group, along with the integrity of the decision-making process, increase when people feel part of a team with the same values. Confidence in one another grows; stress and worry are reduced. People work harder and are more creative because they become fully engaged in what they are doing. We know that when there is solid understanding of how an individual's values and those of the group are aligned, there is considerably greater productivity and success for everyone involved.

Exemplary student leaders spend time with their group talking about values. Too few groups in schools and classrooms spend enough time doing this. It tends to take place as a single occurrence, at the beginning of the school year or when a group is first formed or new members are brought in. Frequent and continuing conversations reminding people why they care about what they are doing renew commitment and help people feel that they are on the same team. When people are clear about the leader's values, about their own values, and about shared values, they know what's expected of them. This understanding increases their ability to make choices, enables them to better handle challenging situations, and enhances understanding and appreciation of the choices others make.

Having frequent and ongoing conversations with the people in your group reinforces what is important to the group as well as to the individuals in it. Think about a time when you joined an organization as a new member. Did anyone talk to you about what the group stood for? Did you ask the question, "What is important to this group?" If you did, was the answer very clear? If you didn't, how did you know what the group was all about? The group's values will guide everything it does, and therefore it is essential to spend time, regularly, talking about those values. We know this can be initially challenging for any leader.

Consider the experience of Kara Koser when she was an RA at a major urban university. She was trying to figure out how she could best meet the needs of her diverse resident population. With so many people on her floor, she wasn't sure what activity she could ever propose that would be of sufficient interest to everyone. She realized that she first had to listen inward, to herself, and then take the time to listen to others. Listening required patience. Kara slowly understood that some people find it intimidating to talk about what is important to them, and it takes time for them to become comfortable sharing. Kara adopted an approach she called "leading out front and leading from the back." What this meant to her was both sharing her own viewpoints *and* intently listening to what others were thinking and talking about, and hearing what was important to them. "The difference in this type of leading was subtle," Kara said, "but both approaches were important because they were done with the interests of the group—in my case, my floor residents—in mind."

Kara didn't give up trying to have conversations with her residents about what they needed and wanted. The more they talked, the more they became comfortable sharing their ideas and visions. Kara regularly worked to create an environment where people could freely and easily contribute. She encouraged her residents, knowing that if she could be respectful of the values of others while at the same time not diminishing her voice, the light would shine on the best solution for all. These conversations enabled the residents to develop a greater sense of community and discover their shared values as they got to know each other better and, subsequently, how they wanted to spend their time together.

Forge Unity, Don't Force It

When leaders seek consensus around shared values, those who follow them are more positive and productive. You cannot mandate unity;

instead, you forge it by involving people in the process, making them feel that you are genuinely interested in their perspectives and that they can speak freely with you. For them to be open to sharing their ideas and aspirations, they must believe that you'll be caring and constructive in searching for common ground.

By encouraging ongoing discussion about the common values of the group, leaders avoid the pitfall of people wasting time and energy trying to figure out what they're supposed to do. When people are unsure about their roles, they tend to lose focus or draw the group off topic; they may stop participating or leave the group altogether. The energy that goes into dealing with incompatible values, through arguments or misunderstandings, takes its toll on both the effectiveness of the leader and the activity level of the group. "What are our core principles?" and "What do we believe in?" are far from simple questions. Even with commonly identified values, there may be little agreement on the meaning of values statements. For example, one study reported 185 different behavioral expectations about the value of integrity alone.[2]

Yi Song told us about one of her class projects at a Chinese university, where she was randomly assigned to a team of people she did not know. Judging from their introductions to one another, Song felt that they had few things in common. They didn't all have the same major, were from different states or countries, and had diverse hobbies and interests. Song suggested that they identify what they valued the most from the team: "Let's each grab a pen and paper and write down five characteristics that we see as most important for working together as a team." After they had finished writing, they shared what they had written and the reasons they had chosen those values, along with examples showing why the values were important. Song told us how this action and discussion affected her and the team:

> Through the individual value-sharing process, we found
> some common characteristics—responsibility, being

punctual, efficiency, good quality of work, and sense of humor—and these shared values served as the guides that led our actions for the rest the semester.

It was a great way to integrate individual values into the group's shared values. Since the shared values were decided by our entire group, everyone understood them, felt like they fit in, and were more willing to follow the shared values.

As Song's experience demonstrates, shared values emerge from a process, not a pronouncement. Leaders can't impose their values on the group's members; instead, they must actively involve people in creating shared values. Ownership of values increases exponentially when leaders actively engage a broad range of people in their development. Shared values are the result of listening, appreciating, building consensus, and resolving conflicts. For people to understand the values and come to agree with them, they must participate in the process. Unity can never be forced.

Fervently shared values are much more than advertising slogans. They are strongly supported and broadly endorsed beliefs about what's important to the people who hold them. People must be able to enumerate the values and have common interpretations of how to practice those values. They must know what their values will look like in action and how their efforts directly contribute to the larger success of the group. On Song's team, for example, *being a responsible team member* meant that each person would put in the best effort on all the work he or she was assigned to do. *Being punctual* meant not being late for team meetings and thus showing respect for one's teammates by not wasting their time.

Having everyone on the same page when it comes to values has many benefits. It ensures consistency in what the group says and what it does. The result is high individual credibility and an excellent reputation for the group, further preparing people to discuss values and expectations when recruiting, selecting, and orienting new members. Whenever new members join your group, whether at the beginning of a term or in the middle of the year, knowing what the group stands for and talking openly about it helps everyone make more informed decisions about their engagement with the group. Having everyone aligned about shared values builds commitment and community, and that is precisely what leaders ultimately hope to do in pursuit of a common vision.

REFLECT AND ACT: CLARIFY VALUES

The very first step on the journey to exemplary leadership is clarifying your values—discovering those fundamental beliefs that will guide your decisions and actions along the path to success and significance. That journey involves an exploration of your inner self, where your true voice resides. It's essential that you take yourself on this voyage because it's the only route to being a credible leader and because your personal values drive your commitment to the organization and to the cause. You can't do what you say if you don't know what you believe. And you can't do what you say if you don't believe in what you're saying.

Although clarity of personal values is essential for all leaders, that by itself isn't good enough. Leaders don't just speak for themselves; they speak for their groups and followers as well. There must be agreement on the shared values that everyone will commit to upholding. These give people reasons for caring about what they do, which make a significant and positive difference in their work attitudes and performance. A common understanding of shared values emerges from a process, not a pronouncement; unity comes about through conversation and debate, followed by understanding and commitment.

Student leaders must hold themselves and others accountable to a set of shared values, which is a topic explored more thoroughly in the next chapter.

Reflect

Model the Way begins with the commitment to *clarify values by finding your voice and affirming shared values.* Think about this commitment and record your responses to these questions:

1. What is the most important idea or lesson about exemplary leadership that you learned from this chapter?

   _____

   _____

   _____

   _____

2. What changes do you need to make in your leadership to better Clarify Values?

   _____

   _____

   _____

   _____

3. Review the suggestions in the following section on what you can do to take action to Clarify Values. After you have reflected on

what you learned and what you need to improve, record your plan here for taking at least one action that will help you become a better leader:

_____

_____

_____

_____

Take Action

Here are some things you can do to solidify your commitment to **Clarify Values:**

- Reflect on the values that guide your actions, and be able to express what they mean in your own words.
- Ask others to describe why they choose to be involved in the things they are and why they care about those things.
- Create opportunities for people to talk about individual values with others in the group.
- Ask the group to identify the common values that are revealed in discussions of individual values.
- Find ways to make the shared values visible, which helps ensure that people adhere to them.
- Periodically review the group's shared values to make certain that they are still salient; make adjustments and reconfirm as necessary.
- Be clear about how you will communicate what the group stands for when someone new comes into the group, and ensure that others in the group are on the same page.

2

Commitment #2: Set the Example

Because he'd been the captain of his high school team, Tyler Iffland thought he'd play football in college. That aspiration soon changed when he realized that committing to football would take too much time away from his studies. Nevertheless, Tyler wanted to find a way to be part of a team. "I realized that I still wanted that leadership experience," Tyler told us, "and that a good way for me to find a new team was to join a fraternity. When I got into the house, I realized that this was no different from leading a team; I was just leading a team of individuals." He joined a fraternity his freshman year, and soon his small acts of leadership and involvement in the community garnered him a reputation as a go-getter.

Fast-forward to Tyler's junior year. Just elected president of his fraternity, Tyler faced a daunting challenge: helping realign his local chapter with the values that were important to them as a national fraternity. For example, the academic rank of Tyler's chapter was sixth out of seven fraternities on campus, and they needed to address this situation. To do that, Tyler knew he had to take radical action.

First, he understood that he had to exemplify the values that his fraternity held dear. Tyler spent time reflecting on the goals and mission of his fraternity and decided that its most important values centered around doing good for the community and achieving academic excellence, all while building strong friendships and relationships among the fraternity members. So Tyler got more involved in the philanthropic aspects of the organization, creating new opportunities for his fraternity brothers to engage in the community. Tyler made sure that he attended every single event, sometimes skipping other social commitments, to demonstrate to his fraternity brothers that he was actively committed to the group's mission. He also searched for ways to become more visibly involved on campus academically. Tyler hosted study groups at the fraternity house, led by himself or other members of the executive team, which emphasized how important it was to be motivated and engaged in their studies. He took on extracurricular academic activities—for example, helping mentor other students at the school. Tyler became involved in a leadership fellowship that met outside of classes and reinforced ways to achieve excellence both in the classroom and in extracurricular pursuits. Tyler pushed himself to become the type of brother he wanted to see in his fraternity.

To motivate his fraternity brothers to contribute academically and philanthropically, Tyler developed an innovative points-based reward system for the group. Points were awarded for reaching certain milestones, such as paying dues on time, attending study hall, getting good grades on exams and papers, and coming to meetings to get more involved in the association that the fraternity supported to help combat amyotrophic lateral sclerosis (ALS, or Lou Gehrig's disease). That way, everyone would stay motivated because each member of the fraternity would have lots of opportunities to earn rewards. "I didn't want anyone to feel like, 'Oh, I've slipped up. I guess I just shouldn't keep contributing because I'm not going to have as many points as my brothers,'" Tyler said. The tiers of rewards in the system Tyler created meant that everyone would have something to celebrate at the end of the year. The members in the top third tier of points would be taken out to dinner, the middle third would have a pizza party, and the bottom third would go to see a movie. "It totally changed the culture of our fraternity," Tyler said.

At the same time, Tyler knew that to effect lasting change in the fraternity, he needed the support and reinforcement of strong leadership from his fraternity brothers. As a junior, Tyler had to engage the class of outgoing seniors, many of whom were more focused on their futures beyond college and didn't want to participate fully in all the chapter's activities. Tyler believed that it was important for the seniors to act as leadership models for the rest of the fraternity, helping promote strong leadership beliefs and behaviors in the underclass members. He said he could've written them off and focused on the brothers who were already more engaged with the values of the fraternity, but he believed in his fellow brothers' potential. Even though it might be hard for them to continue to focus on the works of the fraternity when their time at the university was coming to a close, Tyler didn't want to give up on the idea of having them be actively engaged.

He came up with the idea to sit down with all the seniors and show them why they should remain involved. He brought in alumni brothers who helped demonstrate why getting on board and staying involved in the fraternity was important. "I wanted to show everyone that this was their chance to leave a legacy, to get involved in something bigger than themselves. I wanted them to see that these alumni were the brothers they'd looked up to when they first joined the fraternity, and now they had a chance to be the same type of leader for our underclassmen brothers," Tyler said. At the meeting, Tyler also laid out what he expected of his fellow fraternity brothers to help uphold the values of the organization. He explained:

> I made sure we were very clear on what had brought us together in the first place and what we needed to do to get where we wanted to go—focus on our academics, work hard on our philanthropy.

The strategy worked. By the second semester of Tyler's junior year, the seniors had all assumed the lead-by-example model he'd hoped for. What's more, by the end of his term as president, his fraternity had moved up from its sixth-place academic ranking on campus to third place, based on overall fraternity GPAs. "We were still not where I'd have liked for us to be, but it was a huge jump," Tyler said.

Student leaders like Tyler realize and appreciate that what you do speaks more loudly than what you say. His experience illustrates the second commitment of Model the Way: leaders Set the Example. They take every opportunity to show others, by their own example, that they're deeply committed to the values and aspirations they espouse. No one will believe you're serious until they see you doing what you're asking of others. Either you lead by example, or you don't lead at all. This is how you provide the evidence that you're personally committed. It's how you make your values known and shown.

Our research has consistently revealed that *credibility is the foundation of leadership*. People want to follow leaders in whom they can believe. But what makes a leader credible? When people defined credibility behaviorally, they told us it meant "do what you say you will do." This chapter on Set the Example is all about the *do* part. It's about practicing what you preach, following through on commitments, keeping promises, and walking the talk.

Being an exemplary student leader requires you to live the values you and your organization hold. You must put into action what you and others stand for. You must be the example for others to follow. And, because you're leading a group of people—not just leading yourself—you also must make certain that the actions of your group are consistent with the shared values of the organization. An important part of your job is to educate others on what the team or organization stands for, why those things matter, and how others can authentically serve the organization. As the leader, you teach, coach, and guide others to align their actions with the shared values because you're held accountable for their actions, too, not just your own.

To Set the Example, you need to:

- **Live the shared values**
- **Teach others to model the values**

In practicing these essentials, you become an exemplary role model for what the group or organization stands for, and you create a culture in which everyone commits to aligning themselves with shared values.

LIVE THE SHARED VALUES

Leaders are their organizations' ambassadors of shared values. Their mission is to represent these values and standards to the rest of the world. It's their solemn duty to serve the values to the best of their abilities.

Della Dsouza's leadership challenge was probably not that different from that of most college students who share an apartment with other people: keeping the kitchen clean. From trash piling up to utensils accumulating in the sink, more often than not her place was a mess, she said. This often led to arguments and blaming, and no one was willing to take responsibility for the state of the kitchen. The arguments only added to a "cold war" atmosphere among the roommates. "I always had to remind them to do their bit," Della told us, "and in the beginning, no matter how many times I said it, it didn't work." So Della decided to take the initiative in making sure the kitchen area was clean, if not all the time at least whenever she used the area. This meant that even if there were things lying around that didn't belong to her, she would put them in the right place. She would take out the trash containers when they were full, and whenever she had some time to spare, she made sure she cleaned up the place. What did she notice after a month had gone by? "I realized the arguments got fewer, and there were fewer utensils in the sink. On some days, the trash was already taken out before I could do it. Everybody in the house began to do their part. No instructions, no rules laid down. Just my simple actions produced this outcome!" For Della, this is what it meant to live the shared values:

I had to lead by example. I had to be the doer, not the preacher. I realize that people are constantly observing us. When they see your actions are in sync with your words, you are a more effective leader. And perhaps that is why it was only when I did those things myself that my roommates followed.

As a leader, you always have influence. People watch your every action, and they're determining whether you're serious about what you say. You need to be conscious of the choices you make and the actions you take, because they signal the priorities you have and whether you're doing what you say.

The most significant signal-sending actions you can take to demonstrate that you live the values are how you spend your time and what you pay attention to. Also important is the language (words and phrases) you use, the questions you ask, and your openness to feedback. The actions you take make visible and tangible your personal commitment to a shared way of being. They provide the chance to show where you stand on matters of principle. Simple though they may appear, you should remember that sometimes the greatest distance you have to travel is the distance from your mouth to your feet.

Spend Your Time and Attention Wisely

How you spend your time is the single clearest indicator of what's important to you. People use this metric to judge whether you measure up to espoused standards. Spending time on what you say is important shows that you're putting your money where your mouth is. Whatever your values are, they must show up consistently. They must show up on your calendar if people are to believe they're significant.

Let's say one of your espoused values is teamwork. You're supposed to have a meeting with your capstone project team on Friday afternoon to go over how everyone's research is coming along, and one of your friends invites you to drive down that afternoon to the family's beach home for the weekend. Do you meet your obligations to your classmates because you are committed to being a good team player, or do you go with your friends because you don't want to miss a weekend at the beach? Or suppose that your club decides to run a fundraising car wash. You have an important exam to study for, and you know there will be plenty of people there to help. What do you decide to do? Choices like these are not clear or easy, but ultimately, the things you spend your time on are reflections of your priorities. Are your decisions based on how they reflect your values, or do they indicate that you're distracted or engaged in conflicting interests?

These questions apply to groups as well. Think about the meetings you attend and what's on the agenda. What do you spend most of the time discussing? Being present and consistently aligning your actions with your behaviors say more about what you value than any other message you share, whether it is on social media, in a text, or passed along by someone else. How you behave as a leader signals to others what's important to you and what's merely lip service.

"Even though I was captain of the soccer team," said Alex Golden, "that didn't simply make me a leader. Yet, because I was the captain, all of a sudden I had teammates looking up to me, seeking a role model." For Alex, this meant always being the first at practices and the last one to leave:

> I wanted to demonstrate to the team that just because I am
> the captain, it doesn't mean that I could come and go as
> I pleased. Indeed, when I slacked off during a practice, or
> even a game, I noticed that the rest of the team would also
> slack off. My attitude affected the way the team played.

His actions paid big dividends in developing productive team chemistry. "I knew," said Alex, "that it was my behavior that would earn me the respect I needed and that I had to set an example for the rest of the team."

You can make visible and tangible to others your personal commitment to your group and its values when you seize the kind of signal-sending opportunities that Alex did. Simple though they may appear, actions like just showing up are evidence of where you stand on matters of principle. Leaders like Alex are very mindful that the way they use their time shows others that they are serious about their dedication to the group, the task, and the values shared. You can't just talk the talk. You have to walk it, which often means rolling up your sleeves and being part of, not apart from, the action.

Watch Your Language

Exemplary student leaders understand and are attentive to language because they appreciate the power of words. Words don't just give voice to one's beliefs; they also evoke images of what people hope to create with others and how people expect others to behave. The tradition within fraternities and sororities of members referring to each other as "brother" or "sister" is an excellent example of this. It reinforces the sense of family and loyalty so valued in the fraternal system. The words you choose have a powerful effect on how others see themselves, those around them, and the events you all share.

Researchers have documented the power of language in shaping thoughts and actions. Just a few words from someone can make the difference in the beliefs that people articulate. At an East Coast university, there was a publicized incident of hate mail sent to an African American student. In a study at that institution, researchers randomly stopped students walking across campus and asked them what they thought of the occurrence. Before the student could respond, a research partner impersonating another student would come up and answer with a response like, "Well, he must have done something to deserve it." As you might expect, the first student's response was more often than not just like the student impersonator's. The researchers then stopped another student and asked the same question. This time the impersonator gave an alternative response, something like, "There's no place for that kind of behavior on our campus." Again, the student being questioned replicated the impersonator's response.[1]

This classic study dramatically illustrates how potent language is in influencing people's responses to what's going on around them. Language helps frame people's views of the world, so being mindful of your choice of words is essential. Think about how the phrase "gun control" versus "gun safety" could frame political rhetoric. Frames provide the context for thinking and talking about events and ideas and focus the listeners' attention on certain aspects of the subject. "Watch your language" takes on an entirely new meaning from the times your teacher scolded you in school for using an inappropriate word. It's now about setting an example for others of how they need to think and act.

Consider, for example, the intriguing impact of language on people in experiments in which researchers told participants they were playing either the Community Game or the Wall Street Game.[2] In both scenarios, people played the same game by the same rules; the only difference was that experimenters gave the same game two different names. Of those playing the Community Game, 70 percent started out playing cooperatively and continued to do so throughout. With those told they were playing the Wall Street Game, just the opposite occurred: 70 percent did not cooperate, and the 30 percent who did cooperate stopped when they saw that others weren't cooperating. Again, remember: the name, not the game itself, was the only thing that was different!

This experiment powerfully demonstrates why you must pay close attention to the language you use. You can influence people's behavior simply by giving the task or the team a name that evokes the kind of behavior implied by the name. If you want people to act like members of a community, use language that evokes a feeling of community. If you want people to act like citizens of a village, you need to talk about them that way, not as subordinates in a hierarchy. If you want people to appreciate the rich diversity in their organizations, you need to use language that's inclusive. If you want people to be innovative, you need to use words that spark exploration, discovery, and invention.

Ask Purposeful Questions

When you ask questions, you send people on mental journeys. Your questions chart the path that people will follow, and focus their search for answers. The questions that a leader asks send messages about the emphasis of the group, and they're indicators of what is of most concern to the leader. They're one more tangible indicator of how serious you are about your espoused beliefs. Questions direct attention to the values that deserve attention and how much energy should be devoted to those values.

Questions develop people. They help people escape the trap of their mental models. They broaden people's perspectives and enlarge their responses, which enable them to take responsibility for their answers to your questions. Asking relevant questions also forces you to listen attentively to what those around you are saying, and in doing so demonstrates your respect for their ideas and opinions. If you are genuinely interested in what other people think, then you need to ask their opinion, especially before giving your own. By asking what others think, you facilitate their participation in whatever decision will ultimately be determined and consequently increase support for that decision.

Reflect on the questions you typically ask in meetings, one-on-ones, telephone calls, emails, and texts. How do they help clarify and gain commitment to shared values? What would you like each person in your group to pay attention to each day? Be intentional and purposeful about the questions you ask. The questions you routinely ask model to the group similar questions they should be asking themselves in your absence. What information do you need from the group to show that people are living by shared values and making decisions that are consistent with their values? What questions should you pose if you want people to focus on integrity, or trust, or community service, or safety, or personal responsibility?

The Ask Purposeful Questions Daily box lists a few sample questions that you could purposefully ask every day to demonstrate the importance of various shared values.

ASK PURPOSEFUL QUESTIONS DAILY

- Teamwork: What did you do today to lend a hand to someone else in your group? What's one action you took in the last week as a result of a suggestion someone else made?

- Appreciation: What did you do today to express how grateful you were for something that someone else had done? What's one action you took in the last week to call attention to the good work done by one of your teammates?

- Learning: What's one mistake you made in the last week, and what did you learn from it? What's one action you took in the last week to help someone else benefit from your experience?

- Continuous improvement: What have you done in the past week to practice so that you can strengthen your skills? What's one action you took in the last week to build on something you didn't previously know, in some new way or application?

Whatever the shared values are, come up with a set of questions that will routinely get people to reflect on those values and what they have done each day to act on them. Be clear about how you would answer any of your own questions.

Seek Feedback

Leaders should use questions not only to challenge others to connect their actions with the team's values but also to ask their colleagues and team members about how their own actions as a leader impact both the feelings of others and their performance. You will never know how you are doing if you do not ask for feedback. How can you expect to match your words and your actions if you don't get information about how aligned they are? There's substantial evidence that the best leaders are very aware of what's going on inside them as they are leading and are attuned to what's going on outside them with others. The best leaders are self-aware, and they're very socially aware. They can pick up clues that tell them whether they've done something that has enabled someone to perform at a higher level or whether they have diminished motivation.

It's your responsibility as a leader to keep asking others, "How am I doing?" If you don't ask, no one is likely to tell you. It's not always easy to get feedback. It's not generally asked for, and most people aren't used to providing it. Skills are required to do both. You can increase the likelihood that people will accept honest feedback from you if you make it easier for people to give you feedback. The most effective feedback has these characteristics: it is specific and not general, focused on behavior rather than on the individual (personality), solicited rather than imposed, timely rather than delayed, and descriptive rather than evaluative. For example, instead of asking, "How was that meeting?" you might say, "One thing I am trying to do as a leader is encourage others to contribute ideas. I tried to do that during our meeting today. How do you think it went? What could I have done differently?" Although you might not always like the feedback you get, it is the only way you can know how you're doing as a leader.

How engaged people felt as a result of how their leader "seeks to understand how his/her actions affect other people's performance" is illustrated in Figure 2.1. People's level of satisfaction, pride, and commitment (that is, engagement) is more than eight times higher when they indicate that their leaders very frequently engage in this leadership behavior compared with those who report that their leaders rarely or only once in a while seek feedback.

You invite feedback; you don't demand it. The more frequently that feedback becomes part of the conversation, the easier it will be to hear and deal with it as constructive, especially when everyone

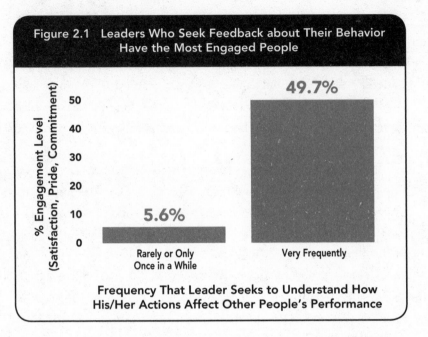

Figure 2.1   Leaders Who Seek Feedback about Their Behavior Have the Most Engaged People

involved shares similar values and aspirations. Setting the right climate for feedback is critical. Remember that there are always two sides to every story. Reviewing past behavior shouldn't be seen as an opportunity to assign blame but as a way to stay curious about what happened and what it says about how you can move forward in line with the group's goals and values. Regularly asking for feedback about "what happened" should be routine, with the focus on "What can we learn?" so that mistakes are not repeated. Keep in mind, however, that if you don't do anything with the feedback you receive, people will stop giving it to you.

A classroom project formed the basis of Alex Golkar's personal-best leadership experience. His group initially wasn't on the same page about the project, and there was a lot of infighting, with people being personally critical of each other. "I was forced to find my voice and act as an exemplar of the values that I wanted my groupmates to emulate," Alex told us. As the group found its way, developing mutual respect and dialogue, Alex asked his colleagues if they had feedback for him regarding his role in the project: "I realized that a good leader accepts feedback just as readily as he or she distributes it." Following this up, they turned to Alex and asked him for his opinions on how the group was progressing and what they could do to work even more productively together on the project. Alex indicated that when conflicts arose, "We established an informal system of feedback with one another to make sure we didn't revert back to unproductive arguments."

Often people fear the exposure and vulnerability that accompanies direct and honest feedback. Those giving the feedback can feel a bit exposed themselves and may even fear retribution or hurting someone's feelings or damaging a relationship. It's a risk, but the upside of learning and growth is far more beneficial than the downside of being nervous or embarrassed. Learning to be a better leader requires great self-awareness, and it requires making yourself vulnerable. Learning to be a better leader requires feedback. Asking for feedback signals to others your openness to doing what's right and makes it easier for others to be receptive to learning about what they can contribute to the common good.

TEACH OTHERS
TO MODEL THE VALUES

You're not the only role model in your group, team, or organization. Everyone, at all levels and in all situations, should be setting the example and aligning their words and deeds. Your role is to make sure that everyone keeps the promises that you and they have agreed on. People are watching how you hold others accountable for living the shared values and how you reconcile deviations from the chosen path. They're paying attention to what others say and do, and so should you. It's not just what *you* do that demonstrates consistency between word and deed. Every team member, partner, and colleague sends signals about what's valued. Therefore, you need to look for opportunities to teach not just by your example but also by taking on the role of teacher and coach.

Kenzie Crane was responsible for the recruitment program for sororities at a large university in the southern United States. In this capacity, she guided nearly two dozen recruitment counselors from sixteen different chapters. Their job was to recruit students and help them find the best fit in a sorority, but because all the recruitment counselors were already members of one of the sororities, it was sometimes challenging for them to be unbiased. Therefore, Kenzie not only had to model what it meant to be neutral but also needed to hold others accountable for doing the same and to teach them how to do that. One action she took each week was to get them all together and do role plays about how they would handle, in an unbiased fashion, various questions from the women being recruited. She also worked with them on changing the perception of sororities as simply social organizations to organizations focused on community engagement, intellectual enrichment, and personal growth. To make this shift credible, they would all have to be able to give examples of the positive experiences sororities offered for personal development. A top priority for Kenzie was making sure that the recruitment counselors knew how to talk about this. "This meant," she told us, "that I always and consistently used this perspective and fostered it in others, not just during the training and role-play sessions."

Exemplary student leaders also know that people learn lessons from how leaders handle the unplanned events on the schedule as well as the planned ones. They know that people learn from the stories that circulate on campus, in classes, in the dining halls, and in social media. Just as Kenzie's frequent role plays helped prepare the recruiters for any circumstance, any attitude, or any questions they might encounter, you need to find ways to show others what's expected and ensure that they hold themselves accountable. You do this by confronting critical incidents, telling stories, and finding every opportunity to reinforce the behaviors you want others to repeat.

Confront Critical Incidents

You can't plan everything about your day. Even the most disciplined leaders can't stop the intrusion of the unexpected. Stuff happens. Critical incidents—chance occurrences, particularly at a time of stress and challenge—are a natural part of the life of every leader. They offer significant moments of learning for leaders and others in the group. Critical incidents present opportunities for leaders to teach valuable lessons about appropriate norms of behavior and what really matters.

When a devastating tornado hit the town of Moore, Oklahoma, it came on fast and literally flattened most of the town, leaving death and widespread destruction in its path. Devin Murphy was working as a resident assistant at a nearby university when the tornado struck. Her first responsibility was to ensure the safety of her residents, but once the storm passed, she immediately reached out across campus to see how she could help. "When we realized the extent of the damage in nearby Moore," she said, "we wanted everyone to go into action." The university had already decided to help by opening student apartment housing to survivors of the storm. Many of the apartments were empty because most of the students had already left for the summer, but all the units needed to be cleaned and readied before families could occupy them. Devin got in touch with her friend Taylor Tyler in Student Life, and together they hatched a plan. "We knew there were a lot of students still on campus, and we knew they would want to help," Devin told us.

This is a campus with a lot of students who study the arts. People in theater know how to pull together to get ready for a show; fine arts people know how to put in the long hours and do what it takes to get their projects done; music majors are used to long hours of rehearsal. This is not a group of people afraid of hard work. We are a campus with a "pull together, work hard, and get it done" attitude, so we looked for ways to tap into that.

Devin and Taylor created a Facebook page, where they asked for volunteers to help clean apartments. In just twenty-four hours, they had enough people to clean sixty-nine apartments and make them ready for the exhausted citizens of Moore. "The support didn't stop there," Devin told us. Another student friend, Kelissa Sanders, was doing an internship at the state capital over the summer. She persuaded a popular barbecue restaurant chain there to donate food for a Memorial Day picnic for the tornado survivors. Continuing to use social media, Devin, Taylor, and the team they assembled sustained their support as the citizens of Moore rebuilt their lives. In the process of initiating and continuing assistance to the community, they exemplified the values of pulling together to get things done that they see on their campus.

Critical incidents are not always as dramatic as an EF5 tornado. They are simply those events in the lives of leaders, and the groups they are a part of, that offer the chance to improvise while still staying faithful to the script. Although these incidents can't be explicitly planned, it's useful to keep in mind that the way you handle them—how you link your actions and decisions to shared values—speaks volumes about what matters to you most. During critical moments, you must put values out on the table and in front of others so that they can return to them as a common ground for working together. In the process, you make clear how shared values compel your actions. You set an example for what it means to take actions based on values. By standing up for values, you show that having shared values requires a mutual commitment from everyone to align their words with their actions.

Tell Stories

Stories are powerful tools for teaching people about what's important and what's not, what works and what doesn't, what is and what could be. Through stories, leaders define culture, pass on lessons about shared values, and get others to work together.

Rana Korayem had just completed her undergraduate work at the American University in Cairo, Egypt. Earning her degree had not been without its trials and tribulations, but she was feeling inspired and ready to begin the next phase of her life. She was aware that many women in her country would face significant challenges in pursuing an education, and she was compelled to try to inspire those she could reach. Rana found that opportunity in a public elementary school for girls.

In Egypt, the public schools serve the poorest young people in the society. The amount of education they get is limited, and many girls stop school at an early age to marry or to care for family. Rana was determined to help the girls see there were other choices and that they could achieve anything they set their minds to. "I came from a family of means," Rana told us, "and when I began to talk about my education, you could tell that they were not relating to me. They saw me as wealthy and therefore not like them. So I told them stories to show that I was not so different from them."

Rana shared stories with them about the risks she had taken to pursue her education and follow her dreams. As she told each story, the girls began to be drawn in, thinking about times they had been scared or lonesome, and recognized Rana as someone not unlike them. "I told them about going to the United States to study and leaving my family and my country for the very first time," she said. "I told them how homesick I was and how nervous to be in a totally new place, not knowing a soul." She talked about how scary it could be to reach out to new people and how she was determined to be brave and believe in herself. She shared with them the prejudice she faced at times, and how frightening that was. She talked about how, by overcoming her fear and reaching out, she had learned so much and gained many new friends and rich experiences. She asked them about times they had been lonesome or afraid and how they had found courage. "The stories were different for each of us," Rana said, "but the human emotion is the same, and by sharing these stories we got closer."

Each week for several months, Rana visited the school and shared her stories with the young girls. "The theme was always the same," Rana said.

> The stories always had to do with how my education had shown me that the sky was the limit if you decided to learn and work hard. I wanted them to see their potential, that no matter what their circumstances, or gender, or how much or little money their family has, they could achieve anything they put their minds to if they were determined and willing to learn. I told them that my college education helped me feel strong, that as a woman I was strong and so were they.

Sharing stories is a powerful way for leaders to make values and visions come alive. The stories that Rana shared reinforced the values of self-reliance and independence that she held dear and hoped to inspire in the young girls she chose to spend time with. Storytelling offers a bridge for people to connect their experiences with your message, and it provides an opportunity to lead through example rather than to come across as lecturing or preaching.

Telling stories has another lasting benefit. It forces you to pay close attention to what is going on around you. When you can write or tell a story about someone your listeners can identify with, they are much more likely to see themselves doing the same thing. People seldom tire of hearing stories about themselves and the people they know. These stories get repeated, and the lessons of the stories spread far and wide.

Reinforce through Systems and Processes

All exemplary student leaders understand that you have to reinforce the fundamental values that are essential to building and sustaining the kind of culture you want. Think about how you recruit new group members, how you make certain selection decisions, when and how you share information, what kinds of assistance you provide, how you measure performance, how you provide rewards, and how you recognize someone when he or she does a great job. These all send signals about what you value and what you don't, and they must align with the shared values and standards that you're trying to instill.

Team sports are full of great examples of this. Consider the stickers added to the helmets of football players to indicate the number of tackles made, or the tradition for every member of the team to suit up in full uniform, even if all they'll be doing is warming the bench. Practices like these speak to the values of being part of a team and evoke a sense of group identity.

Or think about the way different organizations approach new-member recruitment and orientation. Sigma Phi Epsilon (SigEp) is one of the nation's largest fraternities and is committed to changing the negative perceptions of Greek life. Toward that end, the fraternity created the Balanced Man Program, a concept of single-tiered membership and continuous development, offering experiences that don't include some of the destructive traditions often associated with Greek organizations but that focus instead on scholarship, leadership, professional development, and life skills. Members learn to live their best lives through unique, rewarding programming tailored to their distinctive needs and designed to prepare them for the journey of life ahead. The Balanced Man Program is a striking example of student leaders' being more conscious of how they can use systems and processes within programs to reinforce their group's core values in a positive way. The program reinforces the organization's values and demonstrates a willingness to make positive changes. "Being different is hard work, but our colleges and universities need the development-focused, SigEp style of fraternity, especially now," says SigEp's CEO Brian Warren.

As many fraternities draw the glare of the media spotlight for unacceptable behavior, educators and students alike have begun to question the role of Greek life on their campuses. SigEp stands out in the Greek world for aligning its recruiting, its programs, and all its activities with the values expressed in its simple mission, "Building Balanced Men." The fraternity's actions are a striking example of ways to get student leaders to be more conscious of how they can use systems and processes to reinforce their group's core values in a positive way.

REFLECT AND ACT: SET THE EXAMPLE

As a student leader, you're always on stage. People are watching you, talking about you, and testing your credibility—whether you are aware of it or not. That's why it's essential to be mindful of how you Set the Example.

Leaders send signals in a variety of ways, and followers read those signals as indicators of what's okay and what's not okay to do. How you spend your time is the single best indicator of what's important to you, and if you invest your time wisely, you can earn significant returns. What you pay attention to, the language you use, the questions you ask, and the feedback you request are other powerful means of shaping accurate perceptions of what you value.

But it's not just what *you* do that matters. You are also measured by how consistent your followers' actions are with the group's shared values, so you must teach others how to set an example. Critical incidents—those chance occurrences in the lives of all groups, teams, and organizations—offer significant teachable moments. They provide you the opportunity to pass along lessons in real time. Critical incidents often become stories, and stories are among the most influential teaching tools you have. And remember that what gets reinforced gets done. You need to align systems and processes such that they reinforce and reward behavior that is consistent with shared values if you expect that behavior to be repeated. Keeping people informed about how they're doing also provides guardrails to keep them moving forward on the proper path.

Reflect

The second commitment of Model the Way encourages leaders to *set the example by aligning actions with shared values*. Reflect on this commitment and answer these questions:

1. What is the most important idea or lesson about exemplary leadership that you learned from this chapter?

_____

_____

_____

_____

2. What changes do you need to make in your leadership to better Set the Example?

_____

_____

_____

_____

3. In the next section, there are some suggestions on what you can do to take action on Set the Example. After you have reflected on what you learned and what you need to improve, select an action that you can take immediately to become a better leader.

_____

_____

_____

_____

Take Action

Here are some things you can do to act on your commitment to **Set the Example:**

- Be clear about your commitments and follow through on your promises.
- Examine your past experiences to help you identify and confirm the values you actually use to make choices and decisions.
- Request feedback about what impact your actions are having, and make changes and adjustments based on the information you receive.

- Ask purposeful questions that keep people focused on the values and priorities that are the most important.
- Broadcast examples of exemplary behavior through memorable stories that illustrate how people are and should be behaving.
- When you have examples of times when individuals or the entire group has strayed from the shared values, bring those instances up and talk about how you can get back to living your values.
- Reinforce, in every way you can, the behavior you want repeated.

INSPIRE
A SHARED VISION

Leaders look toward the future. They imagine what can be. They have a sense of what is uniquely possible if everyone works together for a common purpose. They also help others see the exciting future possibilities. Leaders breathe life into visions. They communicate hopes and dreams so that others clearly understand and share them as their own.

In the next two chapters, we will explore how you as a student leader must:

➤ **Envision the Future** by imagining exciting and ennobling possibilities.
➤ **Enlist Others** by appealing to shared aspirations.

INSPIRE A SHARED VISION
Reflections from the Student Leadership Practices Inventory

1. Record your overall score from the *Student Leadership Practices Inventory* for INSPIRE A SHARED VISION here: _____

2. Of the six leadership behaviors that are part of Inspire a Shared Vision, write down the statement for the one you indicated engaging in most frequently:

3. Write down the leadership behavior statement that you felt you engaged in least often:

4. On the basis of your self-assessment, complete this statement: When it comes to Inspire a Shared Vision, my areas of leadership competency are:

5. What Inspire a Shared Vision behaviors do you see as opportunities for improving and strengthening your leadership capability? Make a note of these below so that you can keep them in mind as you read this chapter and the next.

3

Commitment #3: Envision the Future

Divya Pari was in the third year of her biotechnology degree program in India when she volunteered to work as one of the editors of *Nucleo,* an annual magazine published by the Biotech Department. The magazine was created, designed, and managed by the members of Biotikos, the biotech students' association, and was very popular among the university's more than twelve hundred biotech students.

In addition to managing the various aspects of magazine content creation and editing that year, Divya initiated the sale of one hundred unsold copies by marketing them in other universities with biotech courses. In total, about six hundred copies were printed and sold. As a result of her experiences, Divya was asked to be the editor-in-chief for the next edition. "I had about eight months' time to lead a team of about thirty biotech students to accomplish this," she told us.

But Divya had a broader future in mind for the magazine than simply getting the next edition created and published in the same fashion as the last. "I saw an opportunity to serve the biotech student community both in my university and in the country at large," she said.

I envisioned a single student magazine immensely popular among all the biotech students in India, a tool that presented opportunities to foster collaboration among all biotech students and a means to raise funds for student biotech projects by generating advertising revenue. The more I saw what was possible, the more I became excited.

I could clearly see all the possibilities end to end, the people who would benefit from this project and how my unique role fit into the whole equation. Every aspect of it excited me, and I looked forward to each new day with enthusiasm. I became intensely inspired by my vision and committed to this goal.

Divya's first challenge was to convince the team of thirty students that this dream was indeed achievable. To do that, she got the team to take stock of what needed to be done to improve the reach and quality of the magazine. To improve the reach, they would have to build their network and enlist students from other universities to aid in the marketing. To improve the quality, the content of the magazine needed to be more student focused—a direction that the team would determine by surveying the magazine's student audience. In addition to soliciting donations from sponsors, selling ad space could help increase revenue. Print quality could be improved by avoiding some of the mistakes made in earlier editions. "By sketching a detailed plan in my mind," Divya said, "I mustered the necessary confidence to talk to my team and take things forward."

Divya organized a meeting of the entire team where she shared her vision for the magazine: a top-notch biotech magazine for students that would be read throughout the country. "I explained what we had done so far, what it would take to make this dream happen, and why it mattered," she told us.

Many reacted, "More than two thousand copies? Sell ad space? Sell *Nucleo* in other universities? You are crazy!"

When your group wonders if you could be crazy, it could make you doubt yourself and your plans. I managed to overcome this with heartfelt persuasive and motivational talk. I said things like, "Only in doing things never done before do we push boundaries, grow in the process, and gain new skills" and "We could either be like all other student magazine teams or do something incredible that we feel truly proud of when we look back."

Divya detailed each step of the plan and said that it was not her logic but the fact that the team "wanted to be a part of a passionate work bigger than them" that inspired them to join in her vision. "They signed up despite knowing that we did not have all the answers to all the problems because we could not foresee all the problems and challenges ourselves," Divya told us. She also believed that her sense of purpose, passion, and excitement, which the team seemed to exhibit with equal intensity, convinced them to subscribe to the new direction for the magazine. "Their sustained motivation for the next eight months ensured that they put in their very best efforts," Divya said.

When the magazine came out the following spring, the registrar and other university officials praised it; students said *Nucleo*'s quality was excellent, its price reasonable—and that it could have been priced higher! "We sold close to two thousand copies," Divya told us. "The team was beyond glad and happy. We felt truly satisfied and fulfilled."

Divya's story illustrates how a new initiative—whether a single project, a campus-wide program, or a student movement—begins with one person's imagination. Call it what you will—vision, purpose, mission, legacy, dream, aspiration, calling, or personal agenda—the intent is the same. If you are going to be an exemplary leader, you must be able to imagine the future you want for yourself and others. When you do that, and when you feel passionate about the difference you want to make, you are much more likely to take that first step forward. But if you don't care about the future or don't have the slightest clue about your hopes, dreams, and aspirations, the chance is slim that you will lead others anywhere beyond where they currently are. In fact, you may not even see the opportunity that's right in front of you.

Exemplary leaders are forward looking. They envision the future and gaze across the horizon, seeing greater opportunities to come. They imagine that noble feats are possible and that something extraordinary can emerge from the ordinary, something that benefits their entire group, team, organization, or larger community. They develop an ideal and unique image of the future for the common good.

But such a vision doesn't belong only to the leader. It must be a shared vision. Everyone has hopes, dreams, and aspirations. Everyone wants tomorrow to be better than today. Shared visions attract more people, sustain higher levels of motivation, and withstand more challenges than those that are exclusive to only a few. You need to make sure that what you can see is also something that others can see and embrace.

The first commitment of Inspire a Shared Vision is to Envision the Future for yourself and others by mastering these two essentials:

- **Imagine the possibilities**
- **Find a common purpose**

You begin with the end in mind by imagining what might be possible. Finding a common purpose inspires people to want to make that vision a reality.

IMAGINE THE POSSIBILITIES

"*The human being is the only animal that thinks about the future,*" writes Daniel Gilbert, professor of psychology at Harvard University (italics his). "The greatest achievement of the human brain is its ability to imagine objects and episodes that do not exist in the realm of the real, and it is this ability that allows us to think about the future."[1] Being forward looking is an essential characteristic that people seek in their leaders, and in our studies, it is selected by a majority of student leaders as a quality they desire in someone they would *willingly* follow. People don't generally expect this characteristic from their peers, yet our global data on leadership characteristics indicates that the quality of focusing on the future most differentiates people who are seen as leaders from those who are not.[2]

Leaders are dreamers. Leaders are idealists. Leaders are possibility thinkers. As Divya's experience illustrates, all ventures, big or small, begin with the belief that what today is merely a yearning will one day be reality. It's this belief that sustains leaders and their constituents through the difficult times. Turning exciting possibilities into an inspiring shared vision ranks near the top of the list of every leader's most important responsibilities.

When we ask people to tell us where their visions come from, they often have great difficulty in describing the process. When they do provide an answer, it's typically about a feeling, a sense, or a gut instinct. There's often no explicit logic or rationale to it. Clarifying your vision, like clarifying your values, is a process of self-exploration and self-creation. It's an intuitive, emotional process.

When Kirstyn Cole reflected on her personal-best leadership experience, she noted that "being a leader often means going out on a ledge; it means being scared sometimes. But you shouldn't be afraid to see things differently, because sometimes your perspective is the one that is necessary and enables you to lead." It can seem difficult, as a leader, to know where you want to take others. You may want to wait for the "right answer" to appear. Yet the right answer, as Kirstyn points out, may well reside within you already. Finding it requires trusting yourself and that gut feeling you have about an idea you can't seem to let go of. You just feel strongly about something, and you feel compelled to explore that sense, that intuition. Visions come from the heart. They are reflections of your fundamental beliefs and assumptions—about human nature, technology, economics, science, politics, art, and ethics.

A vision of the future is much like a literary or musical theme. It's the main message that you want to convey; it's the frequently recurring melody that you want people to remember; and whenever it's repeated, it reminds the audience of the entire work. Every leader needs a theme, something on which he or she can structure the rest of the performance. Recall that for Jacob Philpott, it was preparing low-income students for college; for Bethany Fristad, it was helping underprivileged children; for Kenzie Crane, it was enriching the experiences of women joining sororities; and for Divya Pari, it was publishing a first-rate, revenue-producing student magazine. They could see what they wanted to have happen; they saw how something that didn't exist or wasn't happening now could be possible in the future.

There are several ways you can improve your capacity to imagine exciting possibilities and to discover the central theme for *your* life, and the lives of others. You get better at imagining the future when you intentionally and consciously reflect on where you want to take others. This requires you to *reflect* on your past, *attend* to the present, *prospect* the future, and *express* your passion.

Reflect on Your Past

As contradictory as it might seem, in aiming for the future, you first need to look back into your past. Looking backward before you stare straight ahead enables you to see further into the future. Understanding the past can help you identify themes, patterns, and beliefs that both underscore why you care about certain ideals and explain why realizing those aspirations is such a high priority for you.[3] Student groups often look at those who came before them to see how things are done, and repeat them, finding that the steep learning curve of doing something new themselves is discouraging. But reflecting on the past isn't about repeating prior practices. Leaders don't settle for replicating what was done before. They look to the past as a context from which to learn and a platform from which to spring.

While a student in Ghana, Christian Gbwardo started The Leadership Lab to combat corruption in Africa. The organization was rooted in his reflections about how the dishonesty he saw around him had come to be. As he thought about how this situation had arisen, he realized that those who had come into power had "only been exposed to corruption and greed, and assumed, therefore, that is what government is meant to be."

> My father showed my family that corruption serves few and denies many. I grew up understanding that we are here to help each other, not take from each other. I realized the only way to stop this trend was to expose young people to an alternative as they become young adults, the way I was. They need to see that there is another way.

None of this is to say that the past *is* the future. That would be like trying to drive while looking only in the rearview mirror. It's just that when you look deeply into your entire life's history, even as a young person, you understand things about yourself and about your world that you cannot fully comprehend by looking at the future as a blank slate. It's difficult, if not impossible, to imagine going to a place you've never experienced, either actually or vicariously. Taking a journey into your past before exploring your future makes the trip much more meaningful.

Attend to the Present

The daily pressures, the pace of change, the complexity of problems, and the turbulence in the world can often hold your mind hostage and make you think that you have neither the time nor the energy to be future oriented. But looking to the future doesn't mean you should ignore what is going on in the present. In fact, it means you must be more mindful about it.

You must get off automatic pilot, believing that you know everything you need to know, viewing the world through preestablished categories, and not noticing what's going on around you. To increase your ability to conceive of new and creative solutions to today's problems, you must be present in the present. You must *stop, look,* and *listen.*

Christian looked around at the extracurricular programs that high school students were currently attending, and explored how he might build The Leadership Lab to have some of the same appeal. He looked at college-age programs at his university and such programs in the United States when he was studying abroad. He looked at their purpose, offerings, and popularity, took the best of what he saw for Africa, and began to build his program.

Right now, as you listen to the members of your team, club, or group, what are the hot topics of conversation? What are they saying they need and want? What are they saying should be changed? Is there anything that they have suddenly stopped talking about that seems puzzling? What does all this tell you right now about where things are going?

To be able to envision the future, you need to realize what's already going on. You need to spot the trends and patterns and appreciate both the whole and the parts. You need to be able to clearly see at the same time both the immediate situation your group is in and the greater possibilities available to them. You need to be able to see the forest *and* the trees.

Imagine the future as a jigsaw puzzle. You see the pieces, and you begin to figure out how they fit together, one by one, into a whole. Similarly, with your vision, you need to rummage through the bits and bytes of data that accumulate daily and notice how they fit together into a picture of what's ahead. Envisioning the future is not about gazing into a fortune-teller's crystal ball; it's about paying attention to the little things that are going on all around you and being able to recognize patterns that point to the future.

Prospect the Future

Even as you stop, look, and listen to messages in the present, you also need to raise your head and gaze out toward the horizon. Being forward looking is not the same as meeting the deadline for your current project. Leaders have to imagine what the future will hold. They have to be on the lookout for emerging developments—changes inside and outside their groups, such as new technologies, trends on campus, and neighborhood, national, and world news. They have to anticipate what might be coming just over the hill and around the corner. They have to prospect the future.

There is no hard-and-fast rule as to how far into the future a leader should look. In fact, in school settings, most student leaders might have a time frame that extends through the entire academic term, or perhaps as far out as graduation. Contrast this perspective with supervisors, who typically need to see at least a few years ahead; middle managers, who need to see five or more years into the future; and the most senior executives, who focus on a horizon that's ten-plus years, or even more, into the future. What's critical is not losing sight of the bigger picture while working on whatever it is you are currently doing.

The future is where the opportunity lies; leaders are constantly asking themselves "What's new?" and "What's next?" even while they may be hunkering down in the present. Like Divya, Kirstyn, and their colleagues, you need to make choices today that are consistent with where you want to be in the future and, indeed, choices that tee you up for it. Master chess players study what has happened in the past, and play the game in the present, but make moves designed to get their pieces, and their opponents' pieces, into specific places for a future victory. This is the kind of thinking characterized by great scholars, athletes, video game players, and leaders.

Visions are made real over different spans of time. It may take six months to create a new-member recruitment and orientation process. It may take a couple of years to build your new group into one of the most respected student organizations on campus, just as it may take a decade to build a company that is one of the best places to work. It may take a lifetime to make neighborhoods safe again for children to walk alone. It may take a century to restore a forest destroyed by a wildfire. It may take generations to set people free. Pursuing meaningful change is what matters, not how long it will take to make the change.

As a student leader, you have the opportunity to develop the ability to be forward looking now so that you are experienced with visioning as you move into the workplace. It can seem unimportant to think about the future when you consider the relatively brief amount of time you are in school leading others. Yet we know that leaders must be forward thinking all the time, regardless of the circumstances in which they find themselves. Even if you are leading others on a project that might last only a quarter, semester, or academic year, you can still imagine what you want things to be or look like at the end of that period. It takes practice to develop the ability to envision the future, and it's a skill you will apply throughout your life. Why not start now?

Give greater weight to thinking about what you're going to do after you complete the current problem, task, assignment, project, or program. "What's next?" should be a question you ask yourself frequently. As a student, you are living in a culture where the goals are short term; "If I can just get through this paper [or this exam, or this semester]" is often the prevailing mindset. But if you're not thinking about what's happening after the completion of your longest-term project, then you're thinking only as long term as everyone else. In other words, you're redundant! The leader's job is to think about the next project, and the one after that, and the one after that. This mindset can be very easy for student leaders to ignore. Your time in school, which may seem to last forever, is actually a very short part of your life. An important time, surely, but short in the context of a whole lifetime. It is imperative to create time and space to think about the next things in your life, whether for your immediate school experience or those yet to come in your life beyond school.

Whether it's through reading about trends, attending guest lectures on campus, talking with others outside your campus about issues they face, listening to international news sources, reading a variety of blogs, or watching different types of TED Talks, a significant part of being a leader is developing a deep understanding of where things are going. Those who willingly follow you expect you to have that understanding. You need to spend more of today thinking more about tomorrow if your future is going to be an improvement over the present. And throughout the process of reflecting on your past, attending to the present, and prospecting the future, you also need to keep in touch with what moves you, what you care about, and where your passion lies.

Express Your Passion

Passion goes hand in hand with attention. No one can imagine possibilities when they don't feel passionate about what they're doing. Envisioning the future requires you to connect with your deepest feelings. You have to find something that's so important that you're willing to put in the time, suffer the inevitable setbacks, and make the necessary sacrifices. Everyone has concerns, desires, questions, propositions, arguments, hopes, and dreams—core issues that can help them organize their aspirations and actions. And everyone has a few things that are much more important to them than other things. Whatever yours are, you need to be able to name them so that you can talk about them with others. You have to step back and ask yourself, "What is my burning passion? What gets me up in the morning? What's grabbed hold of me and won't let go?"

This is exactly the thinking you should use to determine what you want to get involved in. Rather than joining groups or seeking experiences because you think it "looks good on your résumé," you should be looking for pursuits you feel passionate about. Leaders want to do something significant, to accomplish something that no one else has yet achieved. What that something is—your sense of meaning and purpose—has to come from within. No one can impose a self-motivating vision on you. That's why, just as we said about values, you must first clarify your image of the future before you can expect to enlist others in a shared vision. As JD Scharffenberger told us about his experience as captain of the baseball team:

> I realized that the easiest way to inspire my teammates was to truly embrace and show my passion for the game. I believe when others saw my dedication toward the future that they were also intrigued by what we could accomplish. They would not have been so inspired if I didn't openly show my excitement on a day-to-day basis.

Researchers in human motivation have long talked about two kinds of motivation—extrinsic and intrinsic.[4] People do things either because of external controls—the possibility of a tangible reward if they succeed or punishment if they don't—or because of an internal desire. People do something because they feel forced or because they want to. People do something to please others or to please themselves. It's no surprise that intrinsic motivators are more likely to produce extraordinary results. The research is very clear on this subject: external motivation is likely to create conditions of compliance or defiance; self-motivation generates commitment and far superior results. There's even an added bonus. People who are self-motivated will keep working toward a result even if there's no reward.[5] You've probably seen examples of this in sports. Even when it's obvious they will lose the game, team members continue to play their hearts out because they are internally motivated. People who are externally driven are likely to stop trying once the rewards or punishments are removed.[6]

Exemplary student leaders have a passion for something other than their personal fame and fortune. They care about making a difference. If you don't care deeply for and about something, how can you expect others to feel any sense of conviction? How can you expect others to feel passion if you're not energized and excited? How can you expect others to suffer through the long hours, hard work, absences from home, and personal sacrifices if you're not similarly committed? When Christine Mielke was asked to describe how she launched Temptalia, now one of the most popular beauty blogs on the web, with over one million unique visitors each month, she replied:

> My career—if you can really call it that; I think I have way too much fun for it to be a career!—began as a hobby, so it was and still is a very organic process. I just started doing something that I loved and was interested in, and by staying dedicated to it and finding ways to make it better, it ended up being much more successful than I ever thought possible.

And if you ask her if she ever gets tired of blogging several times each day, she'll say, "Nope. I just remember why I blog and who I blog for—the readers—and that I never want to let them down!" Christine feels passionately that "every person deserves to feel beautiful and confident from the inside out and free to express themselves," and her passion not only energizes her but inspires others to share this same vision.

When you feel your passion, as Christine clearly does, you know you are on to something meaningful and significant. Your enthusiasm and drive spread to others. Finding something you truly believe in is the key to articulating a vision in the first place. Once you're in touch with this inner feeling, you can look and think beyond the constraints of your current role and view the possibilities available in the future.

FIND A COMMON PURPOSE

Much too often it is assumed that leaders have the sole responsibility to be the visionaries. After all, if focusing on the future sets leaders apart, it's understandable that people would get the feeling that it's the leader's job to embark alone on a vision quest to discover the future of their organization.

This is *not* what people expect. Yes, leaders are expected to be forward looking, but they aren't expected to impose their vision of the future on others. People want to hear more than just the *leader's* vision. They want to hear about how *their* visions and aspirations will come true, how their own hopes and dreams will be fulfilled. They want to see themselves in the picture of the future that the leader is painting. The crucial task for leaders is inspiring a *shared* vision, not selling their personal view of the world. What this requires is finding common ground among the people who will implement the vision. People in the group want to feel part of the process.[7]

Jade Orth began learning about leadership back in middle school. She believes that the lessons she learned then, about giving back, drive what is important to her today. Her earlier experiences helped her define a vision for an event she initiated with a small group of students on her college campus to give something back to their community: a Veterans Day ceremony to recognize local veterans. Jade had several family members who served in the military, and she first brought others along in realizing her vision by sharing with the group why she felt so strongly that it was important to have such a ceremony. Nothing was being done in Jade's college town to honor the substantial number of veterans there who had sacrificed much and gotten very little recognition and appreciation in return. In talking with the people around campus who she thought could help make the Veterans Day observance a reality, Jade shared her vision of making the ceremony an annual event. A group of supporters formed around this kernel of an idea, and people started to share their thoughts about how to sustain the program. Some of the ideas didn't work out and others did, but the group kept talking through their visions. Jade knew that she couldn't just "tell" others what to do. Through this sharing and discussions, they worked to keep the focus on the things that would make the event special rather than being concerned about whose idea was being selected.

What Jade found out is something every leader must understand: nobody likes being told what to do or where to go, no matter how right it might be. People want to be a part of the process of developing a vision. The vast majority of people are just like Jade's team members. They want to walk with their leaders. They want to dream with them, invent with them, and be involved in creating their futures.

This means that you have to stop taking the view that visions come from the top down. Jade said,

> It doesn't always have to be my idea, nor should it be. The more people we have sharing ideas, the better ideas we will get. We accepted that with five or seven heads in a group, we are going to get differing or conflicting views, but we approached our conversations with a give-and-take attitude, and that worked pretty well.

You have to start engaging others in a conversation about the future instead of delivering a monologue. You can't mobilize people to willingly travel to places they don't want to go. No matter how grand the dream of an individual, if others don't see themselves in it, realizing their own hopes and desires, they won't follow freely. You must show others how they, too, will be served by the long-term vision of the future, how their specific needs can be satisfied.

Students were asked about the extent that their leaders "talked with others about how their own interests could be met by working toward a common goal." They were also asked to respond to the statement, "When working with this leader, I feel like I am making a difference around here." The relationships were striking. As shown in Figure 3.1, two-thirds of those students who indicated that their leader very frequently engaged in talking about working toward a common goal strongly agreed that they felt they were making a difference; only about one in ten felt they were making a difference when their leader rarely or only once in a while talked about how working toward a common goal would help them meet their own interests. Similar

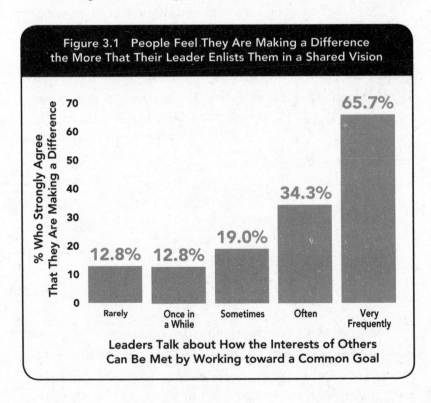

Figure 3.1 People Feel They Are Making a Difference the More That Their Leader Enlists Them in a Shared Vision

results were found in the relationship between motivation levels and the extent that leaders were able to share a long-term vision of the future.

Jade was clear in her mind about what she hoped to accomplish, and she also was careful to make sure that others either shared in her ideas or had their thoughts incorporated into the vision for the ceremony. Jade told us that there were many people involved in launching the Veterans Day celebration, from fellow students to campus officials to local veterans. She said she knew that she had to trust others and their commitment to the cause. Rather than giving orders, Jade told us,

> I regularly checked with the group to be sure we were all still on board with the project and staying true to what our vision was. If we weren't, I knew that I had a responsibility to keep us focused on our vision. I recognized that each person brought something special to the group, and I wanted to trust in and respect their ideas of where we should be going. It was about the collaboration.

Listen Deeply to Others

By knowing the members of your team, group, or organization, by listening to them, and by taking their advice, you are able to give a voice to their feelings. That's what Jade did. You're then able to stand before others and say with assurance, "Here's what I heard you say that you want for yourselves. Here's how your needs and interests will be served by all of us believing in this common cause." In a sense, leaders hold up a mirror and reflect back to others what they say they want most.

One of the challenges Jade faced was being part of two structured groups at her college: she was enrolled in a leadership class and was also a member of student government, both of which had a stake in the event. She was able to help both groups come together and collaborate by understanding how each saw its role in the program. She talked regularly with both groups about their commitment to the program and also about what they were comfortable with and interested in doing. "I wanted to make sure both groups felt as comfortable as possible and felt that they could play the role they wanted in creating the event," she said. "I did that by listening a lot to others."

You need to strengthen your ability to hear what is important to others. The outlines of any vision do not come from a crystal ball. They originate from conversations with members of your team or club. They come from interactions with other students in classes, at campus events, and over meals. They're heard in the hallways, in meetings, and on social media. When Alvin Chen helped launch his university's first international summer academic camp, there were many things that needed to be done, and most of them for the first time in this new venue. Alvin said that "listening is one of the best things any leader can do," and he and his team were, in his words, "learning as we went." His takeaway lesson was an appreciation for how "every stakeholder has a voice, and you should never underestimate or undervalue their opinions."

The best student leaders, as Alvin and Jade attest, are great listeners. They listen carefully to what other people say and how they feel. They ask purposeful (and often tough) questions, are open to ideas other than their own, and even lose arguments in favor of the common good. Through intense listening, leaders get a sense of what people want, what they value, and what they dream about. This sensitivity to others is no trivial skill. It is a truly precious human ability.

Make It a Cause for Commitment

When you listen deeply, you can find out what is meaningful to others. People stay loyal to an organization, research finds, because they like the people they work with, and they experience the work they are doing as challenging, meaningful, and purposeful.[8] When you listen with sensitivity to the aspirations of others, you discover some common themes that bring meaning to work and life. Students—like people of all ages, it turns out—want to:

- Pursue values and goals congruent with their own
- Make a significant difference in the lives of others
- Do innovative work
- Learn and develop professionally and personally
- Engage in close and positive relationships
- Determine the course of their own lives
- Feel trusted and validated

Aren't these the essence of what most leadership challenges are all about? Research in the workplace suggests that people have a strong desire to make a difference. People want to know that they have done something on this earth, that there's a purpose to their existence. Work has become a place where people pursue meaning and identity. The same holds for participating in campus organizations, teams, and clubs. The best leaders satisfy this human desire by communicating both the significance of the group's work and the important role they play in creating it. This is true even at the level of a classroom group project—is there anything beyond passing the assignment that motivates you and others in the group to put your best efforts forward? When leaders clearly communicate a shared vision of an organization, they enrich those who work on its behalf. They elevate the human spirit.

When Ella Tepper served as one of the Campus Governors at her university, the group was charged with developing a program that would inform students about what student government could offer them and how they could get involved. In the past, the publicity for these events had mostly highlighted attending for the free food and giveaways. Ella was determined to make the experience more meaningful, she told us.

> I'm a student too, and I knew that when I attended events like this, I wanted something more. I wanted to leave with more knowledge and have takeaways that were really useful. I wanted to create a way for people to talk about student government, ask questions, and learn.

Ella started by talking to the chief of staff about her ideas and then quickly went to the larger staff with a goal to create a program where students would leave with a good understanding and appreciation of what student government did for them. They quickly focused on how they could transform the event into a space for meaningful conversations about student government. This focus became the cause that the team was committed to, and they generated many good ideas about giveaways that would last and discussions that would truly inform. Together they came up with the idea of a safari. Each student got a passport to different areas where representatives from the different parts of student government were stationed to answer questions. Once the students circled through all the tables, they received a bag of school supplies.

The team, Ella explained, had come up with a way to spark significant conversations about the purpose of student government and provide participating students with useful and lasting souvenirs of the experience.

> There is no way I would have come up with all the great ideas they had, and their commitment to design something that gave the students opportunities to ask questions and have meaningful dialogue was amazing. They were all so

committed to helping students see the value of the student
government they were part of. I may have been the leader,
but they were the ones that made the event successful.

People commit to causes, not to plans. How else do you explain why people volunteer to rebuild communities ravaged by a tsunami; ride a bike from Austin, Texas, to Anchorage, Alaska, to raise money to fight cancer; or rescue people from the rubble of a collapsed building after a tornado? How else do you explain why people work 24/7 to create the next big thing when the probability of failure is very high? People are not committing to the plan in any of these cases. They are committing to something much bigger, something much more compelling than goals and milestones on a piece of paper. That's not to say that executing plans aren't important in realizing great dreams; they absolutely are. It's just to say that the plan isn't the thing that people are signing up for.

Look Forward in Times of Rapid Change

In a world that is changing at warp speed, people often ask, "How can I have a vision of what's going to happen over the next semester or year when I don't even know what's going to happen next week?" This question gets right to the heart of the role that visions play in people's lives. In this increasingly volatile, uncertain, complex, and ambiguous (VUCA) world, visions are even more important to human survival and success than when times are calm, predictable, simple, and clear.

Think about it this way. Imagine you're driving along the Pacific Coast Highway heading south from San Francisco on a bright, sunny day. The hills are on your left, the ocean on your right. On some curves, the cliffs plunge several hundred feet to the water. You can see for miles and miles. You're cruising along at the speed limit, one hand on the wheel, tunes blaring, and not a care in the world. Suddenly, without warning, you come around a bend in the road, and there's a blanket of fog as thick as you've ever seen. What do you do?

We've asked this question many, many times, and here are some of the things people say:

- I slow way down.
- I turn my lights on.
- I tighten my grip on the steering wheel with both hands.
- I tense up.
- I sit up straight or even lean forward.
- I turn the music off.

Then you go around the next curve in the road, the fog lifts, and it's clear again. What do you do? Sit back and relax, speed up, turn the lights off, put the music back on, and enjoy the scenery.

This analogy illustrates the importance of clarity of vision. Are you able to go faster when it's foggy or when it's clear? How fast can you drive in the fog without risking your own or other people's lives? How comfortable are you riding in a car with someone who drives fast in the fog? The answers are obvious, aren't they? You're better able to go fast when your vision is clear. You're better able to anticipate the curves and bumps in the road when you can see ahead. No doubt, there are times in your life when you find yourself, metaphorically speaking, driving in the fog. When this happens, you get nervous and unsure of what's ahead. You slow down. But as the way becomes clearer, eventually you're able to speed up and continue forward along the path.

A very important part of a leader's job is to clear away the fog so that people can see further ahead, anticipate what might be coming in their direction, and watch out for potential hazards along the road.

Simply put, to become a leader you must be able to envision the future. The speed of change doesn't alter this fundamental truth. People want to follow only those who can see beyond today's problems and visualize a brighter tomorrow.

REFLECT AND ACT: ENVISION THE FUTURE

The most important role of vision is to focus people's energy. To enable everyone to see more clearly what's ahead, you must have and convey an exciting, unique, and meaningful vision of the future. The path to clarity of vision begins by reflecting on the past, moves to attending to the present, and then involves prospecting the future. The guidance system along this path is your passions—the ideals that you care about most deeply.

Although you must be clear about your vision before you can expect others to follow, you also need to keep in mind that you can't lead others to places they don't want to go. If the vision is going to attract more than just a few people, it must appeal to all who have a stake in it. Only *shared* visions have the magnetic power to sustain commitment over time, to keep people connected to the group or the cause. Listen to all the voices; listen for people's hopes, dreams, and aspirations.

A shared vision also needs to focus everyone on the future. To do that, it must be about more than a task or job. It needs to be about a cause, something meaningful, and something that makes a difference in people's lives. Whether you're leading a community project, a fraternity or sorority chapter, an athletic team, a campus-wide event, or a national student movement, a shared vision sets the agenda and gives direction and purpose to all those involved.

Reflect

The first commitment of Inspire a Shared Vision requires leaders to *envision the future by imagining exciting and ennobling possibilities.* Reflect on this commitment and answer these questions:

1. What is the most important idea or lesson about exemplary leadership that you learned from this chapter?

   _____

   _____

   _____

   _____

2. What changes do you need to make in your leadership to better Envision the Future?

   _____

   _____

   _____

   _____

3. In the next section, there are some suggestions on what you can do to take action on Envision the Future. After you have reflected on what you learned and what you need to improve, select an action that you can take immediately to become a better leader.

   _____

   _____

_____

_____

Take Action

Here are some things you can do to follow through on your commitment to **Envision the Future:**

- Determine what you most care about, what drives you, and where your passions lie.
- When you think about all the things you want to accomplish, can you say *why* these are so important to you? What makes these aspirations meaningful to you, and to others?
- Identify the important issues and causes about which you and your peers are most concerned. Be curious about what others feel is important to their future.
- When you talk to others in your group about their hopes, dreams, and aspirations for the future, look for patterns and themes in their responses. Determine what their dreams have in common and how they align with your vision for the group.
- Frame what you and others are doing so that it becomes a cause or calling rather than just an assignment, project, or event.
- Come up with ways you can involve others in creating what could be possible; don't make it a process in which you give out orders about what to do.

4

Commitment #4: Enlist Others

There had never been a competitive cheerleading squad at Anita Lim's high school. Instead, there had been a group of cheerleaders, Anita said, "in which a few select individuals had all the power and the rest of the team was not given a voice. There were no consistent processes or scheduled practices, and these same people also choreographed the routine performances, without input from the rest of the team." All of this changed when the school brought a professional coach on board. She took an inexperienced team with nothing in common and transformed it into a unit that worked together to win competitions and establish a name for itself. This coach was able to "bring everyone together in a collaborative way," Anita said. "Our team become extraordinary through the power of sharing her vision and by seeking input from everyone in the group."

Prior to the coach's arrival, the team had never gone to a competition. The old squad had just done its cheerleading on the sidelines of football or basketball games. When the coach arrived, she made it clear to the team that they were capable of much more than waving pom-poms at games and pep rallies. She brought up the idea of participating in a cheer competition. "We were all surprised by the notion," Anita said. "Some of us did not even realize that such a thing existed."

The coach countered a lot of initial hesitation—"What would this cost?" and "How many additional hours would this require?"—by being "transparent in her answers." The coach explained how they would all have to commit to working harder each day in practicing their routines, perfecting their movements, and strengthening their stunts. But, added the coach, the payoff could be huge if they were to succeed in being one of the top finalists. Doing so would make a statement about their dedication and ability, and gain respect from their fellow students. This point in particular struck home because cheerleading was still looked down on as a "girly" activity that did not require a lot of brainpower or athletic ability. The school didn't classify it as a sport, and most people, faculty and students alike, didn't take it seriously. Against these odds, the coach aligned her players so that they could find a common purpose as a team. "We imagined the exciting possibilities," said Anita, "by visually putting ourselves at the forefront of a competition and taking home the prize, gaining the respect of our school and classmates as a legitimate group of athletes. By integrating our goals into her vision of coaching a reputable team, the coach was able to get everyone to stand behind her cause."

As their practice sessions became longer and more arduous, the coach constantly reminded them to keep their eyes on the prize, and she would often ask them to imagine a photograph of the team holding a trophy and being commended in front of the entire student body. She told them stories about her experiences in competitions and how rewarding it felt when she performed in front of the judges. According to Anita, "The rush that she described was exhilarating for us to hear and kept us motivated throughout the next several months." When competition day came, excitement filled the air. The team couldn't wait to get on the stage and show the judges what they had worked so hard for.

> Every person gave 100 percent during the performance, and we fed off each other's energy to put forth our best effort. And it paid off. Out of all the contestants that day, we placed first! No words can describe the emotion that rolled over us as we realized we had not only achieved but had surpassed our own expectations of ourselves.
>
> A few weeks after we took home the grand trophy, our school had its annual end-of-the-year sports awards ceremony. The cheerleading squad was recognized for the first time for its achievements the past year. Over the next few years, as the squad grew and continued to participate in competitions, this activity was officially acknowledged as a sport, and the group of young women who participated in cheerleading became identified as athletes.

None of this would have been possible had their coach not been able to get the team to believe that they could do something that had never been done before. If they signed on for the hard work required, made the commitment to their common purpose, and stood by one another, they would be more successful (regardless, by the way, of where they placed in the competition). "What I learned from this leader," Anita reflected, "is that you must genuinely have a passion for something and be able to convey that passion to your audience in order for them to buy into your idea. It can be very daunting at first when you are faced with pushback, but if you truly believe that your vision is worthwhile, you will be relentless in persuading people to join in your cause."

Fast-forward a few years, and in her current managerial role, Anita has found that those lessons from the cheerleading coach still hold true:

> I must get every team member's buy-in on policies and processes that I implement company-wide. Most people tend to resist change, especially if it pushes them out of their comfort zone. I counteract this pushback by only implementing the processes that I genuinely believe will be of value to the company and the team members in the long run. When I have conversations with people to get their support, I convey my passion. I tie my personal goals in with that of the team to get them to realize why supporting this cause will make their jobs easier and more efficient. I describe to them what I am trying to accomplish so that they can see what the vision is and get behind it.

In the personal-best leadership cases we collected, people talked about the need to get everyone on board with a vision and to Enlist Others in a dream, just as Anita and her coach did. They talked about communicating and building support for their project, idea, or cause. These leaders knew that to make extraordinary things happen, everyone had to believe fervently in a common purpose and commit to it.

Part of the commitment to Enlist Others is building common ground on which everyone can stand. Equally important is the emotion that leaders express for the vision. Our research shows that in addition to expecting leaders to be forward looking, people want their leaders to be *inspiring*. Leaders need to tap into people's vast reserves of energy and excitement to sustain their commitment to a distant dream. Leaders are an important source of that energy because folks aren't going to follow someone who's only mildly enthusiastic. Students actively support those leaders who are *wildly* enthusiastic about what is being pursued.

Whether you're trying to mobilize a crowd in the grandstand or one person with whom you're sharing a class assignment with, to Enlist Others you must act on these two essentials:

- **Appeal to common ideals**
- **Animate the vision**

The commitment to Enlist Others is all about igniting passion for a purpose and moving people to persist against great odds. To make extraordinary things happen, you need to go beyond reason, engaging the hearts as well as the minds of the people in your group. Start by understanding their strongest yearnings for something meaningful and significant.

APPEAL TO COMMON IDEALS

In every personal-best case, student leaders talked about ideals. They expressed a desire to make dramatic changes in the business-as-usual of their environment. They reached for something big, something meaningful and significant, something never done before; and this was true even in what might have been the most mundane of classroom assignments.

Visions are about hopes, dreams, and aspirations. They're about the strong desire to achieve something beyond good, something great and extraordinary. They're ambitious. They're expressions of optimism. Can you imagine a student enlisting others in a cause by saying, "I'd like you to join me in doing the ordinary, doing what everyone else is doing"? Not likely. Visions stretch people to imagine exciting possibilities for their cause, whether it's simply a new approach to an old event or a huge change such as Anita Lim's coach's focus on transforming cheerleading into a competitive, well-respected sport.

When you communicate your vision of the future to your group, you need to talk about how they're going to make a difference, how they're going to have a positive impact on people and events. You need to show them how their long-term desires can be realized by enlisting in a common vision. You need to speak to the higher meaning and purpose of your group's work. You need to describe a compelling image of what the future could be like when people join in a common cause. Consider what 5'1" Cameron McCarthy, captain of her college boxing team and National Collegiate Boxing Association champion, says about recruiting people for the sport:

> I convince people to join the team because of what it does for their confidence and how it enables them to stand out after college. I also explain that it is not easy and it takes courage. Those who are looking for a challenge or a great stress relief have stayed.

Connect to What's Meaningful to Others

Exemplary student leaders don't impose their visions of the future on people; they liberate the vision that's already stirring within them. They awaken dreams, breathe life into them, and arouse the belief that people can achieve something important. When they communicate a shared vision, they bring these ideals into the conversation. What truly pulls people forward, especially in difficult times, is the possibility that what they are doing can make a real difference. People want to know that what they do matters.

Jen Marsh described the time when she volunteered for a special program that helped children learn how to read. On the first day she arrived, as she took a seat in a child-size chair, a little boy came up to her and asked, "Why are you wasting your summer here?" She was initially surprised by the question, but then realized that he just wanted to see if she was going to stay. "I replied by telling him how I genuinely wanted to be there and that I would be his reading buddy for the day. With this reply, his eyes got bigger, and he even let out a tiny smile." Jen realized,

> There was no way I was going to get these second and third graders to read because I wanted them to; instead it was something that I had to help them want to accomplish on their own. I had to get the kids excited about reading and show them how important this achievement would be later in their lives. All the children saw reading as a difficult chore, and they would try to avoid it as much as possible. They didn't know how to read, and it is difficult to persuade someone to partake in an activity that requires dedication. Originally, I got frustrated with the kids and they got on my nerves, but I soon realized that it would take time for my vision to become our vision. I needed to better understand the minds of the children, and this could only be perfected by seeing eye-to-eye with them.

Leaders help others see that what they are doing is bigger than they are and bigger, even, than their instructor, classroom group, school team, or institution anticipates. Their work can be something noble, something that lifts them all up. Leaders believe that the work they're doing makes a difference in other people's lives, that it is work done for the greater good, and that it helps make things better for others. "I will never forget my excitement," recalled Jen, "when I witnessed the young child I met on the first day finish an entire book all by himself."

> When he looked into my eyes and saw how happy I was for him, it finally clicked in him why I had come to volunteer in his school. He could instantly perceive how proud I was, and

in return he extended his learning to his classmates. After we had come together in our common vision, the leading was put into the hands of the students. Collectively we had turned a once impossible chore into a new and enjoyable activity.

Take Pride in Being Unique

Exemplary student leaders also communicate what makes their group, organization, club, team, or project stand out and rise above all others. Compelling visions differentiate, setting "us" apart from "them" in ways that attract and retain group members. People often leave a group because they don't know or understand how the group is different from others that may do similar things. There's no advantage in being just like everybody else. When people understand how they're truly distinctive and how they stand out in the crowd, they're a lot more eager to voluntarily sign up and invest their energies.

Leaders get people excited about signing on to a group's vision by making certain that everyone involved feels that what they do is unique and believes that they play a crucial role, regardless of titles or specific task responsibilities. Feeling special fosters a sense of pride. It boosts the self-respect and self-esteem of everyone associated with the group. When people are proud to be part of your group's effort and serve its purpose, and when they feel that what they are doing is meaningful, they become enthusiastic ambassadors to the outside world. When people are proud to be part of the team, they are more loyal and more likely to recruit their friends to be part of it as well. When the campus and community are proud to have you as a member, they're going to do everything they can to make you feel welcome.

David Chan Tar Wei knows a lot about promoting individual and collective pride. His college decided to start a new system of "houses" intended to spark greater school spirit and add more diversity to school life. David worked with a committee tasked with exploring various ideas for setting the new house groups apart from one another and thereby fostering greater house unity and pride. "The houses originally did not have unique ways to represent themselves," he explained, "and we felt strongly that things like house shirts and house crests could be used and accepted as formal symbols of identification." David and his committee went on to incorporate house outfits, insignia, and other distinguishing devices into almost every school event, from orientation to Teachers' Day, to "create the house vibrancy and culture that we sought."

David's experience shows how feeling distinctive also makes it possible for smaller groups to have their own visions and still serve a larger, collective vision. Although every subgroup within a larger organization—be it a religious institution, school, or volunteer association—must be aligned with the overall vision, each can express its distinguishing purpose within the larger whole.

Align Your Dream with the People's Dream

When Tram Dao started telling us about her leadership experiences, she began by saying, "It is easier for us to share our vision with others when we think about common goals, not our self-interests." With experience as a tutor at her community college, she was asked to train the new tutors for the upcoming semester. She didn't think that this would be so difficult; after all, she would simply show them how she explained the materials to students and answered their questions. When those tutors went to work with students, however, they found that they weren't ready to help the students needing assistance.

Seeing their difficulties, Tram wondered what she had done incorrectly as a mentor and leader. She thought deeply about why she had become a tutor, which was to help students who were having difficulties and to give back and contribute to the school. "I imagined students returning after their tests telling me that they did a good job, that they were able to understand and complete the test with confidence. That I had made a difference."

Tram imagined that the new tutors might share those same beliefs, so she got them all together and asked them why they had become a tutor. She found that "their reasons were similar to mine."

> This was a common purpose for all of us, and I shared my vision with them, wanting them to have the image of successful tutees in their minds. They didn't have to follow my methods if it didn't work for them. I urged them to be creative and follow the methods that were most suitable to their situations. The dream was not about us being great but about how the people we were tutoring would be great, and do well in their exams. We were ultimately able to achieve this desired result by working toward a shared vision.

What is it that gets people engaged? How do student leaders like Tram learn how to appeal to people's ideals, move their souls, and uplift their spirits? How can leaders learn to draw people in and speak to their values and visions, to their dreams? There is no better place to look for an answer than to the late Reverend Dr. Martin Luther King Jr., whose "I Have a Dream" speech tops the list of the best American public addresses of the twentieth century. This speech is replayed on the US national holiday marking his birthday, and young and old alike are reminded of the power of a clear and uplifting vision of the future. If you have never listened closely to Dr. King's stirring words, take a few moments to do so.[1]

Imagine that you are there on that hot and humid day—August 28, 1963—when on the steps of the Lincoln Memorial in Washington, DC, before a throng of 250,000, Martin Luther King Jr. proclaimed his dream to the world. Imagine that you're listening to Dr. King as thousands around you clap and applaud and cry out. Pretend you are a reporter trying to understand why this speech is so powerful and how Dr. King moves so many people.

We've asked thousands of people over the years to do just that: listen to his remarks and then tell us what they heard, how they felt, and why they thought this speech remains so moving today.[2] Here's a sampling of their observations:

- He appealed to common interests. Most anyone in the audience or those who heard this speech afterward could find something personal to which they could relate.
- He talked about traditional values of family, church, and country.
- He used a lot of images and word pictures that the audience could relate to.
- His references were credible. It's hard to argue against the Constitution or the Bible.
- It was personal. He mentioned his own children, as well as struggling.
- He included everybody—for example, different parts of the country, all ages, and major religions.
- He used a lot of repetition—for example, saying "I have a dream" and "Let freedom ring" several times.
- He focused on a theme, but expressed it in different ways.
- He was positive and hopeful, but also realistic.
- He shifted his focus from "I" to "we."
- He spoke with genuine emotion and passion.

These reflections reveal the key to success in enlisting others. To get others excited about your dream, you need to speak about meaning and purpose. You need to *show them* how to realize *their* dreams. You need to connect your message to their values, their aspirations, their experiences, and their own lives. You need to show them that it's not about you but about them and their needs and the communities to which they belong. You need to make the connection between an inspiring vision of the future and the personal aspirations and passions of the people you are addressing. You need to personally believe in what you are saying and have evidence of your commitment. To enlist others, you need to bring the vision to life.

Admittedly, you are not a Martin Luther King. Well, neither is Sheri Lee. As the editor of her school's yearbook, she needed to get everyone on the same page, motivating them to work hard all year long, generally producing smaller pieces of the overall project that would disappear into the yearbook a few days after the work was completed. Think about how many of the same techniques utilized by Dr. King are employed by Sheri in speaking with her peers on the yearbook staff:

> Yearbook is something that I enjoy because we are making something that will be treasured for the rest of our lives. We are in charge of preserving all the memories that occur during this school year, and it is up to us to make sure that there is a yearbook to hand out at the end of the year.
>
> Just think, every time that you look at this year's yearbook, you can see that all your hard work paid off in the pages that you created. When you are older, you can look back at it and be proud that you were responsible for creating something so unique.

Think about how you can communicate using techniques that make a leader's message both memorable and inspirational.

ANIMATE THE VISION

Part of motivating others is appealing to their ideals. Another part is animating the vision and breathing life into it. To enlist others, you have to help them *see* and *feel* how they are aligned with the vision. You have to paint a compelling picture of the future, one that enables your group to experience what it would be like to live and work in an exciting and uplifting future. That's the only way they'll become sufficiently motivated to commit their individual energies to realizing the vision.

Many people don't see themselves as personally uplifting, and certainly few students get much encouragement for behaving this way in most organizations. Despite the acknowledged potency of clearly communicated and compelling visions, our research finds more people uncomfortable with the leadership practice of Inspire a Shared Vision than with any of the other four leadership practices. Most of their discomfort comes from having to express their emotions. You, like many people, may find it hard to convey intense emotions, but don't be too quick to discount your capacity to do it.

People's perception of themselves as uninspiring is in sharp contrast to their performance when they talk about their personal-best leadership experiences or when they talk about their ideal futures—or even when they talk about a vacation they just took or an exciting sports event they just won or witnessed. When relating extraordinary achievements or major successes, people are nearly always emotionally expressive. When they are talking about intense desires for a better future, expressiveness tends to come naturally. When they feel passionate about something, they let their emotions show.

Most people attribute something mystical to the process of being inspirational. They seem to see it as supernatural, as a grace or charm that other people possess, but certainly not them. This assumption inhibits people far more than any lack of natural talent for being inspirational. It's not necessary to be a charismatic person to Inspire a Shared Vision. It is necessary, however, to *believe,* and to develop the essential skills to transmit your belief. If you're going to lead, you must recognize that your enthusiasm and expressiveness are your strongest allies in your efforts to generate commitment in others. Don't underestimate your talents.

Areany Tolentino wouldn't necessarily describe herself as a rousing orator—at least not until the opportunity presented itself. She put together a seminar for the student senators at her university to talk about civil discourse. It was a forum where ideas could be shared outside the scope of hostility that had developed from an ongoing debate about a club that was under scrutiny for the controversies raised by its national organization. Before they broke into small groups, Areany gave a presentation that started out with a bit of her background in student government, from initially being elected as a class senator freshman year, to the projects she had worked on, to the members she worked with. She explained that sharing this background gave her peers a better idea of where she was coming from and allowed her to establish a sense of trust with the other thirty people in the room, some with whom she rarely had a one-on-one conversation.

> I wanted them to know that I was not a random senior who thought I could just tell them what to do based on what I believed, but that I was an equal player on the same field who too had noticed something wrong and wanted our senate to rework our way up to fix it. I believe the picture that I created was critical for their cooperation in the deep conversations that followed.

Use Symbolic Language

Leaders understand the power of symbolic language to communicate a shared identity and give life to visions. They use metaphors and analogies. They give examples, tell stories, and relate anecdotes. They draw word pictures, and they offer quotations and recite slogans. They enable the group to imagine the possibilities—to hear them, to sense them, to recognize them.

Think about just one type of symbolic language: metaphor. Metaphors are everywhere—there are art metaphors, game and sports metaphors, war metaphors, science fiction metaphors, machine metaphors, and religious or spiritual metaphors. They influence what and how people think, what they imagine and invent, what they eat and drink, what they consume and purchase, whom they vote for and rally behind. Learning to use these figures of speech greatly enhances your ability to enlist others in a common vision of the future. For example, you can influence people's behavior simply by giving the task or the team a name that evokes the kind of behavior it implies.

Notice how, as mentioned in an earlier chapter, fraternities or sororities use words like *brothers* and *sisters,* and not simply *members,* to evoke the notion of being closely connected, much like members of a family. If you want people to act like a community, use language that evokes a feeling of community—words like *fellowship, neighborhood,* and *citizens,* for example. If you want them to act like Spiderman, "sticking" with things and working for the good of all, use language that cues those images. Words like these show you why paying close attention to the language you choose to use will serve you well as a leader.

When he was a senior, Robert Quiles was hired as an assistant resident director in a large residence hall. Move-in weekend for the first-year students was one of the most important events. To get his staff mates on board for the arduous work that came with move-in preparation, Robert shared this vision about how the residence hall "was to be more than just a room to sleep in. We wanted these residents to feel safe and truly part of a new community." The challenge now was to view this process not merely as checking residents into a simple "dorm" but rather as a larger welcoming. Instead of simply going about the standard procedures, the residence hall staff were inspired to make this a bigger, more personal moment. Each resident was welcomed to the building with the phrase "welcome home" to signify how the staff aimed to treat this extraordinary living experience. In addition to calling the building home, the staff also used the language of community when referring to the collective residents.

Create Images of the Future

Visions are images in the mind; they are impressions and representations. They become real as leaders express those images in concrete terms to others. Just as architects make drawings and engineers build models, leaders find ways of giving expression to collective hopes for the future.

When talking about the future, people typically use terms such as *foresight, focus, forecasts, future scenarios, points of view,* and *perspectives.* What all these expressions have in common is that they are visual references. The word *vision* itself has at its root the verb "to see." Vision statements, then, are not statements at all. They are pictures—word pictures. They are images of the future. For people to share a vision, they must be able to see it in the mind's eye.

In our classes and workshops, we often illustrate the power of images with this simple exercise. We ask people to shout out the first thing that comes to mind when they hear the words *Paris, France.* The replies that pop out—the Eiffel Tower, the Louvre, the Arc de Triomphe, the Seine, Notre Dame, delicious food, wine, romance—are all images of real places and real sensations. No one calls out the square kilometers, population, or gross domestic product of Paris. Why? Because most of what we recall about important places or events are those things associated with our senses—sights, sounds, tastes, smells, tactile sensations, and emotions.

So, what does this mean for leaders? It means that to enlist others and Inspire a Shared Vision, you must be able to draw on the very natural mental process of creating images. When you speak about the future, you need to create pictures with words so that others form a mental image of what things will be like when you are at the end of the journey. When talking about going places you've never been, you have to be able to imagine what they'll look like. You have to picture the possibilities to make them come alive.

Making the possibilities come alive is precisely what David Mullenburg did when he recruited all the members of his senior class to go on an overnight backpacking trip. When we asked how he got people to sign up, David replied, "I told stories of past camping trips I had been on, how great they were, and painted a picture of how much fun we would all have." This is often the way that the rowing or crew team on campus will convince people to join up: "Imagine how great it will be to get up in the morning before everyone else does, before the sun even rises, get out on a lake, and start rowing with your friends. If you can see this as fun, exciting, and rewarding, then you're a perfect candidate for the crew team!"

Getting people to see a common future does not require some special power. Everyone possesses this ability. You do it every time you take a vacation, go on a road trip, or have a special celebration and share the photos with your friends. If you doubt your ability to paint word pictures, try this exercise. Sit down with a few close friends and tell them about one of your favorite vacations. Describe the people you saw and met, the sights and sounds of the places you went, the smells and tastes of the food you ate. Show them photos or videos if you have them. Observe their reactions—and your own. What's that experience like? We've done this activity many times, and people always report feeling energized and passionate. Those hearing about a place for the first time usually say something like, "After listening to you, I'd like to go there someday myself."

Practice Positive Communication

To foster team spirit, breed optimism, promote resilience, and renew faith and confidence, leaders look on the bright side. They keep hope alive. They strengthen people's belief that life's struggles will produce a positive and more promising future. Students reported feeling most highly productive in direct proportion to how frequently they experienced their leaders as "upbeat and positive when talking about what we can accomplish," as shown in Figure 4.1. There was a threefold gap in the productivity ratings between those interacting with the least and most positive leaders.

Alyssa Giagliani ran track and cross-country on the varsity team in her freshman year and remembers talking with the freshman team

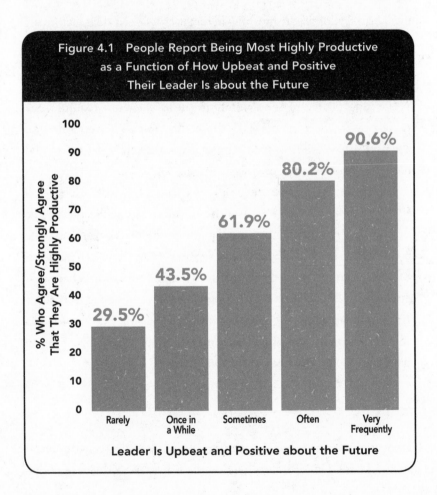

Figure 4.1   People Report Being Most Highly Productive as a Function of How Upbeat and Positive Their Leader Is about the Future

at the end of their first season. They had won the freshman division title race, and Alyssa asked them what they saw in their future. They said they didn't think they had a future in running; winning the title had probably just been a fluke.

The freshmen then asked Alyssa the same question right back, and she told them, "I see a great potential: the potential to be the first women's team in the history of our school to make the championships and win league titles and a division title." These aspirations had never crossed her teammates' minds, Alyssa told us. "I could see that they were enlightened by this idea and that they were willing to put in the hard work to attain those lofty goals."

Fast-forward to the varsity team's senior year. Alyssa lies in a hospital bed after a life-threatening auto accident. Her teammates tell her they don't have the heart to finish the season without her. Alyssa is flabbergasted and tells her team in no uncertain terms what she thinks about their quitting. She says that if they finish the season, she will walk with them to the starting line the day of the championship race. "This way of getting my point across made my teammates realize that I was passionate about the team finishing what we started," she told us. That team didn't quit. Alyssa joined her teammates at the starting line, and they went on to become the first women's cross-country team in the school's history to advance to the championship meet and to win a major title.

People look for leaders who demonstrate an enthusiastic, genuine belief in the capacity of others, who strengthen people's will, and who help support the needs of the group as they take on difficult tasks. They are drawn to leaders like Alyssa who express optimism for the future. People want leaders who remain passionate despite obstacles and setbacks. They want leaders with a positive, confident, can-do approach. Naysayers only stop forward progress; they do not start it. Researchers working with neural networks have documented that when people feel rebuffed or left out, the brain activates a site for registering physical pain.[3] People remember negative comments far more often, in greater detail, and with more intensity than they do encouraging words. When negative remarks become a preoccupation, a person's brain loses mental efficiency. This is all the more reason for leaders to be positive. A positive approach to life broadens people's ideas about future possibilities, and these exciting options build on each other.

Express Your Emotions

In explaining why particular leaders have a magnetic effect, people often describe them as charismatic. However, *charisma* has become such an overused and misused term that it's almost useless as a descriptor of leaders. Being charismatic is neither a magical quality nor a spiritual one. Like being "inspirational," it's mostly about how people behave.

Instead of defining charisma as a personality trait, many social scientists have investigated what people described as charismatic actually do. Individuals who are perceived to be charismatic are simply more animated than people who are not.[4] They smile more, speak faster, pronounce words more clearly, and move their heads and bodies more often. Being energetic and expressive are key descriptors of what it means to be charismatic. The old saying that enthusiasm is infectious is certainly true for leaders.

Conveying emotion has another benefit for leaders: emotions make things more memorable. By adding emotion to your words and behavior, you can increase the likelihood that people will remember what you say. Researchers have shown that "emotionally significant events create stronger, longer-lasting memories."[5] No doubt you've experienced this yourself when something emotionally significant has happened to you. The events don't even have to be real to be memorable. They can simply be stories. For example, in one experiment, researchers showed subjects in two groups a series of twelve slides. The slide presentation was accompanied by a story, one line for each slide.

For one group in the study, the narrative was quite boring; for the other, the narrative was emotionally moving. The subjects didn't know when they watched the slides that they would be tested, but two weeks later, they returned and took a test on how well they remembered the details of each slide. Although the subjects in the two groups did not differ in their memory of the first few and last few slides, they did differ significantly in the recollection of the slides in the middle. People who had listened to the emotionally arousing narrative remembered details better than the group that listened to the boring or more neutral story.[6]

If you want people to remember your message, you have to tap into their emotions; you have to arouse their feelings about the cause to which you want them to commit. Having your messages remembered requires paying attention to adding emotion to your words and your behavior. You don't need a complete narrative, and you don't need slides. Just the words themselves can be effective, as demonstrated in another laboratory experiment in which researchers asked subjects to learn to associate pairs of words. Some of the words in the pairs were used because they elicited strong emotional responses. Two weeks later, people remembered the emotionally arousing words better than they remembered the less arousing ones.[7]

What's more, showing people a concrete example is better than telling them about an abstract principle, which still leaves them on the outside looking in. For example, researchers showed that a story about a starving seven-year-old girl from Mali prompted people to donate more than twice as much money as the message that "food shortages in Malawi are affecting more than three million children in Zambia."[8]

The dramatic increase in the use of electronic technology also has an impact on the way people deliver messages. More and more people are turning to their digital devices and social media—from podcasts to webcasts, social networking to video sharing—for information and connection. Because people remember things that have strong emotional content, social media has the potential for engaging people more than do emails, memos, and PowerPoint presentations. Leadership is a performing art, and this has become even truer as new technologies hit the market. It's no longer enough to write a good script; you've also got to put on a good show. And you've got to make it a show that people will remember.

Whether it's a story, an example, or a word, you're more likely to get people to remember the key messages when you can attach them to something that triggers an emotional response. People are hardwired to pay more attention to stuff that excites them or scares them. Keep this in mind the next time you deliver any kind of presentation. It's not just the content that will make your message stick; it's also how well you tap into people's emotions. People must *feel* something to change. Thinking something isn't nearly enough to get things moving. Your job is to enable them to feel moved to change, and expressing emotions helps you do that.

Speak Genuinely

None of these suggestions about being more expressive will be of any value if you don't believe in what you're saying. If the vision is someone else's and you don't own it, you'll have a tough time enlisting others in it. If you have trouble imagining yourself living the future described in the vision, you certainly will not be able to convince others that they ought to enlist in making it a reality. If you're not excited about the possibilities, you can't expect others to be. The prerequisite to enlisting others in a shared vision is *genuineness*.

Bailey Hamm had been a member of her sorority for three years and each year had run for an officer position. Although she lost those elections to older, more experienced sisters, Bailey told us she never felt discouraged. She was committed to what her sorority stood for and was determined to find a way to continue to make the chapter better for its members. What was most important to her was to serve the women in her chapter regardless of whether she had a position or title or not.

In her senior year, she became vice president for public relations, and she aspired to enhance the image of her sorority. She felt it was important to communicate to her younger sisters, through her work and her words, both who she was and her sincere desire to serve the higher principles of their organization. She made it a point to share her personal story with the younger sorority members and explain why she believed the chapter could do great things and become stronger. Even though she had lost previous elections, she still felt that the sorority had done much for her and had the potential to make a huge difference in the sisters' lives. She explained how important she believed it was for everyone to find a way to contribute to the group.

By being genuine and speaking from the heart about her vision for the chapter, she told us, "I wanted to show the other women that the choices I made after my election experiences were going to be true to who I was and what I thought our chapter stood for." Bailey used her circumstances as an example, not to dwell on the negative, but to speak genuinely and positively in showing her sisters that they could make a difference even when things were difficult. They might not see results in the next day or the next week, Bailey told them, but success would eventually come. And through the stories and insights she shared with her sisters, Bailey found the answers for how to talk to people not affiliated with the sorority system:

> Painting a positive picture of who we are and what we could do set me up to speak to people outside the sorority with conviction about what we stood for and what we could accomplish, and it energized people.

The most believable people are the ones, like Bailey, with deep passion. There's no one more fun to be around than someone who is openly excited about the magic that can happen. There's no one more determined than someone who believes fervently in an ideal. People want their leader to be someone who is upbeat, optimistic, and positive about the future. You can be that someone! It's the only way you can get people to willingly follow you to a place they have never been before.

REFLECT AND ACT: ENLIST OTHERS

Leaders appeal to common ideals. They connect others to what is most meaningful in the shared vision. They lift people to higher levels of motivation and performance, and continuously reinforce that they can make a difference in the world. Exemplary student leaders speak to what is unique and distinctive about the groups, projects, or causes they lead, making others feel proud to be a part of something extraordinary. Exemplary leaders understand that it's not their individual view of the future that's important; it's the collective aspirations of every person that matter most.

To be sustainable over time, visions must be compelling and memorable. Leaders must breathe life into visions, animating them so that others can experience what it would be like to live and work in an ideal and unique future. They use a variety of modes of expression to make their abstract visions concrete. Through skillful use of metaphors, symbols, word pictures, positive language, and personal energy, leaders generate enthusiasm and excitement for the common vision.

Above all, leaders must be convinced of the value of the common vision and share that genuine belief with others. They must believe in what they are saying. If you don't truly believe in what you are doing or in what you want the group to do, how can you ever expect anyone else to believe in the cause or task? Authenticity is the key because people will only follow willingly if they sense that the vision is genuine.

Reflect

The second commitment of Inspire a Shared Vision is to *enlist others in a common vision by appealing to shared aspirations.* Reflect on this commitment and answer these questions:

1. What is the most important idea or lesson about exemplary leadership that you learned from this chapter?

_____

_____

_____

_____

2. What changes do you need to make in your leadership to better Enlist Others?

_____

_____

_____

_____

3. In the next section, there are some suggestions on what you can do to put Enlist Others into practice. After you have reflected on what you learned and what you need to improve, select an action that you can take immediately to become a better leader.

_____

_____

_____

_____

Take Action

Here are some things you can do to act on your commitment to **Enlist Others:**

- Clarify with the team what makes the group unique and how proud they should be about being distinctive.
- Show others why should they persevere and how their long-term interests are served by their enlisting in a common vision, even if there may be some short-term sacrifices.
- Demonstrate that you are listening to what team members are saying by bringing their thoughts and ideas into the vision for the group.
- Generate and share metaphors, symbols, examples, stories, pictures, and words that represent the image of what you all aspire to become.
- Be positive, upbeat, and energetic when talking about the future of your organization.
- Be expressive, using gestures, varying your tone of voice, and speaking with confidence.
- Acknowledge the emotions of others and validate them as important. Avoid dwelling on emotions that discourage people and make them lose heart for the journey.

CHALLENGE
THE PROCESS

Challenge is the crucible for greatness. Leaders seek and accept challenging opportunities and seize initiative to make something meaningful happen. Exemplary leaders look for good ideas everywhere. They turn adversity into advantage and setbacks into successes. They take risks with bold ideas and accept and grow from the inevitable disappointments. They treat mistakes as learning opportunities.

In the next two chapters, you will see how student leaders:

➤ **Search for Opportunities** by seizing the initiative and by looking outward for innovative ways to improve.
➤ **Experiment and Take Risks** by consistently generating small wins and learning from experience.

CHALLENGE THE PROCESS

Reflections from the *Student Leadership Practices Inventory*

1. Record your overall score from the *Student Leadership Practices Inventory* for CHALLENGE THE PROCESS here: _____

2. Of the six leadership behaviors that are part of Challenge the Process, write down the statement for the one you indicated engaging in most frequently:

3. Write down the leadership behavior statement that you felt you engaged in least often:

4. On the basis of your self-assessment, complete this statement: When it comes to Challenge the Process, my areas of leadership competency are:

5. What Challenge the Process behaviors do you see as opportunities for improving and strengthening your leadership capability? Make a note of these below so that you can keep them in mind as you read this chapter and the next.

5

Commitment #5: Search for Opportunities

Rachel Sumekh was a college sophomore when she saw a friend's Facebook post that raised an intriguing question: Would it be possible to collect the unused meal passes from student meal plans and use them to feed students who faced food insecurity?

Rachel was immediately taken with the idea, even though student hunger had never registered as an issue with her. "I saw a way that I could make a difference, and I felt a passion for it, even though I hadn't been passionate about solving student hunger before then," Rachel told us. She fired off an email offering to make up flyers for the project, and from there catapulted herself into the movement called Swipe Out Hunger (SOH).

Rachel and a group of friends worked to persuade the university to conduct a semester-long experiment in food donation. It began with them volunteering during move-out week to transport pallets of donated food into a designated "food closet" to benefit hungry students. Although this experiment was successful in that it was helping feed many students on campus, Rachel had to work continuously to keep the administration on board. "Every semester, the university said to us: let's take a pause this semester. And every semester we had to argue our case over again and prove that this was a good idea. It meant we didn't take anything for granted." By the time she was elected president of SOH her senior year, Rachel had learned that she had to "overpresent" her ideas to the administration again and again.

The day before a student food drive in Rachel's senior year, when students would sign up to donate unused meals on their meal plan, Rachel received a message from the university's dining director that the drive wasn't going to happen. She was told that the school was going to take a break from the program for a semester. Rachel called a university administrator she'd worked closely with in the past, explained the situation, described the impact of the food drives on the students, and asked for advice. Within hours, Rachel received a message from the dining director that the drive was back on. She said,

> I'm so thankful for that experience because it showed me that if you believe something should exist and you present a clear path for it to come into existence, there's no reason anyone should have an excuse for you. To convince a university to give away tens of thousands of dollars of food, you have to show the right leaders how it helps the students and how it benefits the entire campus.

The university-based program became so successful that it transformed from a local student organization into a nonprofit geared toward making a difference at campuses across the country, and Rachel was named the first CEO. With that change came new challenges. For SOH to be truly successful, Rachel knew that she had to be able to train others to replicate her university's success on their campuses. She turned to the success stories of other nonprofits to determine ways to transform SOH into a national movement. From reading about best practices, she decided that the way to make a global impact would be to create a decentralized organization with chapters throughout the country. "I didn't know how to run this organization on my own at first, or the best ways for us to expand and grow," Rachel said. By looking to the wisdom of leaders who had gone before her, Rachel was able to recognize promising strategies for bringing SOH's mission to fruition.

Rachel began to experiment with ways to get students on other campuses ready to start a local SOH chapter. At first, she created a detailed PDF outlining best practices for students. Then, she said, "I realized that no one wants to read a twelve-page PDF," so she abandoned that idea and decided to create a website with the information instead. That meant she had to teach herself how to code. Rachel approached each step with a mindset focused on what would make her organization more successful, and what steps would reach more students, rather than relying on the skill sets she already had and was comfortable with. "There's always been a lot of trial and error in Swipe Out Hunger," she told us. "I continue to ask myself all the time, How do I make this better? What's wrong with what we're doing; how can we do it more effectively?"

Rachel began to spread her message to students across the country through social media messaging and by having members of the organization reach out with personal stories about how they established SOH programs on their campuses. She also broadcasted that she would be personally available to help and talk with students through the entire process, answering questions about how to implement the program on their campus. Rachel provided both a blueprint and customized support for students starting their own chapters, but she said that the most important part of her work was encouraging students to believe in themselves and their ideas, to experiment with changes and innovations to the program that might better suit their campus. Rachel asked them to brainstorm novel ways to improve the SOH campaigns on other campuses and set aside a specific time in their meetings to bounce around ideas. "Don't call me and say, 'Can we do this?' Call me and say, 'We're doing this thing; can I tell you about it and how you can get involved?'"

Rachel had no experience running a nonprofit before taking the job as full-time CEO for SOH. Instead, she looked to her community, reaching out to other nonprofit directors and researching online how to run a board. She arranged conversations with anyone who would meet with her, from local CEOs to entrepreneurs, and gleaned wisdom from each person she talked with, even if their experience wasn't immediately applicable to SOH. Even years later, it's an approach she still follows, looking to meet new people at every opportunity to discover what she can learn from them. She sees each experience as a chance to learn something new and get to know someone new, someone who might help her think of something she hadn't considered before. "Each person that I talk to is another lens that I can put on to understand the world a little more expansively, rather than just seeing the world through my own singular lens," Rachel said.

Challenge opens the doors to making extraordinary things happen. Leaders like Rachel understand that you don't get to anyplace different if you just keep doing the same things over and over again. Getting out of routines and ruts requires treating every project, assignment, or job as an adventure. This involves lifting your head up, looking all around, and being willing to invest your time and energy in finding out about other possibilities.

Sometimes challenges find leaders, and sometimes leaders find the challenges; most often, it's a little of each. What Rachel did is what all exemplary leaders do. She looked outward, keeping up with changing trends and remaining sensitive to external realities. She persuaded others to take seriously the challenges and opportunities they faced. She served as a catalyst for change, challenging the way things were done and convincing others that new practices needed to be incorporated to achieve greater levels of success. This involves a lot more than simply complaining about the way things are, and it's not about pushing back for the sake of pushing back or for the purpose of being controversial. It is about proactively looking for options that might lead to a better way of doing things.

Like Rachel's story, students' personal-best leadership cases are about significant departures from the past, about doing things that have never been done before, about going to places not yet discovered. Change is the work of leaders. In today's world, business-as-usual thinking is unacceptable, and exemplary leaders know that they must transform the way things are done. Delivering results beyond expectations can't be achieved merely with good intentions. People, processes, systems, and strategies all need to change. In addition, all change requires that leaders actively seek ways to make things better—to grow, innovate, and improve.

Exemplary student leaders embrace the commitment to Search for Opportunities to ensure that extraordinary things happen. They make sure they engage in these two essentials:

- **Seize the initiative**
- **Exercise outsight**

Sometimes leaders shake things up. Other times they just harness the uncertainty that surrounds them. Regardless, leaders make things happen. They actively rely on outsight to seek innovative ideas from beyond the boundaries of familiar experience.

SEIZE THE INITIATIVE

When students recall their personal-best leadership experiences, they always think about times of challenge, turbulence, and adversity. Why? Because personal and organizational hardships have a way of making people come face to face with who they are and what they're capable of becoming. Innovation challenges and tests people's values, desire, aspirations, capabilities, and capacities. They require inventive ways of dealing with novel and difficult situations. They also tend to bring out the best in people.

Meeting new challenges always requires things to be different than they currently are. You can't respond with the same old solutions. You must change the status quo, which is what students did in their personal-best leadership experiences. They met challenges with change.

We didn't ask students to tell us specifically about change. They could review any leadership experience. What people chose to discuss were the changes they made in response to the challenges they faced. Their electing to talk about times of change underscores the fact that leadership demands altering the business-as-usual environment. There is a clear connection between challenge and change, and there's a clear connection between challenge and being an effective leader.

The study of leadership is the study of how men and women guide others through adversity, uncertainty, and other significant challenges. It's the study of people who triumph against overwhelming odds, who take initiative when there is inertia, who confront the established order, who mobilize individuals and institutions in the face of stiff resistance. It's also the study of how people, in times of constancy and complacency, actively seek to disturb the status quo and awaken others to new possibilities. Leadership, challenge, and seizing the initiative are linked together. Humdrum situations simply aren't associated with award-winning performance.

Make Something Happen

Alec Loeb joined his fraternity as a freshman. His goal from the start was to hold a leadership position at some point in his fraternity tenure, and he started on that path by accepting the position of philanthropy chair. "I was raised in a family where giving back to the community was a way of life," Alec told us, "so I was well suited to the position. When I took the job, I knew there was a retiring chair who could help me find my way. But then he got an unexpected opportunity to take a semester abroad, and we never got a chance to go over anything. I was left to figure it all out myself."

There were several events that had been traditions with the fraternity that Alec knew he would be expected to continue. The first up was an annual oyster roast. Alec found out that in previous years, the most they had raised from this event was $2,000. He found himself thinking, "I know we can do better than that."

> I started to talk to the brothers about what makes students come to an event like this and asked about how they got the word out. The answers were pretty vague and definitely not adventurous, with suggestions like "We put flyers up, we use word of mouth, we get our friends to spread the word." I decided to try something new. Why not see if some of the local bars and restaurants would be willing to sell tickets for us, or at the very least donate food? What if we could get a few of the past brothers or even famous university alumni to donate to the cause? You never know until you ask, right?

These ideas worked out, and as a result, the oyster roast made $5,600 for charity, almost triple what it had made the year before. This experience taught Alec an important lesson: "If you can think of ways to improve the process, you should take them."

If you are going to lead others, you have to stop simply going through the motions when it comes to the job, project, or assignment you've been asked to do. It's a lesson all leaders need to learn. Even if you're on the right track, you're likely to get run over if you just sit there. To do your best as a leader, you must seize the initiative to change the way things are.

Being an exemplary student leader necessarily means working beyond your job description and seeing opportunities where others don't. For example, some standard practices, policies, and procedures are critical to productivity and quality assurance. However, many are simply matters of tradition. In Alec's example, there was an expectation set by the title to which he had been elected: "philanthropy chair." Certain events had been done every year and were expected to continue, but the bottom line was that it wasn't the particular event that mattered; the point was to raise as much money as possible for good causes. Keeping that goal in mind allowed Alec to try something new. That the previous chair was unavailable to him worked in his favor, he said, freeing his thinking and empowering him to try new approaches.

> There was nobody watching over my shoulder saying, "I did it this way; why are you changing it?" There was just an expectation to plan an event, and it was up to me to make it happen. Once I started thinking about how it could be done and talking to people about those ideas, we got excited about the possibilities and tried some new things.

New jobs and new assignments are ideal opportunities for asking probing questions and challenging the way things are done. They are the times when you're expected to ask, "Why do we do this, and why do we do that?" However, don't just ask this question when you're new to the job or assignment. Make it a routine part of your leadership. Ask questions that test people's assumptions, stimulate different ways of thinking, and open new avenues to explore. Asking questions is how you'll continuously uncover needed improvements, fostering innovation. Treat today as if it were your first day. Ask yourself, "If I were just starting this responsibility, what makes sense about how we do things, and what might I do differently?" If you don't understand why things are done the way they are, ask questions so that you can determine whether an old routine should stay in place or be done differently. Then take action. This is how you'll continuously uncover needed improvements.

And don't stop at what you can find on your own. Ask those around you about what gets in the group's way of achieving its best. Promise to look into what they say and get back to them, then kick the possibilities around with them some more. Keep looking for things that don't seem right or that could be better. Ask questions and then follow up with more.

Leaders want to make something happen, and are often frustrated by the "if it ain't broke, don't fix it" mentality. They earn the respect of the people around them when they question the status quo, come up with innovative ideas, follow through with the changes they suggest, get feedback, understand their mistakes, and learn from failures. Leaders don't wait for permission or specific instructions before jumping in. They notice what isn't working, create a solution for the problem, gain buy-in from constituents, and implement the desired outcome. Research shows that students who rate high on proactivity not only are considered by their peers to be better leaders but also are more engaged in extracurricular and civic activities targeted toward bringing about positive change. Proactivity consistently produces better results than reactivity or inactivity.[1]

As Alec's experience shows, you also need to give everyone on your team the chance to search for better ways of doing things and give them the chance to step forward and take initiative. The data shows that students are significantly more engaged in their organizations when they report that their leader "looks for ways that others can try out new ideas and methods." As shown in Figure 5.1, there is nearly a sevenfold increase in engagement level between those students who report that their leaders rarely engage in this leadership behavior versus those whose leaders engage in it very frequently. Everyone

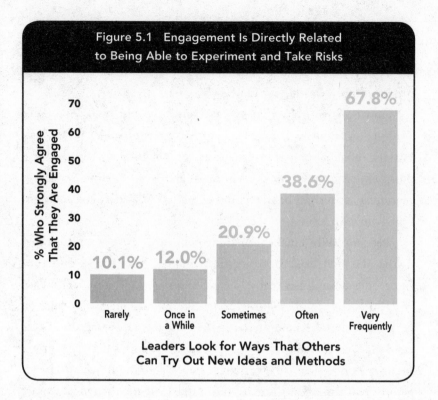

Figure 5.1 Engagement Is Directly Related to Being Able to Experiment and Take Risks

performs better when they take charge of change rather than allow it to buffet them about.

Encourage Initiative in Others

Change requires leadership, and every person in the group, not just the leader, can come up with creative ideas and suggest improvements. This was certainly Kelly Estes's experience. On the first day as summer interns at a law firm, she and her colleagues took part in an orientation and training session about the work they were to do. Many were disappointed with the type of jobs they were assigned: mostly performing data input and simple office tasks. Their reactions: "This sucks!" "This is going to be one long summer." "We should all just quit now and go on vacation." Kelly was determined to remove herself from all the naysayers, and, as she told us, "Right away I decided that I didn't want to make a waste of my summer and, that even in the worst situations, there was always an opportunity to shine."

Kelly started walking around the office, introducing herself to anyone she could. She went the extra mile to meet the staff through-out the firm. Kelly started her assignment correlating data for various attorneys and secretaries and would ask questions when something didn't seem right. Others began to notice her initiative and were happy to have someone on board who would try to resolve issues rather than ignore them, leaving them to turn into bigger problems later.

After a few weeks, the other interns saw that Kelly had developed very positive relationships with many in the firm and started asking her what she had been doing. She explained that she asked questions and offered ideas on what they could do better in their departments. Although she admitted that her direct boss wasn't too excited about her taking the initiative to dive more deeply into the firm's business, Kelly said she wouldn't let that undermine her determination to do a good job. Besides, there were others in the firm who were very appre-ciative of her efforts. Soon many of the other interns began following suit, and the partners noticed how much more efficiently work was completed and that the "status quo" was now quite different in some of the departments. The interns who followed Kelly's lead began en-joying their work and ended up having a great summer experience. They were not only influenced themselves by Kelly's initiative and her drive to try a different approach, but as a group they wound up having a positive influence on the work style within the firm.

Leaders like Kelly take the initiative and in doing so encourage initiative in others. They want people to speak up, to offer suggestions for improvement, and to be straightforward with their perspective and feedback. Yet when it comes to situations that involve high uncer-tainty, high risk, and high challenge, many people feel reluctant to act, afraid they might make matters worse. They get scared.

There are many ways you can create conditions so that others will be ready and willing to make things happen in both good times and bad. Promote a can-do attitude by finding opportunities for people to slowly and steadily gain skills. Help someone learn and talk things through. Use your time together to build people's ability and confidence so that they feel ready to do something about the situations they face. It's tempting to say, "I don't have time to show someone how to do this! It's easier if I just do it myself," or even "If I want it done right, I'll do it myself," but this short-term thinking will cause problems down the road. The best leaders know that taking the time to help someone learn can strengthen the group in the long term. People can't be effective when they don't get the knowledge, skills, or tools they need to perform.

Also, find ways for people to stretch themselves. Give people a chance to learn and grow, but take it one step at a time, at a level where they feel they can succeed. Give people too much too soon and they will fail, and if they fail too often, they'll quit trying. Increase people's challenges slowly but steadily, and as people get better and build their self-confidence, they will continue moving the bar upward regarding their skills, abilities, and confidence. Leaders encourage initiative by providing visibility and access to role models, especially when the role model is a peer who is successful at meeting the new challenges. Seeing them succeed at something new can be an effective way to encourage others to try out new ways of behaving, as long as you put it in a light that is positive and encouraging, rather than demeaning. Comparing people can turn off initiative in a minute, and once it shuts down, it's very tough to restart.

Challenge with Purpose

Doing things differently doesn't necessarily ensure that they will be done better, so leaders realize they must approach change with a purpose in mind. Kathryn Avila knows this principle firsthand, especially, she says, "when existing standards are the biggest obstacles to a leader's success." Her private nonsecular school highly valued tradition, and she knew from the moment she was selected as the yearbook editor that she was expected to uphold those standards, yet she knew that to keep the book current and interesting, they needed to institute some changes. One of the first was moving from black-and-white to an all-color publication, and this necessitated persuading the administration to part with a time-honored tradition. Although the school was very well run, many decisions were based on honoring traditions and what had worked in the past, and this was something the administration hadn't seen before. After multiple meetings, she was able to convince school leadership that converting to color did not mean changing the look of the yearbook to be "avant-garde" (as they originally feared). Kathryn had to convince them that "this change wasn't about destroying tradition, but instead would enhance it."

Leaders don't challenge for challenge's sake. They don't try to change things just to make change. Students who simply criticize new thoughts and ideas, or point out problems with what others have to contribute without offering any kind of alternate options, are not Challenging the Process. They are simply complaining. Leaders challenge, often with great passion, because they want people to live life *on* purpose and *with* purpose. What gets people through the hard times, the scary times—the times when they don't think they can even get up in the morning or take another step—is a sense of meaning and purpose. The motivation to deal with the challenges and uncertainties of life and work comes from the inside, not from something that others hold out in front of you as a reward. Leaders raise challenges to resolve and improve the situation, not simply to complain.

The evidence from our research and from studies by many others is that if people are going to do their best, they must be internally motivated.[2] As we discussed in Chapter 4, intrinsic motivators are more likely to produce extraordinary results than extrinsic motivators. Recall Jen Marsh's teaching experience: "There was no way I was going to get these second and third graders to read because I wanted them to. Instead it was something that I had to help them want to accomplish on their own. I had to get the kids excited about reading and show them how important this achievement would be later in their lives." Leaders get people to see beyond the particular task or project and to focus on the meaning that it fulfills. When it comes to excellence, it's not "What gets rewarded gets done," it's "What *is rewarding* gets done."

Think about your level of engagement when you're doing an assignment that is rewarding rather than when you're working just for the grade. Why do people push their limits to get extraordinary things done? And for that matter, why do people do so many things for nothing? Why do they volunteer to collect toys and clothing, raise money for worthy causes, or help children in need? Why do some risk their lives to save others or defend liberty? Extrinsic rewards certainly can't explain these actions. Leaders understand they must find what motivates people internally; they must tap into others' hearts and minds if they want them to do something difficult or novel.

EXERCISE OUTSIGHT

On a visit to the rugged coast of Northern California, we came across important advice for leaders. Printed at the top of a pamphlet describing a stretch of the Pacific Ocean was this warning: "Never turn your back on the ocean." The reason you can't turn and look inland to catch a view of the town is that a rogue wave may come along and sweep you out to sea, as many an unsuspecting traveler has discovered. This warning holds sound advice for travelers and leaders alike. When you take your eyes off the external realities, turning inward to admire the beauty of your organization, the swirling waters of change may sweep you away. So too with innovation: you must always scan the external realities. Innovation requires the use of outsight. The sibling of insight (the ability to apprehend the inner nature of things), outsight (the awareness and understanding of outside forces) comes through openness. That's because, as researchers have found, innovations come from just about anywhere.[3]

In his senior year of high school, Logan Hall was elected to serve in the leadership group of the 4-H State Council in Pennsylvania, whose role was to advance the purpose and vision of 4-H and to promote it throughout sixty-seven counties in the state. They were also to provide various research-based leadership training programs and curricula to local councils and their officers. Logan knew that his council needed help in identifying and meeting the needs of students from across the state, but instead of jumping right in and possibly reinventing the wheel, Logan and his team looked around to see how other councils had addressed similar issues. For example, they contacted the Tennessee 4-H State Council and reviewed the curriculum and leadership lessons they had created there, identified speakers they had used, and explored what might be adapted to work in Pennsylvania. "The Tennessee students," Logan explained, "put it all on the table for us. We found ways to use many of their ideas, and in the process we began to understand their vision, how it connected to ours, and how we could collaborate. All we had to do was ask them."

According to our research, when students indicate that their leader "searches for innovative ways to improve what we are doing," as Logan and his fellow 4-H leaders did, they are significantly more excited and proud about their organization than students who view their leaders as constrained by current and past decisions. As Logan's experience shows, it's by keeping the doors open to the passage of ideas and information that you become knowledgeable about what is going on around you. Insight without outsight is like seeing with blinders on; you just can't get a complete picture.

Look Outside Your Experience

Studies into how the brain processes information suggest that to see things differently and therefore creatively, you have to bombard your brain with stuff it has never encountered. This kind of novelty is vital because the brain, evolved for efficiency, routinely takes perceptual shortcuts to save energy. Only by forcing yourself to break free of pre-existing views can you get your brain to reorganize information. Moving beyond habitual thinking patterns is the starting point to imagining truly new ideas.[4]

The human mind is surprisingly adroit at supporting its ways of viewing the world. It is also adept at rationalizing away evidence that disproves those views. One way to adjust this limiting lens is by expanding your hands-on experiences. Consider what one North American specialty retailer did in seeking to reinvent its store format while improving the experience of its customers:

> To jump-start creativity in its people, the company sent out several groups of three to four employees to experience retail concepts very different from its own. Some went to Sephora, a beauty product retailer that features more than 200 brands and a sales model that encourages associates to offer honest product advice, without a particular allegiance to any of them. Others went to the Blue Jean Bar, an intimate boutique retailer that aspires to turn the impersonal experience of digging through piles of jeans into a cozy occasion reminiscent of a night at a neighborhood pub. Still others visited a gourmet chocolate shop. . . . By visiting the other retailers and seeing firsthand how they operated, the retailer's employees were able to relax their strongly held

views about their own company's operations. This transformation, in turn, led them to identify new retail concepts they hadn't thought of before, including organizing a key product by color (instead of by manufacturer) and changing the design of stores to center the shopping experience around advice from expert stylists.[5]

The process of moving outside your usual thinking patterns doesn't have to be as elaborate as this retailer's, and it can take place right where you are today, on campus or off. Leaders find ways to look outside the program, department, or chapter they are in to find out, and even experience, what other groups like theirs are doing. Alec Loeb did this when his philanthropy chair predecessor left campus before Alec could get the details of his approach to the traditional oyster roast. Instead of scrambling to recreate an event exactly as it had been done before, Alec relied on a what-if attitude: What if we try something different?

There's also an example of looking outside one's own experience in Kelly Estes's story. She had no experience in legal matters, and in fact her summer internship was her first exposure to the practice of law. She could have just done her assigned work, but she felt that there was more she could do that would help her develop as a person and a leader—not to mention acquiring more skills. By venturing outside her appointed duties and exploring other departments within the firm, Kelly essentially did, internally, the same thing as the employees who sought firsthand experience with different retailing approaches. By lifting her eyes up and looking around her larger surroundings, she found opportunities to make a real difference in the firm's work.

Student leaders like Alec and Kelly understand that innovation requires more listening and greater communication than routine work does. Successful innovations take hard work, constant communication, and the willingness to ask, "What if?" You need to establish relationships, network, make connections, and be out and about.

Listen to and Promote Diverse Perspectives

Demand for change will come from both inside and outside your group. If everything were working perfectly, then perhaps there might not be any urgency to do things differently. But the truth is that if people are going to realize their aspirations, then some things are going to have to change, even before they are broken. Standard operating practices keep things going the way they are, but they are often not well suited for dealing with turbulence, uncertainty, or mandates for better results.

Leaders must be receptive to new ideas if they are to challenge the process effectively. You need to appreciate that one person may have a valid point of view about a problem, but individuals from different backgrounds can come up with diverse views on the same problem. Just as Rachel Sumekh learned when she was expanding Swipe Out Hunger's reach into the national arena, or Logan Hall found out from another state's 4-H experiences, the extra information and perspectives can help you formulate better answers and improve outdated systems. Successful leaders need to encourage the sharing of information from all stakeholders, to be receptive to different ideas no matter the source, and to use the collective knowledge to come up with an effective solution to any challenge.

One of the reasons that people are often afraid to ask around for advice and input from others is that they perceive that doing so means, or at least implies, that they're incompetent, that they don't know something they should already know. However, studies have shown that this fear is misplaced. People perceive those who seek advice as more competent than those who do not seek advice, and this belief is even stronger when the task is difficult than when it is easy.[6] You can enhance others' opinions about your competence by asking questions and seeking advice from people who know what they are talking about. For one thing, doing so makes that other person feel affirmed.

Consequently, when you have a particularly perplexing problem, don't hesitate to talk about it with someone who has dealt with similar situations. There is a good chance that he or she will think more highly of you afterward.

One way to open yourself up to new information is by taking on multiple perspectives. What can you do to take a more expansive view of your present circumstances? Researchers have suggested three approaches:[7]

- Take the perspective of someone who frustrates or irritates you, and consider what that person might have to teach you.
- Listen to what other people have to say; that is, listen to learn rather than to necessarily change their perspective.
- Seek out the opinions of people beyond your comfort zone, folks you don't typically talk with.

Asking questions and seeking the advice of others lead naturally to knowledge sharing across an organization. This inquisitiveness also strengthens interpersonal relationships. It is imperative that you listen to the world outside and ask good questions. You never know where a great idea will come from, which means that you need to acquire an attitude of treating every job as an adventure.

Treat Every Experience as an Adventure

Leaders personally seize the initiative, encourage others to do the same, and actively look everywhere for great ideas. But that doesn't mean you have to wait to be the president of the club or the captain of the team to make things better or change the current environment. When we asked students to tell us who initiated the projects that they selected as their personal bests, we assumed that the majority of people would name themselves. Surprisingly, that's not what we found.

Someone else initiated more than half the cases. If leaders seize the initiative, then how can we call people leaders when they're assigned the jobs and tasks they undertake? Doesn't this contradict all we've said about how leaders behave? No, it does not.

The fact that over half the personal-best cases were not self-initiated should be a relief to anyone who thought they had to start all the change themselves, and it should encourage appreciating that responsibility for new ideas and improvement is *everyone's business.* If the only times people reported doing their best were when they got to choose the projects themselves or when they were the elected head of the group, the majority of leadership opportunities would evaporate—as would most social and organizational changes. The reality is that much of what people do is assigned; few get to start everything from scratch. That's just a fact of being part of a group or organization.

People who become leaders don't always seek the challenges they face. Challenges also seek leaders. Stuff happens on campus, on teams, in communities, and in people's lives. It's not so important whether you find the challenges or they find you. It's the choice you make to address those challenges that matters. So one question is: When opportunity knocks, are you prepared to answer the door? Another question, just as important: Are you ready to open the door, go outside, and look for an opportunity?

Be an adventurer, an explorer. Treat every day as if it were your first day "on the job." Approach every new assignment as an opportunity to start over. Concentrate on ways to constantly improve your whole group. Consider the leadership journey that Kyle Harvey experienced one summer during an internship at a high-end reseller of printers. One of his responsibilities was working in the warehouse, helping with managing the company's inventory.

Historically the company had simply counted the products in stock and logged them in a book. However, there were always hundreds of parts left over or unaccounted for because they had been mislabeled or stocked in an unorganized manner. Kyle began to think about other ways he had learned to organize bits of merchandise and equipment. He wondered if there might not be something he had learned in school and from his other work experiences that would help make his employer's inventory process more efficient and more accurate.

By thinking about how he would approach designing the inventory system from scratch, Kyle came up with the idea of cataloguing the parts by both their part number and the product that they would eventually go into. It took a month for Kyle and his five coworkers to set up the system and reorganize the warehouse. Once installed, the brand-new system gave the technicians quicker access to needed parts, and it helped management keep tighter tabs on the company's property. Had Kyle not treated his internship as an opening to apply his experience with other systems to the inventory-management problem, the company would have stayed stuck in the same old way of doing things, and Kyle would have missed an important opportunity to develop his leadership skills.

Student leaders like Kyle are always on the lookout for opportunities to use new ideas, wherever they are. If you're serious about trying new approaches and helping others be adventurous, make finding new ideas a personal priority. Encourage others to open their eyes and ears to the world outside the boundaries they know. Collect suggestions from everyone you can, in your organizations or outside them. Use social media to draw ideas from an even wider field.

Encourage your group, as Rachel did, to spend some time in meetings thinking about new ways you might be able to do some part of a project or some task or event your group does on a regular basis. If you put on annual events or activities, suspend looking at the notebooks and files from past years and treat an event as if it were the very first time you've ever planned it. If you know groups at other schools or organizations that do similar events, as Logan did, call them to talk about how they do them. Identify groups on your own campus that have a great reputation and meet with their leaders to get ideas about how they are organized. Find out if they have had challenges or faced difficult situations similar to yours. Search around the Internet for ideas and experiences that correspond to what you are addressing in your group. Sometimes new ideas spring from things you come across by accident and aren't even related to what you're working on. Keep your eyes and ears open, no matter where you are. You can never tell where or when you'll come across the next great idea.

REFLECT AND ACT: SEARCH FOR OPPORTUNITIES

Student leaders who make extraordinary things happen are open to receiving ideas from anyone and anywhere. They are skilled at constantly surveying the landscape in search of new ideas. And because they are proactive, they don't just ride the waves of change; they make the waves that others ride.

You don't have to change history, but you do have to avoid the attitude that "we've always done it this way." You need to be proactive, continually inviting and creating new initiatives, and with a purpose greater than just doing something different. Leaders, by definition, are out in front of change, not behind it trying to catch up. This means that your focus needs to be less on the routine and daily actions of your group and much more on the untested and untried. And when you are searching for opportunities to grow and improve, the most innovative ideas are most often not your own. They're elsewhere, and the best leaders look all around them for the unexpected places, and people, in which great new ideas are hiding. Exemplary leadership requires outsight, not just insight. That's where the future is.

Whether you are trying a new approach or taking on a project that's never been done before, change is an adventure. It tests your will and your skill. It's tough, but it's also stimulating. The challenge of change introduces you to yourself. To get the best from yourself and others, you must understand what gives meaning and purpose to your work.

Reflect

The first commitment of Challenge the Process is to *search for opportunities by seizing the initiative and looking outward for innovative ways to improve*. Reflect on this commitment and answer these questions:

1. What is the most important idea or lesson about exemplary leadership that you learned from this chapter?

    _____

    _____

    _____

    _____

2. What changes do you need to make in your leadership to better Search for Opportunities?

    _____

    _____

    _____

    _____

3. In the next section, there are some suggestions on what you can do to put Search for Opportunities into practice. After you have reflected on what you learned and what you need to improve,

select an action that you can take immediately to become a better leader.

_____

_____

_____

_____

Take Action

Here are some things you can do to solidify your commitment to **Search for Opportunities:**

- Always ask: "What's new? What's next? What's better?"
- Make it a daily exercise to reflect on the question, "How can I do better or differently what I did yesterday or plan to do today?"
- If there is something that you feel is not working well, try a different approach. If there is something bugging you, what can you do about it?
- Determine whether you and your colleagues have some routines that are no longer serving a purpose, that have become ruts you need to get out of, and do something about this situation.
- Get firsthand experiences outside your comfort zone and skill set. Put yourself in new situations where you can learn.
- Design tasks and projects so that they are meaningful, which means tapping into the purpose the project serves and not just the fact that it's different.
- Talk with people outside your group; get others around you to do the same. Bring back what all of you learned, share it, and discuss how you can apply this outsight to your assignments and projects.

6

Commitment #6:
Experiment and
Take Risks

Heather McDougall is the founder of Leadership exCHANGE, a student exchange program, and executive director of their Global Leadership Program (GLP). GLP has taught and trained over fourteen hundred students from more than eighty countries and operates programs in ten. "It all started when I went to the Czech Republic as a graduate student," Heather told us.

> The experience was life changing for me. I realized how much we had to learn from other cultures and how that knowledge could inform how we learn to grow and develop as leaders. It seemed such a missed opportunity to learn about leadership on campus and not incorporate the learning I got when I was taken to a different environment and given the opportunity to work with people there.

Heather decided to design a program to do just that. She offered it to her university but received a lukewarm response. Following up after a couple of months, she got more of the same. Months more and still no word, and by then it was too late to engage students for the summer. Later that year, while pursuing graduate studies in London and working part-time for the YWCA, she offered the program to that organization, but the response was again lukewarm.

"I was so frustrated at this point," Heather told us, "that my roommate suggested I stop going through existing entities to find a home for the program and simply do it myself. My response was immediate and clear: 'I can't do that!' But my roommate was so positive, knew the steps needed, and helped me get set up."

When she thought the program was ready, Heather started spreading the word. Living in Prague at the time meant she had to use Internet cafés to reach colleges and universities she thought might be interested. "It was slow and tedious work," she said. "After several months I only had five people signed up, and I thought it might fail again." Heather had gotten married during all this, and when she called her husband one night feeling especially disheartened, he encouraged her to hang in there and also said he'd support whatever she chose to do. "Maybe it was the notion of quitting after all the years of work," Heather said, "but something finally clicked, and I said to myself, 'You're feeling sorry for yourself, and you need to get over it and figure out another way to make this work!' I had experimented with a lot of different approaches, and I knew I was getting closer to a success."

Heather decided that she could run a successful pilot if she could get just eight people to participate. Seven students from the United States eventually signed up, plus one from Finland, which sparked the idea of internationalizing the student body for the next time around. Heather kept revising the curriculum and developing the program from there. If something worked well, she kept it; if it didn't, she changed it, strengthening the program with each iteration. Today each GLP typically includes students from at least ten, and sometimes up to twenty, countries.

"I am so proud of this program and what it has become," Heather said. "I had no idea how hard it was going to be to get off the ground, but I knew I believed in it and the impact it could have. I simply hit a point where I knew I would never give up and just found a way to move past each roadblock, and I am extremely glad I did."

To achieve the extraordinary, you must be willing, just like Heather, to do things that have never been done before. Every single personal-best leadership experience case speaks to the need to take risks with bold ideas. You can't achieve anything new or extraordinary by doing things the way you've always done them. You need to test unproven strategies. You need to break out of the norms that box you in, venture beyond the limitations you usually place on yourself, try new things, and take chances. As Heather told us, "When I created the Global Leadership Program, the term 'social enterprise' wasn't a common term. Without a clear label for 'what' we were or 'guidelines' on how to operate, I had to become comfortable operating in the 'unknown.'"

Leaders not only have to be willing to test bold ideas and take calculated risks but also have to get others to join them on these adventures in uncertainty. It's one thing to set off alone into the unknown; it's entirely another to get others to follow you into the darkness. The difference between an exemplary leader and an individual risk taker is that leaders create the conditions where people *want* to join with them in the effort.

Leaders make risk safe, as paradoxical as that might sound. They turn experiments into learning opportunities. They place a series of little bets, not all-in wagers where they can lose everything in one move. They don't define boldness as primarily go-for-broke, giant-leap projects. More often than not, they see change as starting small, using pilot or test projects, as Heather did, and gaining momentum. The vision may be grand and distant, but the way to reach it is by putting one foot in front of the other. These small, visible steps are more likely to win early victories and gain early supporters. Of course, when you experiment, not everything works out as intended. There are mistakes and false starts. That's part of the process of innovation. What's critical, therefore, is that leaders promote learning from these experiences.

Exemplary student leaders make the commitment to Experiment and Take Risks. They know that making extraordinary things happen requires that leaders:

- **Generate small wins**
- **Learn from experience**

These essentials help leaders transform challenge into an exploration, uncertainty into a sense of adventure, fear into resolve, and risk into reward. They are the keys to making progress that becomes unstoppable.

GENERATE SMALL WINS

Amanda Itliong's personal-best leadership experience was when she became vice president of her college chapter of the National Society of Collegiate Scholars. This organization was, she said, "one of those honor societies that doesn't often do much except induct students with a certain GPA, collect dues from them, and then induct more people the next year." She and her fellow officers quickly realized that the organization had a lot of money from all those years of collecting dues that hadn't been spent on anything.

"We looked to the mission of our organization for ideas about what we could do with the money," she told us. The group had been founded on the concept of supporting academic and service excellence, so they started to brainstorm ways they might be able to fulfill that aspiration. They decided that the arts was an area in which their school didn't offer many opportunities for students to showcase their work and also found that funding for community arts in their city was scarce. They came up with a plan to hold a student-created fashion and arts showcase called Diversion to benefit a nonprofit that taught the arts and entrepreneurship to low-income kids in the area. "Even though we were really excited about the plan," Amanda told us, "we knew it was going to be difficult to get other people on board and involved in the process because our group didn't usually do anything, and all of a sudden we were planning a huge event."

Planning a large arts event was a big risk for the group because it would require a lot of approvals, support, and volunteers from their school and the community at large. So they broke the task down into lots of little pieces. First, they started a forum for people to learn about the general idea for the event and to contribute their personal perspectives on the project. They literally drew a picture detailing the way they envisioned the auditorium during Diversion, and described all the possibilities of what would be there and what it could look like. They then started working with people all over campus to find out how to connect to the interests and values of other groups and individuals they would need for support. Little by little, they got people to say yes, again and again. As Amanda told us:

> The Art Department quickly got on board because we included in our idea a small gallery that was open before the show and during intermission and also gave them space to advertise their academic programs to students. The multicultural groups were excited to showcase their music and dance talents while helping a local good cause at the same time. With the input and brainstorms from so many people, we were able to create a really amazing vision.

From those early small wins, Amanda said, "We went on to host a sold-out event that was fun for everyone! The arts became very visible through the event, and a local charity received significant funding."

Leaders face situations similar to Amanda's all the time. How do you achieve something no one has ever done before? How do you get something new started? How do you turn around a losing team? Or address a campus-wide problem? How do you work to solve even larger problems, such as child trafficking or global climate change? These are such daunting challenges that people can become so overwhelmed that they never even get started.

Build Psychological Hardiness

Problems presented too broadly, or too expansively, can appear daunting and suffocate people's capacity to conceive of what they can do in the future, let alone right now. Leaders want people to reach for great heights but not become fearful of falling. They want people to feel challenged but not overwhelmed, curious but not lost, excited but not stressed. For example, Heather McDougall felt frustrated and ready to give up several times in starting the Global Leadership Program. Her initial battle was with herself. She told us that she had to stop worrying about personal failure and refocus on the mission. Once she made the switch back to focusing on the purpose, it was easier to search a little harder, to give it a bit more time, and to be determined not to give up. She began doing things that would lead, gradually, to the program she had dreamed about.

The tenacious quality that Heather, Amanda, and other student leaders display in their personal-best stories is what social psychologists refer to as *psychological hardiness*: the persistence and resilience that move them forward against the tide. The circumstances weren't always as long and drawn out as Heather's experience, but the conditions people faced during their personal-best leadership experiences were filled with significant uncertainties and stressors. Although 95 percent of the experiences were described as exciting, about 20 percent of student leaders also called them frustrating, and approximately 15 percent said that they felt fear or anxiety.

The very first thing Heather said in relating her story to us was, "My success came after years of setbacks and tears, but out of it came a great experience." Heather faced multiple obstacles in getting started toward her dream of creating a global leadership exchange program. When she felt as though the whole idea was just too much for her, she didn't quit.

> I thought, OK, if you stopped feeling sorry for yourself, what could you do? I was in a small college that often had tiny classes, and I knew I could run a pilot with just a very few students, so I decided to do that. We ended up with just eight students, but it worked, and it was a great experience for them. After that, we simply asked, What next? How can we make this better? We had the momentum and the confidence that we could define and take that next step. Once that class succeeded, things began to change.

Even though in the overwhelming majority of personal-best cases, the emotions are positive, we can't overlook the fact that they were also filled with tension. But instead of being debilitated by the stress of a difficult experience, exemplary student leaders said they were challenged and energized by it. The ability to grow and thrive under stressful, risk-abundant situations is highly dependent on how you view change.

Amanda Rossi told us about one of her fellow swim instructors, Bryan, who was in charge of a junior lifeguard program held at a local pool center. Every year, the program was more and more successful, which eventually led to a long waiting list. The pool supervisors felt that there was no way to expand the program given the limited amount of space in the pool and the cost of adding another lifeguard as an instructor. Not wanting to see kids turned away, Bryan came up with a creative way to increase the enrollment. If they split the children into two separate groups, with one having swim practice in the morning while the other group was doing exercises poolside, more kids could participate. The two groups would meet for lunch and then switch. This arrangement meant that the program could potentially add more children to each group. By adding more children, they could increase their profit and make their clients happy.

Bryan was excited by the possibilities and immediately proposed his idea to his supervisor, who listened but quickly dismissed it, saying there was no way it could be done that summer. Instead of feeling discouraged and worrying about the supervisor's reaction to his idea, Bryan decided to work on a way to convince her of the major benefits of increasing the enrollment for the program, and he figured he had a year to change her mind. His first task was to research the costs involved in running the junior lifeguard program and the costs of adding another instructor. He learned about the program's financial structure and considered ways to make his idea feasible. He chose not to view his supervisor's rejection as the end to his vision; instead, he was motivated by the challenge of convincing her that they could turn this idea for an expanded program into reality.

After calculating the costs of adding another instructor and more children to the program, Bryan worked out the additional revenue coming from the increase in enrollment. He assembled all the necessary information and approached his supervisor again. He showed that the increased revenue far exceeded the added costs, proving that the program could expand profitably. Once again, the supervisor rejected his idea, and once again Bryan didn't stress out. He met the resistance with increased enthusiasm, seeing it as an opportunity to come up with more ways to convince the supervisor to expand the program. He decided to engage the rest of the lifeguards in the discussion. He asked each instructor what they thought of the idea, getting their input and support so that when he spoke to the supervisor again, there would be a unified voice of the very people who would be dealing with the increased workload. It took almost a year, but eventually Bryan's idea succeeded and the program expanded.

Psychologists have discovered that people like Bryan, who experience a high degree of stress, yet cope with it in a positive manner, are psychologically hardy.[1] Whether students, corporate managers, entrepreneurs, nurses, lawyers, combat soldiers, or prisoners, people with a high degree of psychological hardiness are much more likely to withstand serious challenges and bounce back from failure than those low in hardiness.[2] Hardiness is a quality that anyone can develop and that you can support.

There are three key factors necessary to build psychological hardiness: *commitment, control,* and *challenge.* Think back to what Heather, Amanda Itliong, and Bryan did when facing their challenges. To turn adversity into advantage, first you need to *commit* yourself to what's happening. You need to become involved, engaged, and curious. As you saw in Bryan's story, you need to act; you can't sit back and wait for something to happen. When you commit, you'll find the people and the situations much more meaningful and worthwhile to you. You also have to take *control* of your own life, which is what Heather eventually decided to do. You need to make an effort to influence what is going on. Even though it's unlikely that all your attempts will be successful, you can't sink into passivity. Finally, you need to view *challenge* as an opportunity to learn from both negative and positive experiences. You can't play it safe, which was the realization that Amanda came to.

Your ability to cope with change and stress depends on your viewpoint. For you to start that new project, to take that first step, you must believe that you can influence the outcome. You must be curious about whatever is happening, and look for ways to learn every step of the way. With a hardy attitude, you can transform stressful events into positive opportunities for growth and renewal. What's more, you can help your team feel the same way.

Break It Down and Accentuate Progress

How do you get people to want to move in a new direction, break old mindsets, or change existing behavior patterns in order to tackle significant problems and attempt extraordinary performance? You take it step-by-step, one bit at a time. Just as Amanda and her colleagues did in transforming Diversions from concept to reality, you make progress incrementally. Exemplary student leaders appreciate that they need to break down big undertakings into small, doable actions. They also know that when initiating something new, they need to try many little things before they get it right. Not every innovation works, and the best way to ensure success is to experiment with many ideas, not just one or two big ones. Exemplary leaders help others see how breaking the journey down into measurable milestones moves them forward and small wins promote continued progress.

A small win is "a concrete, complete, implemented outcome of moderate importance."[3] Small wins form the basis for a consistent pattern of winning that attracts people who want to be part of a successful group. Although planting one tree won't stop climate change, planting one million trees can make a difference, and it's that first tree that gets things started. Small wins identify the place to begin. For Heather and the Global Leadership Program, the small win was signing up that very first group of eight students. The success of that pilot, and the stories collected and shared, helped in recruiting future groups. The success in one country was also the impetus for programs in other countries. Small wins can make a project seem doable even when time and budget are limited. They minimize the cost of trying and reduce the risks of failing. What's exciting about this process is that accomplishing a small win sets natural forces in motion that favor progress over setbacks.

Exemplary student leaders help others see how breaking the journey into measurable milestones can move them forward. The more often students reported that their leaders "made sure that big projects were broken down into smaller and doable parts," the more they felt satisfied with that individual's leadership, as shown in Figure 6.1. Those viewed as very frequently engaging in this leadership behavior were at least five times more likely to have students indicate that they were satisfied with the leadership of their leader, as compared to students who reported that their leaders rarely or only sometimes engaged in this leadership behavior. Relationships between small wins and the extent to which students felt they were making a difference are similar.

Leaders have grand visions about the future, and they get there one step at a time, building momentum as well as the strength and the resolve to continue forward along the journey. Small wins produce the

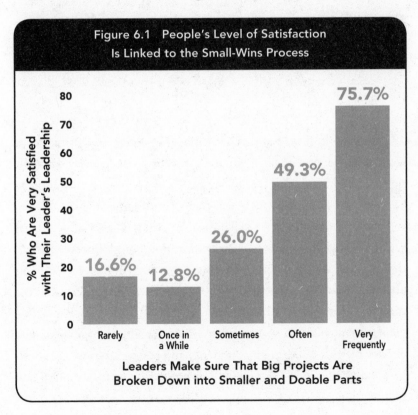

Figure 6.1   People's Level of Satisfaction Is Linked to the Small-Wins Process

kind of visible results that attract people to be connected to a successful group or team. They build people's confidence and reinforce their natural desire to feel successful. A series of small wins, therefore, provides a foundation of stable building blocks. Each win preserves gains and makes it harder to return to preexisting conditions.

For example, Sean Dwyer said he heard the word "no" many times when he set out to fundamentally change the way the school's spring dance was traditionally organized:

> Seeing as I had a limited budget and no real respect from my fellow peers in student government as a freshman, I knew I had to work at it. So I started by getting the vice president of the school to agree to go to lunch. I laid out my plan, and she was very much for it. That was win number one. Then I used her influence to help me get a meeting with the director of student life, which was win number two. I met with the director, showed her the importance of having a food option at the dance, and a budget, and voilà, win number three.

Upon reflection, Sean realized that the sequence of "small wins was crucial because it allows you to slowly eliminate what is seen as the norms and change things for the better. You have to make the effort to go step-by-step, little by little to actually get things changed."

Achieving a small win makes people "winners" and subsequently makes it easier for others to want to continue along. If people can see that you are asking them to do something that they're quite capable of doing, they feel some assurance that they can be successful at the task. By identifying little ways that people can succeed, you create commitment because they see that what they are doing is making a difference. This builds their confidence and creates a positive environment, which, in turn, gives people great reasons to stick around and keep working. Also, as Sean appreciated from his experience with the spring dance, "You have to be constantly learning from your mistakes. You cannot have one without the other."

"Big things are done by doing lots of small things" was a common refrain in the personal-best leadership cases. When you break a big project down into pieces, you're increasing the likelihood of making progress by having multiple experiments. Whatever you call your experiments—a practice, dry run, trial mode, demo, rehearsal, pilot project, test drive—all are methods of trying numerous little things in the service of something much bigger. These are the tactics that continually generate lots of opportunities for small wins.

LEARN FROM EXPERIENCE

When you challenge the status quo, you will sometimes fail. Despite how much you see challenge as an opportunity, how focused you can be, or how driven you are to succeed, there will be setbacks. Not everything will go exactly as planned. That's what experimentation is all about, and, as scientists know very well, there's a lot of trial and error involved in testing new concepts, new methods, and new practices.

People never figure out how to do something new, or something that has never been done before, and get it right the first time—not in the laboratory, the classroom, or the workplace. Yes, it's something that people are told they must do, but it's neither realistic nor useful advice. Some may want and perhaps expect you to get it right *every time*, but when you're doing things you have never tried, doing them perfectly is just not possible. When you engage in something new and different, you will make mistakes. Everyone does.

As part of her school's yearbook staff, Kathryn Avila recalled being "confronted firsthand with a major part of challenging processes: failure." At first, she told us, she hated to fail and thought that it meant that all of her hard work was worthless. With time, however, she came to a different realization:

> Just because I failed, or my staff failed, didn't mean that the work we did had no value. If a layout was created that didn't seem to work, it was worth our time to sit down, critique it, and learn what parts of it worked and what parts of it didn't work as well. Failure was just part of our learning process and something that needed to happen for us to grow, create, and learn, as a team and as individuals.

Repeatedly, student leaders in our studies tell us how mistakes and failure have been crucial to their success, both personally and professionally. Without mistakes, they wouldn't know what they can and cannot do (at least at the moment). Without the occasional failure, they say that they would not have been able to achieve their aspirations. It may seem paradoxical, but many support the idea that the overall quality of work improves when people have a chance to fail. This was precisely the lesson from an experiment one ceramics teacher carried out in his classroom.[4]

At the beginning of the semester, the teacher divided the students into two groups. He told the first group they could earn better grades by producing more pots (e.g., thirty for a B, forty for an A), regardless of the quality. He told the second group that their grades depended solely on the quality of the pots they produced. Not surprisingly, students in the first group got right to it, producing as many pots as possible, while the second group was quite careful and deliberate in how they went about making the best pots. The teacher found, to his surprise, that the students who made the most pots—those graded on quantity rather than quality—also made the best ones. It turned out that the practice of making lots of pots naturally resulted in better quality, because, for example, these students became more familiar with the intricacies of the kiln and how various firing positions affected the aesthetics of their products.

Failure is never the objective of any endeavor. The objective is to succeed, and success always requires some amount of learning. And learning always involves mistakes, errors, miscalculations, and the like along the way. Learning happens when people can openly talk about what went wrong as well as what went right. Leaders don't look for someone to blame when the inevitable mistakes are made in the name of innovation. They ask, "What can we learn from the experience?"

Our research validates the impact of this leadership behavior. From responses about how frequently their leaders "ask what can be learned from this experience when things do not go as expected," the data in Figure 6.2 shows that this behavior is dramatically linked with the extent to which students feel proud to say they are working with this leader. The relationship between this leadership behavior and the

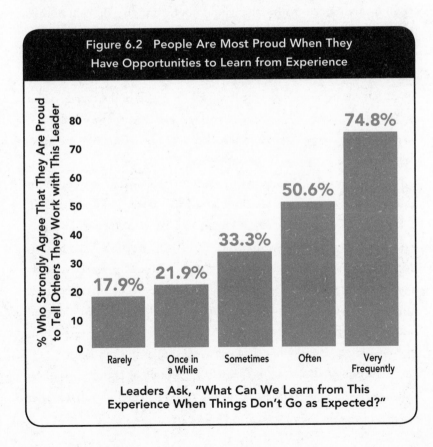

Figure 6.2   People Are Most Proud When They Have Opportunities to Learn from Experience

% Who Strongly Agree That They Are Proud to Tell Others They Work with This Leader

Rarely: 17.9%
Once in a While: 21.9%
Sometimes: 33.3%
Often: 50.6%
Very Frequently: 74.8%

Leaders Ask, "What Can We Learn from This Experience When Things Don't Go as Expected?"

extent to which students feel that their leader values their work mirrors these results.

Be an Active Learner

Marie Jones was one of ten representatives from the United States to Insight Dubai, a conference that paired sixty young women from around the world with Dubai Women's College students for five days of developing global awareness, intercultural understanding, and leadership skills. The experience was so profound that Marie applied and was chosen to return the following year as a facilitator.

Marie knew from her experience the year before that even though she would be leading a group of sixteen women, eight from Dubai and eight from other countries, she would not be standing in front of them lecturing. Her role was to get her group talking, sharing, and eventually shaping the experience themselves if it was going to be meaningful for each of them. "We all learned so much from each other when I was a participant because we were all actively engaged in the conversations we had," she told us. "I was determined to build that same kind of experience as the facilitator, and the key was active listening and active learning."

Active listening started with Marie herself so that she could understand the women's perspective and experience. "I knew it would take some time to get to know them, so I kept an open-door policy, which led to many late-night talks, but it was worth it," she told us. Marie also knew that each woman brought a unique perspective to the conference based on her personality, background, and life experiences. The key to bringing those perspectives into the room, she believed, was to have them actively engaged, drawing on what they knew from their experiences and what they were learning at the conference.

Marie invited people to form small groups, each to work on an issue or topic they needed to think through carefully. From their discussions, each group was to come up with a list of concerns, and recommendations on ways to address them. Marie told us that she "challenged them all to make sure each voice in their group was heard, and to come together as one voice in the end." She also asked the small groups to take time at the end of each session to reflect on what they had learned and what their learning process had been. "The feedback I got was very similar to my own experience as a participant in Insight Dubai. Being fully engaged in your learning helps you understand how you learn. That is so valuable."

Learning is a master skill and is shown to be one of the best predictors of future career success.[5] Concomitantly, our research has found a strong correlation between how engaged a student is in learning and his or her leadership capability.[6] When you fully engage in learning—when you throw yourself completely into experimenting, reflecting, reading, and getting advice or coaching—you are going to experience the satisfaction of improvement and the taste of success.

More is more when it comes to learning. It's clear that exemplary student leaders approach each new and unfamiliar experience with a willingness to learn, an appreciation of the importance of learning, and the recognition that learning involves making some mistakes. Building your capacity to be an active learner begins with developing a *growth mindset*. The foundational belief of this mindset is that people can learn through their efforts. By contrast, those with a *fixed mindset* believe that people's basic qualities are immutable, carved in stone.[7] Individuals with a growth mindset, for example, believe that people can learn to be better leaders. Those with a fixed mindset think leaders are born and that no amount of training is going to make you any better than you naturally are.

In study after study, researchers have found that when working on simulated business problems, those individuals with fixed mindsets gave up more quickly and performed more poorly than those with growth mindsets.[8] The same is true for students, athletes on the playing field, teachers in the classroom, and partners in relationships.[9] Mindsets, not skill sets, make the critical difference in taking on challenging situations.

To develop a growth mindset and to nourish it in others, you need to embrace the challenges you face. That's where the learning is. When you encounter setbacks—and there will be many—you have to persist. You have to realize that your effort, and that of others, is your means of gaining mastery. Neither raw talent nor good fortune leads to becoming the best; hard work is what gets you there. Ask for feedback about how you're doing. Learn from the constructive criticism you get from others. View the success of others around you as inspiration and not as a threat. When you believe that you can continuously learn, you will. Only those who believe that they can get better make an effort to do so.

Create a Climate for Learning

If people are going to grow and thrive, they need to trust one another. They need to feel safe around each other and believe they can be open and honest. They need to support each person's development, have one another's backs, and be there to lift others up when they stumble or fall. They need to be able to collaborate and cheer everyone on. They need to show respect for differences and be open to alternative viewpoints and backgrounds. Studies of top performers strongly demonstrate that people require a supportive environment to become the best they can be. Researchers have found that when there are high-quality relationships in a work group—relationships characterized by positive regard for others and a sense of mutuality and trust—people use more of the behaviors that lead to learning, and hence growth.[10]

As chairperson of the National Society for Black Engineers (NSBE), Matthew Nelson works with public policymakers, corporate executives, nonprofit organizations, and more than two thousand volunteers to increase the number of engineering degrees granted to black students in the United States. "The leadership philosophy I use within NSBE around culture, trust, and building high-quality connections is the same approach I use with our external partners," he told us. He began to form that philosophy when he was a college student, he explained.

> Leadership doesn't magically appear once you attain a high position. The same philosophy and habits you develop as a student will determine if you get the privilege to lead others as well as your degree of success once you get there. It just so happens that student organizations like NSBE give individuals the opportunity to develop and test their assertions about leadership early in their career.

As an undergraduate NSBE chair at his university, Matthew worked to create a supportive network and learning environment for his board members, believing they would be future leaders in the field of engineering. At the beginning of every semester, Matthew would meet with board members to map out areas of personal development. Throughout the semester, Matthew helped each person set goals, identify learning opportunities, and track whether or not they felt they were meeting their targets. For example, one individual wanted to improve his skills and confidence in public speaking. "I gave him the opportunity to be the face of NSBE's newly minted partnership with the Biomedical Engineering Society," Matthew said. "That gesture solidified the trust he had in me as a leader and true friend."

Another way that Matthew worked to develop his team was to give them constructive feedback. "I never tell NSBE members that they're not doing a good job," Matthew told us.

> I always ask them if they think they're living up to the example they want to set and then we have a conversation—a two-way

dialogue—about whether or not that's true. I've never had to ask anyone to leave the board. We always have a conversation, and sometimes people come to the conclusion on their own that this isn't the right fit for them. But that's because I give them the chance to discuss it first and search their own consciences.

You can't create a climate for learning instantly. "People have learned to trust that I have their best interests in mind," Matthew said.

People know that they don't always get it right the first time they try something and that learning new things can be a bit scary. They don't want to embarrass themselves or look incompetent in front of their peers. To create a climate for learning, you have to make it safe for others to try, to fail, and to learn from their experiences. Make it a habit to ask, "What can we learn?" as often as you can from each project experience, and build on people's experiences so that mistakes are not repeated but are learned from.

It's a fact of life that failures and disappointments cannot be completely avoided. It's how you handle them that will ultimately determine your eventual effectiveness and success. You need to be honest with yourself and with others. You need to own up to your mistakes and reflect on your experiences so that you gain the learning necessary to be better the next time around. It's true for you and true for members of your team or group.

Strengthen Resilience and Grit

It takes determination and strength to deal with the adversities of life and leadership. You can't let the setbacks get you down or allow the roadblocks to get in your way. You can't become overly discouraged when things don't go according to plan. You can't give up when the resistance builds or people criticize your ideas. Nor can you let other tempting new projects divert your attention. You can't lose focus or move on too quickly. You have to stick with it. You must never give up. Heather's and Bryan's successes would never have happened if they had allowed the frustration they were feeling to shut them down. In both situations, resistance from others actually spurred them on to do what was needed: to build the teams necessary to make their programs come about.

The ability to recover quickly from setbacks and continue to pursue a vision of the future is often referred to as *resilience*. Others have called it *grit*. Grit is defined as "perseverance and passion for long-term goals," and it "entails working strenuously toward challenges, maintaining effort and interest over years despite failure, adversity, and plateaus in progress."[11] Showing grit involves setting goals, being obsessed with an idea or project, maintaining focus, sticking with things that take a long time to complete, overcoming setbacks, and the like. Empirical studies, whether with students, cadets in the military, working professionals, artists, teachers, and others, document convincingly that people with the most grit are the ones most likely to achieve positive outcomes. The more grit you demonstrate, the better you do.

Resilience and grit can be developed and strengthened, much like a growth mindset. People with resilience bounce back, and those with grit simply don't give up. These folks interpret setbacks as temporary, local, and changeable.[12] Essentially, people who are resilient, even in times of considerable stress and adversity, remain committed to moving forward by believing that what has happened isn't going to be permanent and that they can do something about the outcome the next time around. As every basketball player knows, 100 percent of the shots *not* taken don't go in. So you'd better keep shooting if you want to make a basket.

When a failure or setback occurs, don't become obsessed with blaming yourself or the people working on the project. Instead consider situational circumstances that contributed to the failure and convey the belief that this particular situation is likely to be temporary, not permanent. Emphasize that the failure or setback is a problem in this instance and not in every case. Even in times of high stress and extreme adversity, resilient people remain committed to moving forward by believing that what has happened isn't going to be permanent and that they can do something about the outcome.

Breed a growth mindset when reaching milestones and achieving success by attributing these to the hard work and effort of the individuals in the group. Convey a belief that many more victories are at hand and be optimistic that good fortune will come eventually and be with your team for a long time. You can bolster resilience by assigning people tasks that are challenging but within their capabilities, focusing on rewards rather than punishments, and encouraging people to see change as full of possibilities.[13]

The Personal-Best Leadership Experience cases all involved change and stressful events in the lives of student leaders, and nearly everyone described the experience in terms consistent with the conditions for psychological hardiness, resilience, and grit. They experienced commitment rather than alienation, control rather than powerlessness, and challenge rather than threat. They had passion. They persevered. They didn't give up despite the failures and setbacks. They showed that, even in the toughest of times, people could experience meaningfulness and mastery. They could overcome great odds, make progress, and change the way things were.

REFLECT AND ACT: EXPERIMENT AND TAKE RISKS

Change is the work of leaders. They are always looking for ways to get it done *better*—continuously improving, innovating, and growing.

They know that sticking to the way things are done today won't get people to the better tomorrow they envision. So they experiment. They tinker. They shake things up. They ask, "What can we change that might make things better?"

Exemplary student leaders view change as a challenge that can be successfully overcome. They believe—and get others to believe—that everyone can influence outcomes and control their own lives. They make sure that the meaning and purpose of change are clearly understood, and they create a strong sense of commitment to the mission.

To get things moving in the right direction, you need to break tasks down into small wins, setting short-term goals or milestones. Take it one step at a time. And whenever you try new things, big or small, stuff happens. People make mistakes, and failures occur. That's why exemplary student leaders create an environment that encourages learning. People need to know that when they experiment and take risks, they won't be punished for failure. Instead, it'll be treated as a learning experience.

You need to create a learning climate—one in which everyone is encouraged to share successes and failures and views continuous improvement as a routine way of doing things. Exemplary student leaders make it a practice to create a climate in which others feel strong and proficient, capable of flourishing even under the most adverse circumstances.

Reflect

The second commitment of Challenge the Process requires leaders to *experiment and take risks by consistently generating small wins and learning from experience.* Reflect on this commitment and answer these questions:

1. What is the most important idea or lesson about exemplary leadership that you learned from this chapter?

    _____

    _____

    _____

    _____

2. What changes do you need to make in your leadership to better Experiment and Take Risks?

    _____

    _____

    _____

    _____

3. In the next section, there are some suggestions on what you can do to put Experiment and Take Risks into practice. After you have reflected on what you learned and what you need to improve, select an action that you can take immediately to become a better leader.

    _____

    _____

    _____

    _____

Take Action

Here are some things you can do to follow through on your commitment to **Experiment and Take Risks:**

- Keep people focused on the tasks or work they all do together and what they can control in their lives, not what they can't.
- Ask yourself what's holding you and your group back and whether there are any obstacles you are putting in your own way.
- Emphasize how personal fulfillment results from consistently challenging yourself to improve. How can you use that to motivate yourself and others?
- Break big projects down into achievable steps. What are some of the "little things" in a project that people can do and succeed at, and consequently see the difference those make in the bigger picture?
- Remind people of the progress they are making every day and how any setbacks are not only temporary but also opportunities for learning.
- Continuously experiment with new ideas. Test them out in a way that will build people's confidence, marking both progress and learning.
- Discuss and reflect on successes and failures; record the lessons learned and make sure that they can be applied in subsequent initiatives.

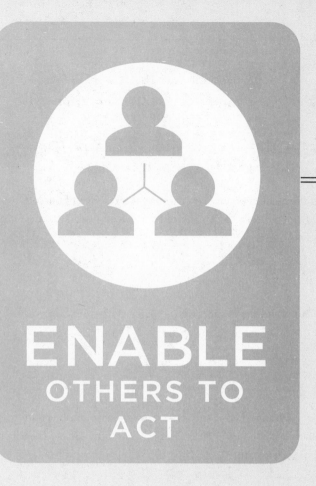

ENABLE
OTHERS TO
ACT

Leaders know they can't do it alone. They need partners to make extraordinary things happen. Exemplary leaders invest in creating trustworthy relationships and building spirited and cohesive teams. Exemplary leaders make others feel strong, capable, and confident to take initiative and responsibility. They build the skills and abilities of their constituents to deliver on commitments. They create a climate where people feel in control of their own lives.

In the next two chapters, we will explore how student leaders:

➤ **Foster Collaboration** by building trust and facilitating relationships.

➤ **Strengthen Others** by increasing self-determination and developing competence.

ENABLE OTHERS TO ACT

Reflections from the *Student Leadership Practices Inventory*

1. Record your overall score from the *Student Leadership Practices Inventory* for ENABLE OTHERS TO ACT here: _____

2. Of the six leadership behaviors that are part of Enable Others to Act, write down the statement for the one you indicated engaging in most frequently:

3. Write down the leadership behavior statement that you felt you engaged in least often:

4. On the basis of your self-assessment, complete this statement: When it comes to Enable Others to Act, my areas of leadership competency are:

5. What Enable Others to Act behaviors do you see as opportunities for improving and strengthening your leadership capability? Make a note of these below so that you can keep them in mind as you read this chapter and the next.

7

Commitment #7: Foster Collaboration

Soon after Attiya Latif became the chair of the Minority Rights Coalition (MRC) at her university, there was a spate of hate crimes on campus, including spray-painted hate speech and swastikas. For Attiya the trouble hit home—literally—when a racial slur was spray-painted across the door of her passkey-protected on-campus apartment. It was time to act, she said.

Attiya mobilized the MRC to reach out to other student organizations to create a campaign in response to on-campus hate crimes. Called Eliminate the Hate, the program was envisioned as a way to curb the hate crimes and to provide a united front of peace and tolerance. She brought together members of the MRC, Black Student Lives Matter, the Latina Student Alliance, and seven other minority student organizations to figure out what to do. Everyone knew that something had to be done, but there was no one clear vision for what needed to happen. Each group came with different priorities and solutions for the best way to make a statement against the hate crimes. Some students wanted to put together something to launch the next day. Attiya and others figured that to make the most impact, the coalition would have to formulate a longer-range plan.

Attiya wanted to make sure that as many visions and voices as possible were heard and considered. She explained:

> I knew that having an immediate reaction to the hate crimes was important, but I also knew that we needed time to plan something that would gain momentum. Our team was split on how things should be handled, but we came up with a solution that honored everyone's ideas.

By creating a forum in which everyone's concerns would be heard and understood, Attiya was able to encourage an open exchange of ideas and knowledge and build a sense of trust among the ten groups with sometimes-competing interests. Her approach eventually led to a greater vision for the Eliminate the Hate campaign than the MRC had at the beginning. "I didn't allow my personal opinions to overshadow what other people wanted," Attiya told us.

> There are ten different organizations, all with different needs and priorities, and it's my job to facilitate a conversation that makes sure that we all come to a consensus about what's important. It's essential to be a facilitator and guide people to a mutual decision. If you're not doing that, then you're not leading anyone. You're just doing what you want to do.

In the end, the group decided on a combined approach of a quick social media response as well as a longer, more strategic person-to-person campaign for the school. First, they would put together an immediate statement proclaiming their mission and what they stood for, which they would post on their social media profiles at noon the next day.

Each organization reached out to other organizations, both on campus and in the community. By noon the next day, when the statement went viral, one hundred different organizations had posted the statement online in a show of solidarity. At the same time, all ten organizations collaborated to create a single new Facebook page on which the statement would live. The first day, the Facebook page generated one thousand new likes. By the evening of the first day, the page had had thirty thousand views.

"I knew then we had the momentum for our weeklong in-person project," Attiya said. She capitalized on that momentum by forming a committee to organize events for each day of the weeklong campaign. Attiya also created an online forum where everyone involved in the campaign could propose ideas. At the end of a day of planning, the top eight ideas, chosen by everyone on the committee, were each given a day for the Eliminate the Hate campaign.

Each day of the campaign featured a different event on campus, open to participation by anyone and live-streamed on Facebook. The first event of the week generated over four hundred thousand views on Facebook. By week's end, the live stream was capturing close to a million audience members. Attiya attributes this success to the way the group's members had evolved a spirit of cooperation. "Everyone felt ownership of the campaign, because everyone felt like their ideas could be heard," Attiya said.

The final event of the Eliminate the Hate campaign broke down the walls between the different MRC organizations. Attiya and a planning committee organized a diversity town hall in the university's multipurpose center, where each minority group on campus had its own room for gathering and discussion. In these conversations, professional experts spoke on different topics, and anyone could offer ideas on solutions for diversity-related issues, such as on-campus housing, orientation needs, and transgender bathrooms.

The Eliminate the Hate campaign significantly raised student awareness of diversity issues. "Since the campaign, we have seen less hate crime and increased awareness on campus," Attiya told us. What's more, there has been "a cultural shift of how students feel ownership over the university space." She explained:

> When we were organizing the campaign, we purposefully made it a campaign that anyone could take and feel ownership of. In the past, students were very apathetic about these issues because they didn't feel like it was about them. We wanted to make sure everyone knew that this campaign was for all students on campus, and I think that started with getting so many other organizations involved

In the end, Eliminate the Hate was a bigger success than Attiya and the other members of the MRC had ever imagined. Attiya believes it's because she worked hard to bring together all the minority student organizations on campus. She showed that she was willing to incorporate their concerns and needs into the MRC's plans and proved she listened to other people's ideas and handed over the reins of leadership, resulting in a bigger, more inclusive project than if she'd only organized it herself. When you create a climate of cooperation and trust, as Attiya and her team did among the school's minority organizations, you create an environment that allows people to freely contribute and innovate. You nurture open exchanges of ideas and honest discussions of issues. You motivate people to go beyond compliance and inspire them to reach for the best in themselves. And you nurture the belief that people can rely on you to do what's in everyone's best interests.

Attiya's experience is a good illustration of something that all exemplary leaders know: leadership is not a solo pursuit. It's a team effort. When talking about personal bests, and when talking about leaders they admire, people speak passionately about teamwork and cooperation as the interpersonal route to success, especially when conditions are extremely challenging and urgent. Leaders of all ages, from all professions and economic sectors around the globe, consistently acknowledge that "you can't do it alone."

Exemplary leaders understand that to create a climate of collaboration, they must determine what the group needs in order to do its work and must then build the team around a common purpose and with mutual respect. Leaders make trust and teamwork high priorities.

Extraordinary performance isn't possible unless there's a strong sense of shared creation and shared responsibility. Exemplary leaders make the commitment to Foster Collaboration by engaging in these essentials:

- **Create a climate of trust**
- **Facilitate relationships**

Collaboration is always an indispensable element for success in any extraordinary endeavor. Leaders, no matter what age, must find a way to invite and encourage collaboration and teamwork. They must be trustworthy themselves, and build relationships with others and between people based on mutual trust and respect.

CREATE A CLIMATE OF TRUST

Trust is the central issue in human relationships. Without trust, you can't lead. Without trust, you can't accomplish extraordinary things. Individuals who are unable to trust others fail to become leaders, precisely because they can't bear to be dependent on the words and works of others. They end up doing all the work themselves, or supervising work so closely they become micromanagers. Their lack of trust in others results in others' lack of trust in them. For you and your group to build and sustain social connections, trust must be reciprocal and reciprocated. Trust is not just what's in your head; it's also what's in your heart.

"The achievement of dreams and ambitions is rarely the product of contributions from a single person," reminds Stephanie Sorg, who went on to tell us:

> Exemplary leaders enlist the help of others and build a team to embark upon the path that achieves mutual success. However, people can only apply themselves to the greatest extent when mutual trust between themselves and the leader is evident.

When she was captain of her club soccer team in high school, Stephanie realized that she had not deeply understood the importance of trust. Then, she said, "I had the pleasure of playing college soccer under the leadership of one of the most inspiring individuals I've ever met." That individual was Dani Weatherholt, who now plays professional soccer for the Orlando Pride. Dani was elected to be one of the team's captains, Stephanie says, "because she exhibited the qualities that would bring out the best in each player. The secret ingredient in her recipe for success was trust. Her initial mission as a leader was to let others know what she stood for, communicate her values and goals, and disclose information about herself." For example, one evening early in the preseason, the team took some time to open up and share something about themselves that a typical person would not know. Dani was the first to put herself in a vulnerable place and share an aspect of her life with which she was uncomfortable. With each person who shared something about herself, Dani made it clear through her words and actions that she fully supported and appreciated the player for having the bravery and trust to disclose those secrets. "After having that experience with her," Stephanie said,

> I felt a greater sense of trust between the two of us, as well as with the rest of the group. It takes a lot of courage to open yourself up to others, making yourself vulnerable,

and through the initiatives that Dani took, I learned that
the benefits of taking the necessary steps to building trust
significantly outweigh the risks and reservations.

With a greater sense of belonging and mutual trust, Stephanie felt
that she worked harder out on the field and was significantly more
invested in the goal that the team was working toward. "The bottom
line," she said, "was that I possessed a greater sense of commitment to
both the environment and the people involved."

When trust is the norm, people make decisions efficiently and
swiftly, and they innovate more quickly and effortlessly. When you
create a climate of trust, you create an environment that enables people
to contribute freely and to innovate. You nurture an open exchange
of ideas and an honest discussion of issues. You motivate people to go
beyond compliance and inspire them to reach for the best in themselves. You foster the belief that people can rely on you to do what's in
everyone's best interests. To get these kinds of results, you must ante
up first in the game of trust. You must listen and learn from others,
and you have to share information and resources with others. Trust
comes first; following comes second.

Be the First to Trust

Samantha Malone spent a good deal of her time outside the classroom working with a free SAT prep class for minority students. She
understood that building trust is a process that begins when someone
(either you or the other party) is willing to risk being the first to open
up, being the first to show vulnerability, and being the first to let go of
control. She explained:

If you want your team to trust you, you need to give a little
to get anything back, meaning you should trust them before

you expect them to trust you. This practice sets reciprocity standards for the group, showing that trust is expected and allowing trust between members to spread as they work toward their collective goal.

Generally, it is you, the leader, who goes first when it comes to trust, demonstrating your trust in others before asking them to trust you. Going first is a scary proposition. You're taking a chance. When Dani Weatherholt went first, she was betting that others wouldn't betray her confidence and that they'd take good care of the information she communicated and of the feelings she shared. You're risking that others won't take advantage of you and that you can rely on them to do what's right. This requires considerable self-confidence, but the payoff is huge. Trust is contagious. When you trust others, they are much more likely to trust you. However, when you choose not to trust, distrust is equally contagious. If you exhibit distrust, others will hesitate to place their trust in you and their colleagues. It's up to you to set the example and be willing to overcome the need to hide all your vulnerabilities.

When Jordan Goff started working with a project team, he quickly had to develop the confidence that he could trust others. As many students know, working on class projects as a group can be stressful, frustrating, and challenging because of the various levels of commitment of the people in the group. Jordan knew that he couldn't do the project all alone and that he needed his classmates to complete the task successfully, but he was concerned that they wouldn't live up to his expectations.

Eventually, Jordan was overwhelmed by the work required, and he decided to take a chance on his classmate Stanley and ask him to take over an important piece of the project. Stanley did not disappoint Jordan, turning in great-quality work and ahead of schedule. That's when it dawned on Jordan that he needed to give up control and create an atmosphere where people can count on others to meet their responsibilities. As Jordan began to trust others with carrying out important details of the project—taking into account their individual skills, abilities, needs, and interests—their trust in him grew. By going first, by showing that he trusted Stanley to succeed, Jordan demonstrated to his classmates that he was confident that they could learn from and support one another.

Self-disclosure is another way that you go first, as Dani demonstrated with Stephanie and her soccer teammates. Letting others know what you stand for, what you value, what you want, what you hope for, and what you're willing (and not willing) to do reveals information about yourself. You can't be certain that other people will appreciate your candor, agree with your aspirations, or interpret your words and actions in the way you intend. But once you take the risk of being open, others are more likely to take a similar risk and be willing to work toward mutual understanding.

Trust is built in many ways, but it can't be forced. If someone refuses to understand you, viewing you as neither well intentioned nor competent, there may be little you can do to change his or her perceptions and behavior. However, keep in mind that placing trust in others is the safer bet with most people most of the time. Trust begets trust. It's a reciprocal process. When you are first to trust, others are more likely to trust you.

Show Concern for Others

Ike Opara was a sophomore on his college soccer team when he was heavily pursued to enter the Major League Soccer draft at the end of the year as a projected top-three pick. Although Ike acknowledged that it was a terrific honor, he just didn't feel quite right about it. He had been part of his university's team that had taken the national championship the year before, and if he entered the draft, he would be leaving when they were all deeply connected and thriving as a team. They had an excellent opportunity to win another national title, and Ike felt as though his departure might jeopardize the team's chances of achieving that goal. "I wanted to help us win again if we could," he told us. "These were my best friends; I counted on them, and they counted on me."

When Ike talked with his teammates and his coach, everyone was very supportive of whichever decision he might make. "That's the thing about a team," he said, "we're all connected." He also knew he was taking a risk financially and professionally by not going pro after his sophomore year. Uncontrollable factors, such as a serious injury, could hinder his development or even end his career prematurely. After taking all these factors into account, Ike chose to embark on his professional journey one year later. "I'm grateful it all worked out," he said. "I got to spend another year as part of a great team with great people, many of whom I still consider good friends, and I got a year further in my academics."

The concern you show for others is one of the clearest and most un-ambiguous signals of your trustworthiness. When others know you will put their interests ahead of your own, they won't hesitate to trust you.[1] However, this is something people need to see in your actions. Ike's decision to stay in school and play on the soccer team for another year was a crystal-clear expression of his values, demonstrating that he could be trusted and how he had placed his trust in his teammates. He listened to others, paid attention to their ideas and concerns, and was open to their influence. When you show your openness to the ideas of other people and your interest in their concerns, people will be more open to *yours*.

The simple act of listening to what other people have to say and appreciating their unique points of view demonstrates your respect for them and their ideas and earns their trust. Being sensitive to what others are going through creates a bond between people that makes it easier to accept another's guidance and advice. These actions build mutual empathy and understanding, which in turn increase trust. Leaders demonstrate how powerful both listening and empathy can be in building trust. You need to see the world through others' eyes and make sure that you consider alternative viewpoints. Those who follow you need to feel they can talk freely with you about their difficulties. They need to believe that you'll be caring and constructive in your responses if they are to be willing to share their ideas, their frustrations, and their dreams with you. They won't do that if they don't feel that you are open with them in return.

Those students with the highest levels of engagement were those who found it most true that their leaders "actively listen to diverse points of view." There was an astounding gap in this regard; those students who reported that their leader was a very frequent active listener were over ten times more engaged than those who said this was a leadership behavior which their leader rarely demonstrated. Not surprisingly, as shown in Figure 7.1, how students viewed the skill level of their leader also increased dramatically as they observed more and more listening on the leader's part.

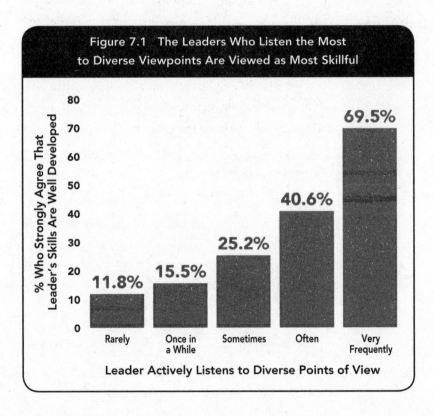

Figure 7.1 The Leaders Who Listen the Most to Diverse Viewpoints Are Viewed as Most Skillful

Share Knowledge and Information

Competence is a vital component of trust and confidence in a leader. As our studies have demonstrated, people want to believe that their leaders know what they're talking about and what they're doing. One way to demonstrate your competence is to share what you know and encourage others to do the same. You can convey your insights and know-how, share lessons learned from experience, and connect team members to valuable resources and people. Student leaders who play this role of knowledge builder set an example for how team members should behave toward each other. As a result, team members' trust in one another and in the leader increases, along with their performance.[2]

That's what happened with Gregory Smith's university debate team. The team had grown so fast that it didn't have enough coaches to help all the students adequately prepare and compete. Gregory and another senior on the team stepped in to assist by sharing lessons from their more extensive debate experience and by coaching the younger competitors. "I led practice every Thursday night, working with anyone who wanted to improve their performance," Gregory told us. He also began teaching an undergraduate-level public speaking class.

Gregory saw the teaching and coaching he was doing not just as a one-way transfer of his knowledge and skills to the debate team but as a matter of "building communication bridges" within the team. He told us:

> One of the greatest needs I filled on my team was being
> a sounding board for teammates—whether critiquing an
> event or just listening and encouraging teammates with their
> problems, because even nonspeech difficulties can distract
> them from their best performance or infect the team when
> ignored.

Gregory also pointed out that "I was certainly not alone in seeing and acting on this need on my team." Others began to follow his lead, and people started to open up with one another and share information and insights about what they were learning from their practice and tournament experiences. All this, combined with the team's already high motivation and "willingness to work together," Gregory said, "catapulted us from being a mediocre debate team into being one of the best in the country."

Student leaders like Gregory know that trust among team members goes up when people share knowledge and information, and the fact that performance increases as a result underscores how important it is for leaders to stay focused on the needs of their team. If you show a willingness to trust others with information, they will be more inclined to overcome any doubts they might have about sharing information. However, if you display a reluctance to trust—or if you're overly concerned about protecting your turf and keeping things to yourself—you'll dampen their trust and their performance. And trust, once lost, is very difficult to regain.

FACILITATE RELATIONSHIPS

When we asked college senior Samantha Malone what she would teach someone about leadership based on her personal-best experience, she said, "I would tell them to understand that the experience is not all about you—it is about your followers. Take each person's thoughts into consideration; go out of your way to ask what they think. You cannot lead a team, without a team to lead."

Samantha's lesson was a common refrain. As we noted previously, "You can't do it alone" is the leader's mantra. You really can't be much of a leader if no one wants to follow in the same direction with you. What defines leaders, quite simply, is that they have followers. And what makes people willing to follow is, paradoxically, that leaders turn their followers into leaders. Leaders have the best interests of others in their hearts, and trusting in any other person is evidence of a caring relationship. Leadership is a relationship that needs to be nurtured and treasured. When leaders can get the people on their team, in their class, or in their community to trust one another, the strength of these relationships facilitates the ability of everyone to work together for the collective good. When this is the case, asking for help and sharing information come naturally, and working toward a common goal becomes the norm.

Kerrin McCarthey was a sophomore when she got involved in a peer advisory board for the college's first-generation student mentoring program. She was responsible for helping guide the program and the other mentors who worked with a small group of students throughout the year. The previous boards' practice had been to have all the students attend a retreat to kick off the program and then meet with their mentors on a regular basis to talk about all sorts of things related to the college experience and how to be academically successful. Kerrin immediately saw that one of the program's difficulties was that after a few months, students didn't seem as excited and involved as they had been right after the retreat. She felt that this had a great deal to do with the fact that neither the mentors nor the students they served had developed solid relationships. There also was a general lack of trust in the mentoring process and even in the value and worthiness of the program itself.

Kerrin talked with her fellow board members to get their perceptions, and then she started consulting the mentors. "It was very awkward at first to talk with others and get them to open up about what they were feeling and thinking," she told us. "I realized that maybe we hadn't developed much trust yet so that everyone could feel comfortable sharing their thoughts." In her conversations with the board members and the mentors, Kerrin communicated first that she "felt honored to have their trust" and that she would do whatever it took to help them believe in her and in the program.

She often went first in sharing some of her personal experiences, both during times when she was mentored and when she served as a mentor, thinking that this would help others feel more relaxed in sharing what was on their minds. She believed that if they thought she wasn't trying to judge or criticize, they might open up and talk about what was on their minds. She asked probing questions about their experiences, what they thought the program needed, and how the mentors could better help and work with their mentees. They also talked about what might be keeping other students from getting more involved.

The result of Kerrin's probing seemed to come down to the core issue that folks hadn't taken the time to develop genuine relationships with one another. After the sense of camaraderie from the kickoff retreat wore off, the mentees didn't care about much else because they didn't see their mentors caring. Kerrin continued seeking out stories and ideas of what would help both the students and their mentors realize what they wanted from the program and began to get everyone more personally involved in regular gatherings. As a result, the mentors grew more committed to the program because they wanted to be a part of it and make a meaningful difference rather than just going through the motions. Seeing the mentors' newfound dedication, the students grew more enthusiastic and started gaining more value from the mentoring experience. Soon they became advocates for the program, encouraging their friends and other students to participate.

Leaders like Kerrin understand that facilitating relationships is how leaders build a climate of trust. To collaborate, people must be able to rely on one another. They must appreciate that they need each other to be most successful. To create an environment in which people know they can count on each other, student leaders need to develop cooperative goals and roles, support norms of reciprocity, structure projects to promote joint efforts, and encourage face-to-face interactions. All these practices played a big part in the turnaround of the peer mentoring program.

Develop Cooperative Goals and Roles

For a team of people to have a positive experience together, they must have shared goals and a clear reason for being together. Otherwise, why not just do it all by yourself?

Have you had a group assignment that caused you to think to yourself, "Holy cow, I could do this whole project by myself and be better off. This is taking forever and going nowhere." That was precisely Tommy Baldacci's thinking when he began working with two classmates on their yearlong civil engineering senior design project. It didn't take too long for him to find himself not seeing eye-to-eye with one of his colleagues and saying to himself, "I will *never* work with this person again!" Then, he told us, he realized that he still had six months to go, working with that person on this project.

> Something needed to change, and I could not wait for him to change; I had to be the one to adjust. It took every bit of me to swallow my pride and admit that I needed him to succeed at the project. I looked at the aspects of each of my group members and considered what each member did best. By laying out each of our strengths, I made it apparent to the group that we each were a crucial part of the project.
>
> The culture of fighting for who was going to make the decisions was gone. We each saw our roles and worked together toward a common goal. There were many times when the hours were long and adversity was met, but by feeling that we were all in it together, we were able to stay grinding. We ended up finishing first in our section and celebrated this achievement together as a group.

Tommy told us that this experience taught him that working toward a common goal is the easiest way to create a collaborative culture, and that trusting others to do what they said they would do is an essential part of the process. "It's that trust which empowers each individual to perform at the best of his or her abilities," Tommy said. "The energy and power that each member of a group feels from each other are the synergistic strengths of a collaborative culture."

The most important ingredient in every collective achievement is a common goal. Common purpose binds people into cooperative efforts. It creates a sense of interdependence, a condition in which all participants know that they cannot succeed unless everyone else succeeds, or at least that they can't succeed unless they coordinate their efforts. Without a sense that "we're all in this together"—that the success of one depends on the success of all—it's virtually impossible to create the conditions for positive teamwork. If you want individuals or groups to work cooperatively, you have to give them a good reason to do so, such as a goal that can only be accomplished by working together.

Keeping individuals focused on a common goal promotes a stronger sense of teamwork than emphasizing individual objectives. For cooperation to succeed, determine how to design roles so that every person's contributions are both additive and cumulative to the outcome. Individuals must clearly understand that unless they contribute whatever they can, the team fails. For two people in a fishing boat, one can't say to the other, "Your side of the boat is sinking, but my side looks just fine."

Fostering collaborative goals and roles means making sure that there aren't any in-groups or out-groups, any "us versus them," or competition for attention among members. People have to identify with the group they are part of in order to work together. Schools create identity with mascots, uniform colors, unique gestures, and songs. Fraternities and sororities do it with Greek letters, handshakes, special symbols, ceremonies, and rituals. Project teams do it with special names for product versions, insider jokes, swag, badges, and the like. Make sure you get everyone feeling that they are part of one team. It multiplies the strength of their feeling that it's "all for one and one for all."

Support Norms of Reciprocity

In any effective long-term relationship, there must be a sense of reciprocity. If one partner always gives and the other always takes, the one who gives will feel taken advantage of, and the one who takes will feel superior. When this happens, cooperation is virtually impossible. University of Michigan political scientist and National Medal of Science recipient Robert Axelrod demonstrated the power of reciprocity in a series of studies involving the Prisoner's Dilemma paradigm.[3] The dilemma is this: two parties (individuals or groups) are confronted with a series of situations in which they must decide whether to cooperate. They don't know in advance what the other party will do.

There are two basic strategies: cooperate or compete. Each party has to make a selection without knowing in advance what the other party will do. The maximum individual payoff comes when one player decides to compete and the other party decides to cooperate. In this "I win, but you lose" approach, one party gains at the other's expense. If both parties choose not to cooperate and attempt to maximize individual payoffs, then both lose. If both parties choose to cooperate, both win, though the individual payoff for a cooperative move is less than for a competitive one.

Scientists from around the world submitted their proposals for winning in a computer simulation of this test of win-win versus win-lose strategies. "Amazingly enough," says Robert, "the winner was the simplest of all strategies submitted: cooperate on the first move and then do whatever the other player did on the previous move. This strategy succeeded by eliciting cooperation from others, not by defeating them."[4] Simply put, people who reciprocate are more likely to be successful than those who try to maximize individual advantage. Cooperation wins over selfishness in the long run.

The dilemmas that can be successfully solved by this strategy are by no means restricted to theoretical research. Similar predicaments arise every day: "What price might I pay if I try to maximize my personal gain?" "Should I give up a little for the sake of others?" "Will others take advantage of me if I'm cooperative?" Reciprocity turns out to be the most successful approach for such daily decisions, because it shows both a willingness to be cooperative and an unwillingness to be taken advantage of. As a long-term strategy, reciprocity minimizes the risk of escalation: If people know that you'll respond in kind, why would they start trouble? If people know that you'll reciprocate, they know that the best way to deal with you is to cooperate and become beneficiaries of your cooperation.

Reciprocity leads to predictability and stability in relationships—in other words, trust. It's less stressful to work with others when you understand how they will behave in response. Treat others as you'd like for them to treat you, and it's likely they'll repay you many times over. Once you help others succeed, acknowledge their accomplishments, and let them shine, they'll never forget it. The norms of reciprocity come into play, and people are more than willing to return the favor and do what they can to make you successful. Whether the rewards of cooperation are tangible or intangible, when people understand that they will be better off by cooperating, they're inclined to recognize the legitimacy of others' interests in an effort to promote their own welfare.

Structure Projects to Promote Joint Efforts

People are more likely to cooperate if the payoffs for working together are greater than those associated with working by themselves. Many people who grow up in Westernized countries that emphasize individualistic or competitive achievement have the perception that they'll do better if each person is rewarded based solely on his or her individual accomplishments. They're wrong. In a world that's trying to do more with less, competitive strategies lose to strategies that promote collaboration.[5]

The motivation for working diligently on one's job, while keeping in mind the overall common objective, is reinforced when the team's outcome—not simply individual effort—gets rewarded. Certainly, each individual within the group has a distinct role, but on world-class teams, everyone knows that if they only do their separate parts well, they are unlikely to achieve the group's goal.

Cooperative behavior requires people to understand that by working together, they will be able to accomplish something that no one can accomplish individually. You wouldn't necessarily think of fencing as a team sport, but that's what college senior and nationally ranked fencing champion Zachary Chien told us he got the students he coaches to realize in their practice sessions. "My first and probably most difficult challenge as a coach," explained Zach, "was creating an environment that fostered collaboration amongst all my students. Even though everyone represents the same club, at the end of the day, fencing is an individual sport, so athletes often prioritized their own development."

Although he had personally developed cooperative, respectful, and growth-oriented relationships with all of his students, most of them didn't have that type of relationship with each other. They were often competitive and didn't socialize and bond as much as other athletes in traditional team sports. To rectify this, Zach created skill games and drills that required teamwork and cooperation to succeed. For example, students fenced each other, and after each touch, whoever scored told their partner exactly how they set up their point; their partner described what was happening, why it was happening, and how to correct it. These activities brought a new energy to practice, and athletes began fixing each other's form and sharing personal strategies and tactics to help those who were struggling, Zach told us.

> Once athletes began showing more support toward one
> another, I was able to get them to buy in to the larger idea
> that fostering collaboration and sharing growth is in every-
> one's best interest. I told my athletes that they couldn't get
> to the top on their own, and I alone couldn't help get them
> there. They need the support from the people they practice
> with. In order to be the best, you have to beat the best.
>
>   That being said, it's incredibly helpful if the people you
> train with are the best. When your toughest competition
> is the people you practice with five days a week, tourna-
> ments become so much easier. This lesson was understood
> quickly, and after a few weeks, we created an environment
> of respect and communal support. Having these types of
> relationships allows people to compete freely and without
> worry, which over the last eighteen months resulted in at
> least one podium finish for all twenty-five of my students.

Joint efforts reinforce the importance of working collaboratively and helping one another. Figuring out how to take as much as possible from others, while contributing as little as possible, has the opposite effect. You need to make sure that the long-term benefits of joint efforts are greater than the short-term benefits of working alone or competing with others.

Support Face-to-Face and Durable Interactions

Group goals and roles, shared identity, reciprocity, and promoting joint efforts are all essential for collaboration to occur. Also vital are positive face-to-face interactions and durable interpersonal relationships.

People trust their friends and work together with them more easily, and innovatively, than they do with strangers or people they never expect to interact with again. This is true not only in the classroom but also in globally distributed relationships. Getting to know others firsthand is vital to cultivating trust and collaboration. It's the leader's responsibility to provide frequent and lasting opportunities for team members to connect between disciplines, across groups, and among peers. "My best class in college," Kim Chi Hoang told us, "was when the teacher made us learn the names of everyone else in the class and find out some things about them."

> He also had us sit next to someone new in each class, and encouraged us to come early to class and spend a few moments just chatting about "whatever" with the people around us. He was constantly mixing around the people in our group discussions, so we had a chance to interact with everyone in the class and not just the people who were seated next to us. All of this made it much easier for us to eventually work on an entire class project assignment; we felt more accountable to one another in meeting our individual commitments. Another payoff was that I formed relationships in this class which easily extended to working with these classmates in subsequent courses.

It's often challenging to find the time for everyone to meet. Technology and social media can certainly enhance communication. Virtual connections abound, and in a global economy, no organization could function if people had to fly halfway around the world to exchange information, make decisions, or resolve disputes. That said, the stroke of a key, the click of a mouse, or the switch of a video doesn't get you the same results as an in-person conversation does. There are limits to virtual trust. As Viet Doan told us about his experience working with a group of high school friends to open a bar and grill in Ho Chi Minh City:

> You have to build trust, and the most effective way is to get everyone on the same page as soon as possible. The first session should not be so much about planning as it should be about getting to know one another. The time "wasted" getting everyone on the same page is still many times better than the cumulative time wasted dealing with frustration among people who don't know each other or feel they don't have anything in common.

For example, rather than texting a person across the hall, talk face-to-face first and then, if necessary, you can continue that communication online. Work as hard as you can to get the members of your group together in person as often as possible. Firsthand experience with another human being is simply a more reliable way of creating identification, increasing adaptability, and reducing misunderstandings than virtual connections.[6]

Virtual trust, like virtual reality, is one step removed from the real thing. Human beings are social animals; it's in our nature to want to interact, and bits and bytes or pixilated images make for a very fragile social foundation.[7] If you mainly know the members of your group virtually, you probably don't know them well enough to trust them with extremely important matters. You will have to reconcile the benefits of virtual meeting time and the costs of bringing people together face-to-face with the knowledge that building trust depends on getting to know one another on a personal level.

People who expect their interactions to be more than a single incident, who believe they will continue to interact with one another in the future, and who like being in a relationship are more likely to cooperate in the present. Knowing that you'll have to deal again with someone tomorrow, next week, or in another class next term ensures that you won't easily forget about how you've treated one another. Durable relationships make the impact of today's actions on tomorrow's contacts that much more pronounced. Also, frequent interactions between people promote positive feelings about one another. If you wish to maximize your leadership effectiveness, begin with the assumption that you'll be interacting in some way with these people again and that these relationships will be critical to your mutual success in the future.

REFLECT AND ACT: FOSTER COLLABORATION

"You can't do it alone" is the mantra of exemplary student leaders—and for good reason. You can't make extraordinary things happen by yourself. Collaboration is the key skill that enables classrooms, clubs, teams, and communities to function effectively. You sustain collaboration when you create a climate of trust and facilitate effective long-term relationships within your group. You need to promote a sense of mutual dependence—feeling part of a group in which everyone knows they need one another to be successful.

Trust is the lifeblood of collaborative teamwork. To create and sustain the conditions for long-lasting connections, you must trust others, they must trust you, and they must trust each other. To build that trust, you must share information and knowledge freely with people in your group, show that you understand their needs and interests, be open and receptive to their ideas, make use of their abilities and expertise, and—most of all—demonstrate that you trust them before you ask them to trust you.

The challenge of facilitating relationships is making sure everyone recognizes that they are interdependent and need each other to succeed. Cooperative goals and roles contribute to a sense of collective purpose, and the best incentive for people to work to achieve shared goals is the knowledge that you and others will do the same. Structure projects to reward joint efforts. Get people interacting and encourage communication through face-to-face dealings as often as possible to reinforce the durability of relationships.

Reflect

The first commitment of Enable Others to Act is to *foster collaboration by building trust and facilitating relationships.* Reflect on this commitment and answer these questions:

1. What is the most important idea or lesson about exemplary leadership that you learned from this chapter?

   _____

   _____

   _____

   _____

2. What changes do you need to make in your leadership to better Foster Collaboration?

   _____

   _____

   _____

   _____

3. In the next section, there are some suggestions on what you can do to put Foster Collaboration into practice. After you have reflected

on what you learned and what you need to improve, select an action that you can take immediately to become a better leader.

_____

_____

_____

_____

Take Action

Here are ways you can live out your commitment to **Foster Collaboration:**

- Identify someone you can extend your trust to, even if he or she hasn't already shown it to you. Take the initiative and seek reciprocity.
- Share information about yourself—your hopes, your strengths, your fears, your mistakes—the things that make you who you are.
- Spend time getting to know those in your group and learning what makes them tick. Similarly, find ways to engage people in meaningful conversations where they can get to know each other.
- Listen, listen, and then listen some more.
- Share with others what you know, answer their questions, connect them to resources they need, and introduce them to others who might be helpful.
- Clearly and frequently communicate the common goal that you are all striving to achieve, the shared values that are important, and the larger purpose everyone is a part of.
- Structure projects and assignments so that there is a common goal that requires people to cooperate and help each other out. Make visible the fact that people are interdependent with one another for success.

8

Commitment #8: Strengthen Others

L earning is just knowledge until you put it to use and reflect on it. You have to be able to turn it into something that you can use in the future," Amy Lebrecht and Zachariah Karp told us. That was the philosophy of the alternative spring break program they developed as students at a southeastern university.

The alternative spring break was a weeklong trek where all the participants were paired up, and each pair had to plan a service learning event, each in a different city along the way. Over the course of the eight days, the group volunteered for three-hour service stops at a variety of different service-based organizations, including homeless shelters, a Salvation Army store, and a Habitat for Humanity construction site, all chosen and arranged by the students.

It was up to each team of students to find an organization whose purpose resonated with them and then to coordinate with its leaders to provide a service learning experience for the entire group. Amy and Zachariah assigned the teams the cities in which they'd be leading an activity and provided some examples of where to search for service organizations to partner with, but the proposal for the specific project, as well as the logistics of each learning experience, was left up to the participants. In that way, the entire alternative spring break activity rested on the shoulders of the students themselves.

"We wanted to give them an opportunity to take ownership and find agencies that provided services they were really passionate about," Amy said. She went on to say:

> I don't believe the trip would've had the same impact if we had been arranging every stop and telling them to get involved in different causes—we wanted them to explore the things they really cared about and then find a way to transform that passion into action.

Given the opportunity to take responsibility of one small piece of the trip, without having to plan the entire trip themselves, each team had a sense of personal ownership over the entire alternative spring break experience.

In addition to taking charge of one of the service learning activities, everyone on the trip was responsible for handling some of the everyday logistics, such as cooking dinner for the group. Even this activity turned into a learning process that evolved throughout the trip. Zachariah recalled that at one stop, there was only a single microwave available to prepare food for seventeen hungry people. The team responsible for dinner that night decided to have baked potatoes. "They put together a toppings bar in their room and cycled us in and out, cooking the potatoes in the microwave and allowing us to dress the potatoes ourselves," Zachariah said. "It was a pretty unique solution."

"When we hit the ground running on spring break," Amy said, "there was some learning curve at each stop, but we wanted them to be able to learn from their experiences, so we did our best to keep our hands off. We wanted them to know, this is on you, this is about becoming the leader that you want to be, the leader that we know you can be."

Amy and Zachariah facilitated discussions in which the whole group would sit down after dinner and reflect on the successes of the day, talk about its challenges, and celebrate the hard work of the team in charge of the activities for the day. "We asked them to reflect on the experience that they'd been through and pick out specific ways that each experience made them a better leader," Amy told us. "I actually think that was one of the most important parts of the trip, really solidifying all of the things they'd gone through and what they learned."

At the end of the evening reflection, Amy and Zachariah recognized what behavior and actions had made that day a success, whether it was planning and leading the volunteer activity; handling an unexpected request, grocery shopping; or creatively preparing dinner. They publicly acknowledged each team member, giving specific examples of what he or she did well. This was a way to help the team develop from their experiences and cement the lessons learned throughout the alternative spring break. Amy said, "We really depended on each other to get through each stop—we're a team, but that team is made up of different people, each of whom had to do his or her job to get us to the end of a successful day of volunteering."

Exemplary student leaders like Amy and Zachariah make a commitment to Strengthen Others. They enable people to take ownership of and responsibility for the group's success by enhancing their competence and their confidence in their abilities, by listening to their ideas and acting on them, by involving them in important decisions, and by acknowledging and giving credit for their contributions. As leaders, Amy and Zachariah gave each team a sense of personal ownership over the entire alternative spring break program in a way that would not have been possible if they had simply planned each stop and let the team members execute the work. The team members were able to explore and try new things, learning new skills and strengthening their overall capability and self-assurance.

Creating a climate in which people are fully engaged and feel in control of their own lives is at the heart of Strengthening Others. Exemplary leaders build an environment that develops people's abilities to perform their tasks and bolsters their self-confidence. In a climate of competence and confidence, people don't hesitate to hold themselves personally accountable for results; they feel profound ownership for their achievements and contribute all they can to make extraordinary things happen.

To Strengthen Others, exemplary student leaders engage in two essentials. They:

- **Enhance self-determination**
- **Develop competence and confidence**

Leaders significantly increase people's belief in their own ability to make a difference. They move from *being in control* to *giving over control* to others, becoming more like their coach. They help people learn new skills and develop existing talents, and provide the institutional supports required for ongoing growth and change. In the final analysis, leaders realize that their responsibility is not to create more followers but to develop more leaders.

ENHANCE SELF-DETERMINATION

Leaders accept and act on this paradox of power: you become most powerful when you give your power away. Long before *empowerment* entered the mainstream vocabulary, exemplary leaders understood how important it was for their constituents to feel strong, capable, and efficacious. People who feel weak, incompetent, and insignificant will consistently underperform; they are disengaged, hoping they can flee the situation, and are ripe for disenchantment, even revolution.

Individuals who are not confident about their power, regardless of their organizational position or place, tend to hoard whatever shreds of influence they have. We've asked thousands of people over the past thirty years to tell us about their experiences of feeling powerless as well as powerful. Think about actions or situations that have made you feel powerless, weak, or insignificant, like a pawn in someone else's chess game. Are yours similar to what others have reported?

REPRESENTATIVE ACTIONS AND CONDITIONS THAT STUDENTS SAY MAKE THEM FEEL *POWERLESS*

- "No one was interested in, listened to, or paid attention to my opinion or questions."

- "The leader argued with me in front of my peers—even called me derogatory names."

- "My decisions were not supported by others, even though they had said they would back me up."

- "Someone else took credit for my hard work and results."

- "Information I needed to know was not forthcoming, and I wasn't part of the conversation on things that mattered to what I was doing."

- "I was given responsibility but no authority to actually make decisions or hold others accountable."

- "Our leader played favorites, and I wasn't one of them!"

Now think about what it's like during times when you feel powerful: strong, efficacious, like the creator of your own experience. Is what you remember similar to what others recall?

> ## REPRESENTATIVE ACTIONS AND CONDITIONS THAT STUDENTS SAY MAKE THEM FEEL *POWERFUL*
>
> - "All the important information and data were shared with me."
>
> - "I was able to make choices and use my own judgment about how we would handle a situation."
>
> - "People asked for my opinion and listened to what I had to say; in fact, my ideas often carried the day."
>
> - "The leader had my back, and supported the decisions that I made."
>
> - "I was given the chance to learn new skills and the opportunities to apply them."
>
> - "I was appreciated for my accomplishments, especially from people I respected."
>
> - "Our leader made time to let me know how I was doing and where I could be improving."

As you examine what people say about powerless and powerful times, there is one clear and consistent message: *feeling powerful—literally feeling "able"—comes from a profound sense of being in control of your life.* People everywhere share this fundamental need. When you feel able to determine your own destiny, when you believe you can mobilize the resources and support necessary to complete a task, then you will persist in your efforts to achieve. However, when you feel controlled by others, when you believe that you lack support or resources, you naturally show little commitment to excel. Even though you may comply, you still realize how much more you could contribute if you wanted to.

What students have told us about the actions and conditions that make them feel powerful and powerless is consistent with what Yi Song told us about an internship she had in the international department of a major Chinese bank. It was a terrible experience, Song explained, because her supervisor did not provide any of the conditions that would make her feel powerful:

> She thought that I was just a junior undergraduate student, and so she did not trust me to do anything. Instead of trusting and enabling me, she chose to put me aside. In our first conversation, she told me, "I am not going to teach you anything here. If you want you can help them type and print documents, but do not ask me anything." When I tried to explain to her that I had enough knowledge to contribute, she asked me to shut up. The way she talked to me on the first day also made me avoid face-to-face interactions with her. I kept my meeting time with her as minimal as possible. I felt stressed and unhappy every day at work.
>
> In my case, she did not give me respect and was not willing to share knowledge and information with me. When my leader does not show respect to me, I tend not to try my best to finish my work. Thus from the very beginning, I was not motivated to perform at my best.

What Song experienced was not unique to her. She noticed that the supervisor's lack of trust permeated the entire working group. "Team members did not communicate with each other, and because she failed to create norms of reciprocity, they rarely shared information with each other," Song explained. "We did not build trust with others or facilitate relationships. No one cooperated as a team; we all worked as individuals. If there was a problem, it was typically ignored, and instead of asking for help, we tried to find out a solution on our own." Given this environment, Song was afraid to ask her supervisor or colleagues any questions, didn't learn very much, and, to no surprise, wasn't all that efficient. "I felt powerless when working with this supervisor," Song explained. "I wanted to perform better, but was not able to figure a better way out."

Consequently, after several weeks Song asked to join another team and the contrast in her experience, and performance, could not have been more profound. Her new supervisor trusted her and was willing to educate and share information with her. The working environment was friendly; people talked with one another, shared information, and wanted to be helpful. Consequently, says Song, "I learned more from them. I had chances to do similar tasks that I could not do in the old team. My new supervisor gave me more authority to access more information, and I felt I performed much better, compared to the previous one."

The most effective leaders, as Song's experience documents, exemplify the actions that make people feel powerful.[1] They realize that leadership actions that increase peoples' sense of self-determination, self-confidence, and personal effectiveness make people more powerful and significantly enhance the energy and commitment they put forward.[2] Through actions that make people powerful, both figuratively and literally, they are not actually giving their power away but enhancing their sphere of influence. Self-determination is enhanced when people are given the opportunity to make choices, exercise latitude, and feel personally accountable.

Provide Choices

Freedom is the ability to make choices. People who perceive that they don't have any choices feel trapped; and, like rats in a maze, when left with no alternatives, they typically stop moving and eventually shut down. By giving people genuine autonomy, leaders can reduce the sense of powerlessness and accompanying stress that people feel and increase their willingness to exercise their capabilities more fully. You want people to take initiative and be self-directed.

What impact do leaders have when they "give others a great deal of freedom and choice in deciding how to do their work"? Students whose leaders very frequently provide this latitude evaluate their leader's skills over three times more favorably than students whose leaders do so only rarely. In addition, as shown in Figure 8.1, the gap in productivity between those students who feel empowered and those

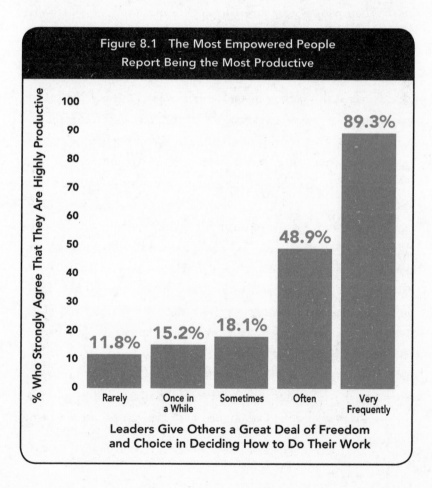

Figure 8.1 The Most Empowered People Report Being the Most Productive

who don't is dramatic. Students feel significantly more productive as a result of their leader's providing an opportunity to use their judgment and to have discretion in how their work is completed.

Francis Appeadu-Mensah served as director of his school's drama club in South Africa and felt that it had great potential for helping his classmates find new avenues for personal expression. He promised them that they could participate in any activity they wished (for example, writing, directing, or performing) in order to discover their passions and their abilities. He gave them choices, telling them that "this is a place where you can explore and decide where your talent lies." When people were new to the club or simply not sure what part of the club they wanted to explore, Francis would pull them aside, often after rehearsals, and ask, "What did you think?" or "What would you do if you were directing this scene?" or "How would you have delivered this passage if you were the actor?" Clearly, Francis left spaces open for people to choose for themselves, and in this process of exploration, they learned new skills, strengthening their overall capability and confidence, and increasing their commitment to both their individual projects and the overall success of the performance and the club.

Leaders want people to think for themselves and act, not continually ask someone else, "What should I do?" You can't develop this ability if you tell people what to do and how to do it. People can't learn to act independently unless they get to exercise some degree of choice. The only way to create an efficient and effective group of people who can meet the challenges that are part of trying new things is by giving them the chance to use their best judgment in applying their knowledge and skills. This implies, of course, that you've prepared them to make these choices and that they feel well-grounded and aligned with the values and the vision of the group.

Structure Tasks to Offer Latitude

Every year, the students in a leadership development program at a large eastern university participate in the annual homecoming week festivities. One of the major events of the week is the parade, for which groups across campus build floats based on the theme for the year. Designing and building their parade float had always been a group effort for the students, but the process was not always well planned out, and their floats seldom measured up to what the other student groups put in the parade.

The year Dan Samuels was cochair, he and his float committee recalled how challenging it had been building the floats in previous years. Conversations at the beginning of previous float projects typically progressed from talking about what had been created in prior years to tossing around new ideas with great enthusiasm. It was common to start with a high level of energy, Dan said, but then the momentum would quickly wane as confusion set in around who would play what role, who would oversee the work, how the subcommittees would get more students involved, how much time would be required, and on and on.

Dan was determined not to repeat history, and set out to make the group's float for that year—and the process of creating it—the best one yet. "I'd been involved in the homecoming float project a couple of times," he told us, "and people getting confused and losing interest didn't make sense to me because as construction on the float progresses, it gets to be even more exciting and fun." When Dan began talking to students who had started strong in years past and then dropped off, he learned that this was because they just didn't feel as though they were contributing in a significant way, that there were plenty of others who could do what they had been assigned to do. "That made me realize," he said, "that I needed to help people feel like their unique contribution was valued and that we were counting on each and every one of them."

As in the past, the float committee spent a lot of time brainstorming designs and choosing one they thought best fit that year's homecoming theme. Dan decided that the traditional process needed something else to engage students. So he asked some members of the committee to build a model of the float they envisioned. They could then use the model to encourage students to sign up for specific parts of the float project rather than having people show up night after night and just jump in for sawing, hammering, and painting as they had done in years past.

Once the students had signed up for the portion of the float they wanted to work on, Dan led a smaller group to create a list of the specific tasks that needed to be done. The students could then pick from the list the work they wanted to do, factoring in the time they realistically had to contribute and what they thought they'd be good at doing. This strategy made a huge difference in how everyone engaged in the project. With everyone having a choice about what they would do and being asked to be honest about the time they had to contribute, Dan and his committee were able to spread the work out more efficiently and avoid the chaos and disengagement that had characterized their float building in the past. "There was no way people could fade away, because they had signed up for the job they wanted and had committed to it," Dan explained. "Students signing up for the float also really liked the fact that they weren't assigned something, but had a chance to provide input on what they wanted to do."

By providing them latitude in the roles they would play, Dan was able to influence the attitude students brought to the project. As a result, most kept their commitments. In addition, because Dan gave people the opportunity to sign up for as much or as little as they realistically could afford, their commitment was stronger. The float committee had far fewer no-shows than in any previous year. People weren't overcommitted, and they knew what they were doing, so nobody bailed. There was much less frustration and much more efficiency and organization in the planning and construction process. "Everyone seemed to simply enjoy their work much more," Dan told us. "The enthusiasm kept on going, and the whole process was fun."

Having latitude in how they do their work strengthens people. They grow when they're allowed to try new things and make decisions that affect how they do their work without having to check with someone else.[3] Effective leaders are not control freaks. Nor are they wedded to a standard set of rules, procedures, or schedules. You need to give people sufficient freedom and choice in deciding how to do their work. The payoff will be significant. Our research shows that when student leaders more frequently "support the decisions that people make on their own," people are significantly more engaged in their organizations, feeling more productive and appreciated.

Foster Accountability

When people take personal responsibility and are held accountable for their actions, their colleagues are much more inclined to work with them and are more motivated to cooperate in general. Individual accountability is a critical element of every collaborative effort. Each person must do his or her part for a group to function effectively.

Mykell Bates had played soccer from the age of fourteen and was chosen captain of the US Under-17 national team when he was just fifteen years old. When he went on to college, his soccer playing continued, and in his sophomore year, Mykell was chosen captain of his school's team. Being captain entailed many more organizational duties than Mykell was used to, both on and off the field. "At first I tried to do it all," Mykell told us, "but then it occurred to me, since we depend on each other on the field, shouldn't I depend on them off the field too?"

Mykell began to reach out to his teammates to take on some of the communication duties for the team, he told us.

We all play an important part in our success on the field,
so all I was asking for was that same level of accountability
and connection to the team off the field. When I'd ask a
player, "Hey, can you text the guys about the team meeting
tonight?" they always stepped up.

Slowly Mykell began passing on responsibilities to more members of
the team. Ultimately, it became clear that spreading out some of the tasks
was a much more efficient way of doing things, and it helped all those
who contributed feel accountable for the successful operation of the team.

What Mykell was doing with his team is what student leaders do
to foster accountability: they consciously create an environment where
team members count on one another to get done what needs to get
done. This doesn't mean they are autocratic or controlling. His teammate Brandon Zimmerman told us,

Mykell was not directive in handing out tasks; he would
simply ask for your help, and you would want to help him.
He trusted that I could do the job that needed to be done,
and I didn't want to break that trust. It was mutual respect,
for each other and for the good of the team.

Leaders like Mykell appreciate a fundamental truth about
strengthening others: the power to choose rests on the willingness to
be held accountable. They know that the more freedom of choice people have, the more personal responsibility they must accept. There's
also a bonus: the more that people believe that everyone else is taking
responsibility for his or her part of the project—and has the competence to do it—the more trusting and the more cooperative they're
going to be with one another. People will be more confident and committed to doing their part when they believe others will do theirs.

Some students believe that groups, teams, and other cooperative
experiences minimize individual accountability. They argue that if

their classmates are encouraged to work collectively, somehow they'll take less responsibility for their actions than if they are encouraged to compete or to do things on their own. Think about a group project for a class. If there are a lot of individuals in the group, do you think that people are less likely to worry about what happens if they don't do their part? It's true that some people become social loafers when working in groups, slacking off while others do their jobs for them. However, this doesn't last for long, because their classmates quickly tire of carrying the extra load. Either the slacker steps up to the responsibility, or the team wants that person removed—provided the team has shared goals and shared accountability.[4]

Enhancing self-determination means giving people control over their lives. It means you need to give them something of substance to control and to be accountable for. Define roles broadly—as projects, not tasks—and find ways to ensure that everyone is part of the decision-making process. Make certain that everyone in your group, no matter the task or job, has someone they are serving (that is, someone they feel accountable to). Ask group members to do things that are not part of their regular routine and to stay up-to-date on what is going on. Keep in mind that you also need to provide the necessary resources—for example, materials, money, and time, as well as information—for people to perform autonomously. There's nothing more disempowering than to have lots of responsibility for doing something, but nothing to do it with.

DEVELOP COMPETENCE AND CONFIDENCE

Choice, latitude, and accountability give people control over their lives and fuel their sense of powerfulness. However, as necessary as enhancing self-determination is, it's insufficient. Without the knowledge, skills, information, and resources to do a job expertly, and without feeling competent to execute the choices required, people will be overwhelmed and possibly even discouraged. Even if they have the resources and skills, there may be times when people don't have the confidence that they're allowed to use them, or that they will be supported if things don't go as well as expected. There may be times when they just lack the self-confidence to do what they know they need to do.

What Mykell did, when he asked his soccer teammates to step up and take over some of the operational tasks for the team, had another benefit beyond fostering accountability. When responsibilities were spread among the group, each teammate could specialize in one activity and perfect it, which wouldn't happen if only one person took on all of the tasks.

Mykell learned that giving others responsibilities enhanced their skills and self-confidence. One of his teammates told us that this was precisely what Mykell did for him: "I have a part-time construction job, and Mykell's leadership showed me that one thing I can do is pass on some of the building responsibilities to others. I have always liked doing everything myself, but I am sure the guys I am working with can do just as well as I can, if not better in some cases. I can coach them through it, and that will build their capabilities and confidence, eventually making us a much stronger and more productive work team."

It's no secret that sharing power the way Mykell did results in higher performance for the group as a whole. Developing competence and building confidence for all members of the group are essential. To make extraordinary things happen, you must invest in strengthening the capacity and the resolve of every single person in your group.

Think about a time when the challenge you faced was greater than the skills you had. How did you feel when the challenge was high, but your skill was low? If you're like most people, you felt anxious, nervous, scared, and the like. Now think of a time when your level of skill was greater than the level of challenge in the job. How did you feel? Bored and apathetic, most likely. Do you do your best work when you're anxious or bored? Of course you don't. You do it when the challenge you face is just slightly greater than your current level of skill. That's when you feel stretched but not stressed out. What's true for you is just as true for the other people you work with.

Exemplary student leaders strive to create the conditions that make it possible for others to perform effortlessly and expertly despite the difficulty of the task or project. That means you need to continuously assess the capacity of individuals and the group to meet the challenges they face, which in turn requires attention to the skill power and the willpower of each person you lead.

Educate and Share Information

People can't do what they don't know how to do. Therefore, when you increase the latitude and discretion of your team members, you also need to increase training and development opportunities. When people aren't sure about how to perform critical tasks or are fearful of making mistakes, they may be reluctant to exercise their judgment. Developing the competence and confidence of each member in a group is a virtuous cycle that makes everyone involved feel more qualified, more capable, more effective, and more like leaders themselves. It's your job as a leader to instill these feelings. That was the job that Christina Beige took on when she was selected, along with faculty and staff across the campus, to serve on her university's Energy Task Force.

The year before Christina joined the task force, there had been an initiative led by the Student Alliance for a Green Earth (SAGE) to institute a "Green Fee," but the university president felt that there was insufficient evidence of overall student support and did not enact the fee. Christina's task force had come up with numerous green projects, policy plans, and publicity efforts to make the school more environmentally friendly. "This was a fantastic effort," Christina said, "but I knew it would go nowhere if there was no funding. I had to take action." She wrote a resolution for a $10 Green Fee designed to fund various projects and promotional efforts to boost environmental awareness and responsibility on campus. She presented the Green Fee resolution to the school's student senate, with a detailed outline of how to spend the $200,000 assessment.

The student senate was hesitant, feeling that the previous student body survey needed to be conducted again to provide solid evidence of support. So Christina and SAGE, along with other supportive students across campus, reached out again to educate the student body about the fee. They were competing at the time with a proposal from athletics to raise the athletic fee and appeared to be outnumbered and outspent every step of the way. "But we didn't stop," Christina told us. "We had a lot of good information on something we believed the student body really cared about, and we believed that if we could share it with the students, we'd have a fair shot." Their knowledge sharing paid off big-time. Armed with facts and figures about the impact of the projects the Green Fee would fund, students overwhelmingly supported it, with 75 percent of them eventually approving the fee increase.

Christina's experience demonstrates that sharing information with others is a crucial task for leaders who want to make extraordinary things happen. Recall that sharing information shows up consistently on the list of what makes people feel powerful, whereas the lack of information makes them feel powerless. For leaders, developing the competence and confidence of the people on their team so that they are more qualified, more capable, and more effective—and so that they are leaders themselves—reflects their appreciation of the truth that they can't get anything extraordinary accomplished all by themselves. Making people smarter is the job of every leader. If the people in your group aren't growing and learning from the projects and activities they are involved in, they're likely to leave and find more fulfilling opportunities elsewhere.

Organize Work to Build Competence and Ownership

A leader's job is to enrich the responsibilities of the group members so that they experience variety in their tasks, and opportunities to make meaningful decisions about how things get done. Do as exemplary student leaders do and organize assignments so that people feel that their work is relevant to the group's or organization's pressing concerns. Make sure that everyone feels well represented on the committees, teams, and problem-solving groups dealing with the important matters in your organization. Involve them in programs, meetings, and decisions that have a direct impact on what they are being asked to do. Actions like these build competence and promote a sense of ownership and accountability.

This was another lesson that Dan Samuels learned from his personal-best leadership experience in the homecoming float project. Traditionally, the job assignments had been organized by general tasks: construction, painting, decorating, and so forth. Students would sign up for one type of task, and that was it. Dan had a different idea about how to organize things. "In the past, people were encouraged to sign up for something they felt they knew how to do or had done before, like painting," Dan explained. "The result was that often people just got sick of painting; they felt pigeonholed." Dan thought, why not let people try a new skill? If they are good at painting, they could do that, but maybe they want to learn how to do some of the construction. "If we helped people get some new experience and skill," Dan told us, "that would put us in a better position for getting the work done, and make it easier in future years too."

This approach increased everyone's ownership in the project. It meant that the subgroups had to coordinate their efforts for the project to be successful. Everyone needed to take ownership of the section of the float they signed up for so that the whole project would come together at the end and look like a coherent construction. By organizing the project in this way, the students would be dependent on each other to get the final project done. This approach also demanded that the quality of each section be consistent, so the groups had to coordinate to meet one another's standards. Altogether, the students' work on the float was done in a way that built their confidence and encouraged ownership; more people were fully engaged in the project than ever before. And there was another payoff: the float took first place in the judging competition.

Student leaders like Dan know how important it is to turn tasks, assignments, and projects into opportunities to increase people's knowledge and skills and to build ownership. For people to feel like owners, they need to be able to understand what is going on to the extent that any "owner" would expect. If they are going to work together effectively, your team needs to be able to know the answers to such questions as: Who are the people we serve, and for whom do we exist? How do they perceive us? How do we know whether we're doing what we should be doing for them? How have we done recently? What can we do that is new and better in the next six months?

Foster Self-Confidence

Even if people know how to do something, a lack of confidence may stop them from doing it. Without sufficient self-confidence, people won't have the commitment required for taking on tough challenges. Low self-confidence manifests itself in feelings of helplessness, powerlessness, and often crippling self-doubt. By building people's belief in themselves, you are bolstering their inner strength to forge ahead in uncharted terrain, to make tough choices, to face opposition, and the like because they believe in their skills and decision-making abilities, as well as yours.[5]

Encouraging self-confidence is what Amy and Zachariah did when they structured the alternative spring break so that the whole experience rested on the participants' shoulders. It's what Francis did when he provided people the opportunity to participate in various parts of the drama club's activities, and what Dan did in letting people work on any part of the homecoming float they wanted to. It's what Mykell was doing when he started spreading around the tasks and responsibilities that traditionally had belonged to the soccer team captain. "When Mykell asked me to do something, it instilled confidence in my abilities," teammate Brandon Zimmerman told us.

> When he would ask me to take on some of his day-to-day responsibilities, it gave me the confidence and competence to perform those tasks. All Mykell did was give me the authority to use the skills that he believed I already had, but maybe I wasn't acknowledging in myself. The more he did this, the more it worked to the advantage of the group as a whole because each of us became stronger.

People's having confidence and believing in their ability to handle the job, no matter how difficult, are essential in promoting and sustaining consistent efforts. By communicating to your group that you believe they can be successful, you help people push themselves beyond their self-limiting boundaries.

Coach

Although it's true that exemplary student leaders communicate their confidence in others, you can't just tell people they can do something if they can't. Leaders need to provide coaching, because no one ever got to be the best at anything without constructive feedback, probing questions, and active teaching by respected coaches. In strengthening others, you must not only have high expectations for them but also gently guide them by expressing your confidence in their ability to make good choices, backing them up when they make mistakes, helping them learn from experiences, and supporting their decisions. Often this is incremental, in the fashion of small wins, so that people don't feel overwhelmed and stressed out by the gap between their abilities and skills and their initial performance.

Anthony Gochenour worked throughout college as one of the building managers of the student union at his midwestern college, eventually becoming the senior building manager and leader of the student employment team. His greatest challenge, he told us, was getting the staff, comprising three different teams of student employees, to appreciate how important their work was and to be motivated to develop their ability to do their jobs better.

Anthony saw their day-to-day apathetic attitudes and their lack of commitment to the job as major problems because the student union was probably the most used building on campus. He began to think about the routine work the staff had to do and looked at these tasks from the perspective of how important they were in serving students who used the building. From there, he began to guide different members of the teams to focus on particular tasks so that the many things they had to do wouldn't seem so overwhelming.

After breaking the whole job down and connecting the student workers to responsibilities that appealed to them, Anthony coached them one by one, working alongside them to give pointers and feedback on how they were doing. Over time, team members could see how progress in their smaller assignments contributed to the bigger picture, and they could see the impact each of them had on what happened in the building. With Anthony's support, the student teams came to appreciate that their work didn't just keep the building running but shaped the experience of everyone who used the building.

Student leaders like Anthony never take control away from others. They leave it to their group members to make choices and assume responsibility for them. When leaders coach, educate, enhance self-determination, and otherwise share power, they're demonstrating deep trust in and respect for others' abilities. When leaders help others grow and develop, others reciprocate. People who feel capable of influencing their leaders are more strongly attached to those leaders and more committed to effectively carrying out their responsibilities.[6]

Good coaches understand that strengthening others requires paying attention and believing that people are smart enough to figure things out for themselves when given the opportunity to make choices, provided with support, and offered feedback. Coaching stretches people to grow, develops their capabilities, and provides them with opportunities to both hone and enhance their skills in challenging assignments.

Good coaches also ask good questions. The benefits of asking questions are numerous. For one, it gives people both the room to think and to frame issues from their perspective. Second, asking questions indicates an underlying trust in individuals' abilities by shifting accountability, and it has the benefit of creating almost immediate buy-in for the solution. (After all, it's *their* idea.) Asking questions puts leaders in a coaching role, more of a guiding role, which, in turn, frees them up to be thinking more strategically.

The success of every group or undertaking is a shared responsibility. As we said in Chapter 7, you can't do it alone. You need a competent and confident team, and the team needs a competent and confident coach. While you're at it, think about getting a coach yourself. There's no better way to model the behavior you expect from others than by doing it yourself.

REFLECT AND ACT: STRENGTHEN OTHERS

Strengthening others is essentially the process of turning everyone into leaders—making people capable of acting on their own initiative. Leaders need to bring others along *as* leaders. Leaders strengthen people when they make it possible for them to make choices, designing options and alternatives to the ways that things get done, and when they encourage accountability and responsibility that lead to action.

Leaders develop in others the competence, as well as the confidence, to act and to succeed. They make certain that people have the information they need to understand how the group operates and what is going on. They help build skills, and they coach people on how to put what they know into practice, stretching and supporting them to do more than they might have imagined possible. Exemplary student leaders use questions to help people think on their own, and coach them on how to be at their best.

Reflect

The second commitment of Enabling Others to Act requires leaders to *strengthen others by increasing their self-determination and developing competence.* Reflect on this commitment and answer these questions:

1. What is the most important idea or lesson about exemplary leadership that you learned from this chapter?

_____

_____

_____

_____

2. What changes do you need to make in your leadership to better Strengthen Others?

   _____

   _____

   _____

   _____

3. In the next section, there are some suggestions on what you can do to put Strengthen Others into practice. After you have reflected on what you learned and what you need to improve, select an action that you can take immediately to become a better leader.

   _____

   _____

   _____

   _____

Take Action

Here are ways you can follow through on your commitment to **Strengthen Others**:

- Let people make choices about how they do their work. Structure tasks so that individuals have opportunities to use their judgment about how the job can be completed.
- Find a balance between people's skills and the work you are asking them to do. Provide opportunities that stretch them just outside their comfort zones, but not so far that they lose their confidence.

- Promote accountability by making sure that people have the necessary resources to complete their task or project.
- Share your personal influence and any organizational authority with others.
- Demonstrate in visible and concrete ways that you believe in the abilities of the people in your group.
- Set aside time to coach others, which begins by learning enough about the skills, interests, and aspirations of the people you are working with to determine how you can enable them to make the most of their talents.
- Solicit ideas from people and get them to take initiative in implementing them.

ENCOURAGE
THE HEART

Making extraordinary things happen is hard work, and leaders need to encourage others to continue the quest. Leaders strengthen people's courage by visibly recognizing contributions to the common vision. Leaders express pride in the accomplishments of their teams. They make a point of telling the rest of the organization about what has been achieved. They make people feel like heroes. Leaders find ways to celebrate accomplishments and are personally involved with them. They take time out to rejoice in reaching a milestone.

In the next two chapters, we see how student leaders:

➤ **Recognize Contributions** by showing appreciation for individual excellence.
➤ **Celebrate the Values and Victories** by creating a spirit of community.

ENCOURAGE THE HEART

Reflections from the *Student Leadership Practices Inventory*

1. Record your overall score from the *Student Leadership Practices Inventory* for ENCOURAGE THE HEART here: _____

2. Of the six behaviors that are part of Encourage the Heart, write down the statement for the one you indicated engaging in most frequently:

3. Write down the leadership behavior statement that you felt you engaged in least often:

4. On the basis of your self-assessment, complete this statement: When it comes to Encourage the Heart, my areas of leadership competency are:

5. What Encourage the Heart behaviors do you see as opportunities for improving and strengthening your leadership capability? Make note of these below so that you can keep them in mind as you read this chapter and the next.

9

Commitment #9: Recognize Contributions

Throughout her college career, Kadesha Zimmerman had been academically successful—earning a place on the dean's list and honor roll, as well as a leadership award her senior year—but it wasn't always as easy for her as it looked. As a young black woman looking to go into the field of finance, she didn't see many other students like her when she first arrived on campus. The support and mentoring of a senior faculty member, who was also African American, significantly contributed to her academic achievements. That experience inspired her to become what her school called a *success coach* for her peers on campus during her senior year.

Even though she received good grades, Kadesha had often struggled and needed help from others to achieve her academic goals. She told us that she wanted to show other students that "just because it looks like academic success comes naturally to some people, sometimes those people are really struggling too. I learned a lot that I wanted to be able to pass on: study habits that worked for me, how to deal with certain professors, time management. I think there's a lot that goes into being successful in your studies that we don't talk about."

Kadesha had come to understand the importance of coaching and peer support for academic success and wanted to find a way to pass that on to others. Becoming a success coach was her way to demonstrate how students can help each other do well in school and become future leaders.

Success coaches at Kadesha's university work with students who have been placed on academic probation or have been flagged from placement exams as potentially having difficulty adjusting to college-level academics. Although students in the program are assigned a success coach, it's up to the student whether to utilize the success coach's services or not. "I can't force anyone to want to work with me, but I can try to get them excited to work with me," Kadesha said.

During her first semester as a success coach, Kadesha convened a meeting for all her assigned students to talk about goals and set up individual meeting times to identify things that she could work with them on, one on one. During the meeting, Kadesha noticed that there was one first-year student who was quiet and attentive but didn't speak up or make a follow-up appointment.

Afterward, Kadesha learned that this young woman (let's call her Akira), a very talented graphic artist, was one of the students flagged as having potential difficulties in college courses. Kadesha reached out to her several times via email but got no response. Finally, she tried one last route: social media. Kadesha sent her a message on Facebook, letting her know how much she liked the art Akira had posted and ways she thought it might be used to enrich the environment and experience of college life for her fellow students. She also suggested ways that Akira could get more involved in the artistic community on campus. That did the trick. Akira made an appointment to discuss her artistic ambitions and what she wanted to do with her artwork while on campus. "I think there was a lot of shame associated with having been assigned to a success coach, but I made her feel like she had something valuable to offer to our campus community. Instead of just focusing on things she needed to work on, we were able to build a relationship," Kadesha said.

At those meetings, Kadesha outlined the courses that Akira would need to take and demonstrated several different career paths she might consider, including becoming a graphic artist. Kadesha told her how talented she thought she was, and how the other courses that she was taking (for example, geometry and composition) would be important to her future. She also gave Akira suggestions about organizations she could join on campus that would appreciate and stretch her artistic talent, including a group who displayed their artwork at an on-campus café.

Kadesha also made clear the expectations she had for Akira. They would continue to meet on a regular basis to discuss her schoolwork, and Akira would set academic goals for herself—for example, a grade-point average goal that she and Kadesha would continue to review over the course of the year. Their meetings would also allow Kadesha to give feedback to Akira on her targets. "Early on, she set a goal of just making a 2.0 her first semester, and I thought she could do better. I urged her to aim a little higher; maybe we could set up more appointments if she needed, but I believed she should aim for at least a 2.5 because she was more than capable of achieving that," Kadesha explained, adding that she had asked Akira to consider the more challenging goal "from a place of faith and belief in her abilities." Kadesha explained, "I didn't want her to think that I didn't believe her difficulties in her classes weren't real, but I also wanted her to know how much I believed in her academic potential." Akira ended up earning a 2.8 GPA her first semester, and improved that to 3.0 her second semester.

Toward the end of the school year, Kadesha held another meeting with all the students she had worked with, to showcase what they had accomplished and experienced that year. Everyone brought with them something they were proud of having created or worked on during the year, whether it was a paper, a project, or a grade on a final exam. "It was the highlight of the year," Kadesha said, "all of us getting to acknowledge the things we were proud of. For me, I was most proud of all of my students and how hard they had worked together." After the celebration, Kadesha sent thank-you notes to everyone she worked with for bringing in their personal contributions.

Kadesha's year of success coaching showed her the importance of seeing and acknowledging the individual talents and contributions that each person has to offer, and how simply doing that can help build meaningful relationships. "That experience taught me a lot," Kadesha said.

> It taught me how much it meant to people to be found valuable for what they're good at and how much my experience as a success coach was about the relationship being a two-way street—the students I work with have a lot to teach me, too.

Like Kadesha, exemplary student leaders know how important it is to connect with the people around them, not taking anyone for granted and appreciating folks for both who they are and what they do. All exemplary leaders make the commitment to Recognize Contributions. They do it because people need encouragement to function at their best and to continue to persist when the hours are long, the work is hard, and the task is daunting. Getting to the finish line of any demanding journey demands energy and commitment. People need emotional fuel to replenish their spirits.

To Recognize Contributions, you need to utilize these two essentials:

- **Expect the best**
- **Personalize recognition**

By putting these essentials into practice, you uplift people's spirits and arouse the internal drive to strive. You stimulate their efforts to reach for higher levels of performance and to aspire to be faithful to the visions and values of the group. You help people find the courage to do things they have never done before.

EXPECT THE BEST

Belief in others' abilities is essential to making extraordinary things happen. Exemplary student leaders elicit high performance because they firmly believe in group members' abilities to achieve even the most challenging goals. That's because positive expectations profoundly influence not only the aspirations of people in your group but also, often unconsciously, how you behave toward them. You broadcast your beliefs about people in ways you may not even be aware of. You give off cues that say to people either "I know you can do it" or "There's no way you'll ever be able to do that." You can't realize the highest level of performance unless you let people know in word and deed that you are confident that they can attain it.

Social psychologists refer to this as the "Pygmalion effect," from the Greek myth of Pygmalion, a sculptor who carved a statue of a beautiful woman, fell in love with the statue, and appealed to the goddess Aphrodite to bring her to life. Aphrodite answered his prayers. Leaders play Pygmalion-like roles in developing others. Ask students to describe the best leaders they've ever had, and they consistently talk about individuals who brought out the best in them. They say things like "She believed in me more than I believed in myself" or "He saw something in me even I didn't see." The same is true when students describe why they took on the assignment that became their personal best—"because someone believed that I could do it, even if I had never done something like this before."

Exemplary leaders bring others to life, figuratively speaking. If the potential exists within someone, they always find a way to release it. They dramatically improve others' performance because they care deeply for them and have an abiding faith in their capacities. They nurture, support, and encourage people they believe in.

People do respond positively to these expectations. Research on the phenomenon of self-fulfilling prophecies provides ample evidence that people act in ways that are consistent with others' expectations of them.[1] When you expect people to fail, they probably will. If you expect them to succeed, they probably will. Think about this from a personal perspective. Can you recall a time when you were feeling overwhelmed by something you were asked to do? Perhaps it was a crucial game your team had to win against a team that hadn't lost all season. Maybe it was being asked to take over a project about which you knew very little but for which you were to be held accountable. Maybe it was an exam that would earn you the grade you needed to get into college. If you were successful, chances are there was someone who reinforced your sense of self, someone who said without a doubt, "I believe you can do this." Words like those send a powerful message to people's brains, one that helps them step up to match the image others hold of them.

Alex Golkar wasn't initially very excited about the team he would be working with for his masters of finance capstone project. After all, he only joined them because they needed one more member and this group was his and their only option. He was even more skeptical when he found out that one team member, though quite smart, was pre-occupied with the rigorous demands of his job and announced that he was unable to devote his full energy to their project. The other member of the group was an amicable fellow who enjoyed socializing. However, he was in the midst of family problems, so his attention to the project was also compromised. The team performed poorly over the next five weeks, with the teacher rejecting all four of their initial project proposals.

With the deadline looming, Alex decided that he had to take the initiative and enact some changes to redirect the team's focus and restore their sense of optimism and possibility. "The first impediment that I addressed," he said, "was personal. I had to change my manner of thinking about my group mates. Rather than viewing them as unproductive and ineffectual, I decided to have some faith in their abilities. After all, they were professionals working in reputable companies."

There's substantial evidence that leaders who create an affirmative orientation, foster high standards, and focus on achieving outcomes beyond the norm are quite successful.[2] Alex told us that when he decided to have confidence in the expertise and motivation of his teammates, he also began to alter his thinking and behavior.

> Initially I was somewhat withdrawn because I believed that my efforts would be wasted due to the unfocused nature of the group. However, with a renewed interest in the group's success, I openly expressed to them my beliefs in their abilities and what we could accomplish together. By communicating in a way that exhibited confidence, we were able to share information and work cohesively as a unit more effectively.

The best student leaders, like Alex, bring out the best in others, as well as themselves.

Show Them You Believe

Tiffany Lee was doing an internship in the vice mayor's office of a major city. As the youngest and most inexperienced person in the office, she was given much of the grunt work, including taking messages for return phone calls, filing, writing thank-you letters, and responding to the routine correspondence sent to the office. She felt out of place in the office where staff members had close relationships based on a history of working together. "I was not seen as a vital part of the staff," she said, "but just an intern who did their leftover work."

At the end of each week, she was required to sit in on staff meetings during which each staff member would share an item that they were currently working on. Each week, as her coworkers stated important issues that they were a part of, such as helping to author legislative bills or working with the health board, Tiffany's response was always the same: "Correspondence." "I would feel almost embarrassed as I hurriedly stated my 'contribution,'" she told us, "and in comparison to my coworkers' responses, I felt insignificant and not a very important part of the team."

A short time later, at one of the meetings, the chief of staff praised the team for their contribution to another successful week. Then the chief of staff told everyone that due to the way correspondence was being handled, the vice mayor's office was now receiving thank-you letters from residents who felt that their concerns and welfare were not being ignored and that the office genuinely cared about them. Knowing that Tiffany was the person responsible for handling this correspondence, her coworkers turned to her and told her what a wonderful job she was doing. The chief of staff went on to say that each member in the office had something valuable to bring to the group, and that their joint efforts were the reason the office was so highly respected and valued. In telling us about this experience, Tiffany explained how the chief of staff, and her coworkers, demonstrated that they believed in her and made her feel that she was not the most insignificant person on the team, and that this, she said, "is something I will take with me forward into every situation."

That is precisely what she has done. Tiffany now supervises other interns, and she makes it a point to expect the best from them, giving them opportunities to make a difference and watching carefully for the contributions they make to the team, no matter how small or seemingly insignificant. "I make it a rule to help people see how even the small tasks contribute to our collective success," Tiffany says. "People need to know they matter."

Leaders' positive expectations aren't fluff.[3] They're not simply about keeping a positive outlook or getting others psyched up. The expectations you hold as a leader provide the framework into which people fit their realities. They shape the way you behave toward others and how they behave on the task. Maybe you can't turn a marble statue into a real person, but you can draw out the highest potential of the members of your group. Tiffany's experience, like Kadesha's, is a clear example of how showing people you believe in them, even when they are down, helps them acknowledge that they still have their best to give. Holding positive expectations of high performance and motivation in others, along with recognizing them for their contributions, easily beats the alternative of the "just do what I tell you" approach. People need to feel they belong, are accepted and valued, and have the skills and inner resources needed to be successful.

Believing in others is an extraordinarily powerful force in propelling greater performance. If you want people to have a winning attitude, you have to do what Tiffany's supervisor did: show you believe that the people in your group are already winners. It's not that they will be winners someday; they are winners right now! When you believe that people are winners, you behave in ways that communicate to them that they are precisely that—not just in your words but also through tone of voice, posture, gestures, and facial expressions. No yelling, frowning, cajoling, making fun, or putting them down in front of others. Instead, it's about being friendly, positive, supportive, and encouraging.

Our research shows that students who work with student leaders who regularly "praise people for a job well done" and "express appreciation for the contributions that people make" are most highly engaged. As illustrated in Figure 9.1 there's a direct relationship between students' levels of engagement and the extent they report their leaders engaging in these two leadership behaviors. There is a statistically significant increase in each of the adjacent engagement categories.

It's a virtuous circle: you believe in your group members' abilities; your favorable expectations cause you to be more positive in your actions; and those encouraging behaviors produce better results, reinforcing your belief that people can be successful. Another virtuous circle begins as people see that they are capable of extraordinary performance; they develop that expectation of themselves.

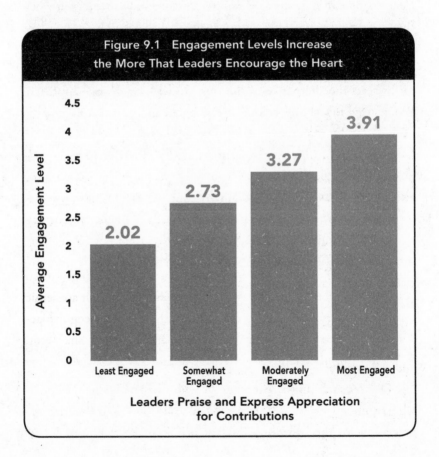

Figure 9.1 Engagement Levels Increase the More That Leaders Encourage the Heart

Be Clear about the Goals and the Rules

Positive expectations are necessary to generate high performance, but that level of performance isn't sustainable unless people are clear about ground rules and outcomes. When you were a kid, you might have read Lewis Carroll's *Alice's Adventures in Wonderland.* Do you remember the croquet match? Flamingos were the mallets, playing-card soldiers were the wickets, and hedgehogs were the balls. Everyone kept moving, and the rules kept changing all the time. There was no way of knowing how to play the game or what it took to win. You don't have to fall down a rabbit hole to know how Alice felt.

Believing that people can succeed is only part of the equation. If you want people to give their all, to put their hearts and minds into their work, you must also make certain that they know what they're supposed to be doing. You need to clarify what the expected outcomes look like. You need to make sure there are consistent norms governing how to play the game and score points. Have you ever been involved in a class assignment for which the objective wasn't clear? If you have ever found yourself asking "Why are we doing this?" you have experienced the frustration, apathy, fear, and resentment that can surface when you are asked to do something but don't know the reasons why.

Liz Eilen was working in the tutoring center at her college when the center's director suggested to her that greater encouragement might influence the commitment that students being tutored would have to their study groups, and as a result affect their academic improvement. Liz decided to come up with ways to recognize active and involved students for their work at the center. She began by challenging the students to involve themselves more fully in the study-group process, setting high expectations for what each of the groups needed to do. She discovered that setting the expectations was just what the individual members needed to feel motivated and enthusiastic about participating and improving their academic standing. "It was as though the high expectations had a way of creating a self-fulfilling prophecy," Liz said. She also noticed students pushing themselves harder to ensure they wouldn't let their colleagues down. "Students started accomplishing so much, showing improvement in new and different areas," Liz told us. "They surprised everyone, including themselves."

As Liz learned, expectations play an essential role in developing people, drawing out their highest potential and their desire to achieve the extraordinary. And, as Liz also discovered, expectations can address goals, including a certain level of group participation, and values, such as the importance of academic achievement.

Goals and values provide people with a set of standards that concentrates their efforts. Goals are typically short term, whereas values (or principles) are more enduring. Values and principles serve as the basis for goals. They're your standards of excellence, your highest aspirations, and they define the arena in which to set goals and metrics. Values mediate the path of action. Goals release the energy.

But what do goals have to do with recognition? They give recognition context. Goals give people something to strive for, something important to attain—such as coming in first, breaking a record, or setting a new standard of excellence. Goals enhance the significance of recognition because the acknowledgment is for something a person set out to accomplish or exemplify. Recognition is most meaningful when you reward appropriate behaviors and achievement of something everyone knows is highly desirable.

Goals focus people's attention on shared values and standards. They help people keep their eyes on the vision. Goals enable people to makes choices about the kinds of actions they need to take, to know when they are making progress, and to see when they need to course-correct. They help people put their cell phone in do-not-disturb mode, appropriately schedule their time, and focus their attention on what matters most. Goal setting also affirms the person. Whether you realize it or not, goals contribute to what people think about themselves.

Provide and Seek Feedback

People need to know whether they're making progress toward a goal or simply marking time. Their motivation to perform a task increases only when they have a challenging goal *and* receive feedback on their progress.[4] Goals without feedback, or feedback without goals, has little effect on people's willingness or motivation to put discretionary effort into the task.

With clear goals and detailed feedback, people can become self-correcting and can more easily understand their place in the big picture. With regular feedback, they can also determine what help they need from others and who, in turn, might be able to benefit from their assistance. Anyone who has been a part of a fundraising event that has a set goal knows the power of seeing progress toward that target.

Take it from one group of student athletes we talked to that held a "Miles for Kids" event over several months. They got people to sponsor their virtual "trip across the nation" and demonstrated how their journey was going by collecting dollars per miles logged and tracking their progress on a giant map. There was a little friendly competition too, with a bonus incentive for the first person to reach the West Coast. They told us that completing the trip, coast to coast, got to be a real focus of pride for them, and everyone's commitment to a daily run or walk went way up.

The Miles for Kids group understood that feedback is at the center of any learning process. For example, consider what happens to your self-confidence without feedback. Think how you might feel in a class when you don't receive timely feedback on assignments or receive a grade on a paper without any explanation of why or about what is needed to be more successful in subsequent efforts. Wouldn't you agree that this is frustrating and demotivating?

Saying nothing about a person's performance doesn't help anyone—not the performer, not the leader, and not the group. People want useful feedback. They prefer to know how they are doing, and no news generally has the same negative impact as bad news. In fact, people would prefer to hear bad news rather than no news at all. Most stressful is not knowing, because it leaves the person in a state of limbo, unable to determine what steps to take next.

Moreover, without feedback there is no learning. Getting feedback about how they are doing is the only way people know whether they're getting close to their goal and whether they're executing properly. Although most people realize intellectually that feedback is a necessary component of self-reflection and growth, they are often reluctant to make themselves open to it because feedback can be embarrassing, even painful. People often want to look good more than they want to get good! Researchers consistently point out, however, that the development of expertise or mastery requires receiving constructive, even critical, feedback.[5]

Feedback should create dialogue. Your goal as a leader is to encourage the best in others, to find out what they need in order to feel more confident and competent to meet the challenges they face as a member of the group. Giving feedback in a way that encourages dialogue will create a learning opportunity for you both.

When leaders provide a clear sense of direction and feedback along the way, they encourage people to reach inside and do their best. Information about goals and about progress toward those goals strongly influences people's abilities to learn and to achieve, and this applies to leaders themselves. Encouragement is more personal and positive than other forms of feedback, and it's more likely to accomplish something that other forms cannot: strengthening trust between a leader and members of the group. Encouragement, in this sense, is the highest form of feedback.[6]

PERSONALIZE RECOGNITION

One of the more common complaints about recognition is that it's far too often highly predictable, mundane, and impersonal. Genuine recognition cannot be industrially manufactured and distributed en masse. There is no cookie-cutter solution or template for effective acknowledgment. A one-size-fits-all approach to recognition feels insincere, forced, and inconsiderate. Over time, it can even increase cynicism and damage credibility. What's more, generalized statements of encouragement fail to produce a significant effect because no one is very certain about either to whom the comments are directed or for what actions.

Clay Alm put together an intramural softball team at his university, consisting of a group of friends, some coworkers from his job in the student union, and even a faculty member. No matter how well they played or how poorly, Clay told us, "I knew this season was going to be extremely interesting purely because of the wide variety of personalities we had on our roster." The season went well, and the day before their first playoff game, Clay invited everyone on the team to his house for a surprise he had organized:

> I had prepared tie-dyed baseball shirts for each of my teammates. We then spray-painted numbers onto the back of everyone's shirt, and they got to choose their favorite number. Finally, I had purchased an iron-on patch for each person on the team. Each patch was different, and each patch had a short story behind it. Some of them ranged from things that each specific teammate was interested in, to personal jokes, to representations of their hometowns.

I took the time to present everyone with their patches individually, and in front of the entire team I told the story of why I got each of them their specific patches. It was a proud moment for me not only because the gesture was well received but also because everyone on the team got to see some of the personal bonds we had formed with one another. The single most important part of the uniforms was that they were entirely genuine. It was not an act.

People appreciate knowing that you care about them, and they are more caring about what they are doing as a result. When recognition is not personalized, it will quickly be forgotten and discounted. The entire softball team was brought closer together by experiencing a unique mixture of team spirit and individuality embodied in the personalized recognition Clay provided. Recognition is most effective when it comes from and is expressed from your heart.

When students tell us about the most meaningful recognition they've received, they consistently say that it's personal. They say that it feels special. You get a lot more emotional bang for your buck when you personalize recognition and rewards. That's why it's so important for student leaders to pay attention to the likes and dislikes of every individual in their group. Step into the shoes of other people and ask yourself, "What do I wish someone would do to celebrate and recognize my contribution?" Let your answer to this question guide your own thinking about how to acknowledge the contributions of others, while also being sensitive to the fact that not everyone is just like you. This means that you must get close enough to others to know what makes recognition meaningful to them.

Get to Know People

Think back to Liz's experience in her school's tutoring center, where she learned that students were more productive when they had a clear understanding of the goals of the program and the expectations of them. That experience also taught her that students were much more motivated and encouraged when they felt someone expected great things from them and was watching to see how they were doing. Liz said she couldn't have helped foster those feelings without making a point of getting to know as many students in the groups as possible: "The time spent connecting with each student, sharing our expectations, helped motivate each student to succeed, not just for themselves but for the group as well." That time proved to be well spent when Liz wrote a weekly note of appreciation to students who had met or surpassed expectations, occasionally even finding a special little gift that acknowledged their individual progress or their contribution to the group. By getting close to her students, Liz gained insight into the challenges they faced and the efforts they were putting forth, enabling her to recognize their accomplishments in a genuine and significant way.

To make recognition personally meaningful, as both Liz and Clay did, you first need to get to know people. If you're going to personalize recognition and make it feel genuinely special, you'll have to look past the organizational diagrams and roles people play and see the person inside. You need to get to know who they are, how they feel, and what they think. As a leader, this means you need to find a way to get close to people.

Because proximity is the single best predictor of whether two people will talk to one another, you have to get physically close to people if you're going to find out what motivates them, what they like and don't like, and what kinds of recognition they most appreciate. The payoffs are significant. For example, over a five-year period, researchers observed groups of friends and groups of acquaintances (people who knew each other only vaguely) performing motor-skill and decision-making tasks. The results were clear. The groups composed of friends completed, on average, more than three times as many projects as the groups composed merely of acquaintances. Regarding decision-making assignments, groups of friends were over 20 percent more effective than groups of acquaintances.[7]

Another payoff from meaningfully connecting with team members is that it will be reciprocated with loyalty. In other words, paying attention, personalizing recognition, and creatively and actively appreciating others increase their trust in you. If others know that you genuinely care about them, they're more likely to care about you.

People are more willing to follow someone with whom they have a relationship. And the foundation of any relationship is trust. An open door is a physical demonstration of a willingness to let others in. So is an open heart. To become fully trusted, you must be open to and with others. This means telling others the same things you'd like to know about them—talking about your hopes and dreams, your family and friends, your interests and your pursuits.

Be Creative about Incentives

Can you think of an acknowledgment you received for something you did that makes you smile or feel proud every time you look at it? It may be a picture of your team celebrating after a major victory, a small gift that was a symbol of what you did or what you love, or a simple handwritten note. Whatever it is, somehow it is attached to a feeling of self-worth and being a part of something significant. As a student leader, you can provide that same meaningful connection with the rewards you give. It is not the size or expense of the token; it's the meaning the recipient associates with it. All it takes is a little thought. If you've done your homework and you know the members of your group, it doesn't take long at all. Let yourself be creative.

Spontaneous, unexpected acts of recognition are often more meaningful to people than expected ones. Recognition is most effective when it is highly specific and given close to the time the appropriate behavior occurred. One of the most important results of spending time with people on your team and being out and about as a leader is that you can personally observe people doing things right and then recognize and possibly even reward them either on the spot or at your next public gathering.

You can't be a broken record when it comes to recognizing and appreciating others, praising people the same way again and again. People respond better to a variety of recognitions and rewards.[8] That's the beauty of being creative and personalizing your recognition. You have lots of options. You can give out stuffed giraffes, rainbow-striped zebra posters, T-shirts, mugs with team photos, crystal apples, classic car rides, clocks, pens, plaques, and hundreds of other creative expressions of appreciation. You can provide recognition verbally and nonverbally, elaborately and simply. There are no limits to kindness and consideration, as Kara Koser knows. Kara talked to us about how she used what she called "small token surprises" when she was a residence hall adviser at an East Coast urban university. Those "tokens" were all the little things she would do to recognize the students who lived on her floor.

> I tried to surprise people with little things, maybe a small handmade gift. It doesn't have to be a big expensive deal. It's a simple gesture. I liked to do it when it was least expected. That's what makes it fun.

It's important to understand that genuine recognition does not have to include anything tangible. Exemplary leaders make extensive use of intrinsic rewards—rewards built into the task itself, including such factors as a sense of accomplishment, a chance to be creative, and the challenge of the assignment—all directly tied to an individual's effort.

It's often the simple, personal gestures, like Clay's patches and Kara's small surprises, that are the most powerful rewards. It's all about being considerate. The techniques you use are less important than your genuine expression of caring. When you genuinely care, even the smallest of gestures reap huge benefits.

Just Say "Thank You"

There are few more basic human needs than to be noticed, recognized, and appreciated for one's efforts. It's true for everyone—classmates, teachers, volunteers, and staff. Extraordinary achievements bloom more readily in climates marked with a high volume of positive and appreciative comments. Studies show that work teams in which the ratio of positive to negative interactions is greater than three to one are *significantly* more productive than those teams that haven't achieved this proportion.[9]

"Saying thank you is easy to do, is powerfully important, but often easily forgotten or put off," Cameron McCarthy told us. Growing up, she said she hated it when her parents asked her to write thank-you cards. "I'd argue," she said, "that I had already said thank you in person." However, as captain of her school's boxing team, Cameron realized,

> I missed the point, which is common in my generation, especially with the ease of the Internet. It's more than the card, or those two words, but rather it's the sensation of receiving a personal note of appreciation. The key point is to illuminate their individual excellence so they continue to do their best. Praising accomplishments along the way allows individuals to continue to raise the stakes and strive for greatness.

It is always worthwhile to recognize someone's hard work and contributions. All too often, people forget to extend a hand, a smile, or offer a simple thank you. People naturally feel a little frustrated and unappreciated when someone takes them for granted. Sometimes these feelings can be set aside because people are under the pressure of deadlines, and the mandate to deliver on time overtakes expressing gratitude. However, it's critical that you stick around for that extra minute or two to say thanks. This is because letting people know why you appreciate them and their efforts reinforces the vision and the values of the group, strengthening everyone.

And, by the way, don't think you need to be the leader to provide recognition. Andy Ramans, while a student at a small private West Coast university, wondered whether you had to be "the person in charge" to Encourage the Heart. He questioned whether his efforts at saying "Good job" or "Thank you" would be wasted. Would his classmates value these words from a fellow student? We asked him to think about how he felt when his classmates thanked or praised him. He thought about this, smiled, and then had that "aha realization" about the importance of recognizing and appreciating others: "It always made a big difference to me," he said.

Or take it from JD Scharffenberger, who was part of a five-person community-based consulting team in one of his marketing classes. He says that a large part of their success was that they celebrated certain milestones and never failed to praise one another. For example, throughout the weeks leading up to the due date for their proposal, JD said,

> I went out of my way to text or call my teammates and thank them for their dedication. I figured that praising them for a job well done was one of the easiest ways to keep group morale high. Giving a simple "Thank you" or "Great work today" to my classmates made them feel that their accomplishments were meaningful and not overlooked. This also incentivized them to keep producing quality work, knowing that their contributions were being recognized and celebrated.

Making a point of regularly saying thank you goes a long way in sustaining high performance. Personalized recognition comes down to being thoughtful. It means knowing enough about another person to answer the question "What could I do to make this a memorable experience so that this individual will always remember how important his or her contributions were?" As Cameron learned from her experience, "Encouraging my teammates was one of the easiest and most beneficial things I could do to make each person on the team better."

REFLECT AND ACT: RECOGNIZE CONTRIBUTIONS

Exemplary student leaders have positive expectations of themselves and their group. They expect the best of people and create self-fulfilling prophecies about how ordinary people can take extraordinary actions and produce exceptional results. Exemplary leaders have clear goals and standards, helping people fully understand what needs to be done. They provide timely feedback and reinforcement. By maintaining a positive outlook and providing motivating feedback, you stimulate, rekindle, and focus people's energies and drive.

Exemplary leaders recognize and reward what individuals do to contribute to the vision and shared values. They don't limit their expressions of appreciation to formal events but look to be both timely and imaginative in saying thank you. Personalizing recognition requires knowing what's appropriate individually and culturally. Though it may be uncomfortable or embarrassing at first, recognizing someone's efforts is not all that difficult to do. And it's well worth the effort to make a connection with each person. From many small and often casual acts of appreciation, learn about what works for each person in your group and how best to personalize recognition. Take part in the celebrations yourself. After all being present is a tangible signal to others that showing up and sharing in the festivities is important for everyone.

Reflect

The first commitment of Encouraging the Heart requires leaders to *recognize contributions by showing appreciation for individual excellence.* Reflect on this commitment and answer these questions:

1. What is the most important idea or lesson about exemplary leadership that you learned from this chapter?

    _____

    _____

    _____

    _____

2. What changes do you need to make in your leadership to better Recognize Contributions?

    _____

    _____

    _____

    _____

3. In the next section, there are some suggestions on what you can do to put Recognize Contributions into practice. After reflecting

on what you learned and what you need to improve, select an action that you can take immediately to become a better leader.

_____

_____

_____

_____

Take Action

Here are ways you can follow through on your commitment to **Recognize Contributions:**

- Elevate expectations about what individuals and teams can accomplish.
- Create an environment that makes it comfortable to receive and give feedback, including feedback about your actions.
- Link recognition and rewards with what your group states it wants to achieve, and be sure that only those individuals who meet or exceed these goals receive them.
- Connect with people on a personal basis. Find out the types of encouragement that make the most difference to them.
- Be creative when it comes to recognition. Be spontaneous. Have fun.
- Make saying thank you a natural part of your everyday behavior.
- Identify anyone you might be taking for granted and do something that acknowledges who he or she is and what he or she contributes.

10

Commitment #10:
Celebrate the Values
and Victories

While in college, Kevin Straughn and Kaitlyn Morelli spent a summer working together as head coaches for a swim league team in their local community. With swimmers ranging in age from six to eighteen, and an eight-week season giving them a relatively short time together, they needed to build bonds and a sense of community within the team right from the beginning. They started the season with a get-together where they clarified their goals for the summer: improvement of each swimmer on the team and success for the whole team in the Summer Swim League Championship. "The team had won the championship in previous years," Kevin and Kaitlyn told us, "and we wanted to build off of that right from the start, giving swimmers something to set their sights on."

The team's name was the Hurricanes, and the coaches used this name as a metaphor to reinforce its values and the potential victories ahead. At their kickoff get-together, Kevin and Kaitlyn had all the swimmers paint the back wall of the clubhouse with slogans like

"Hurricanes—we blow you away" and "Hurricanes—we make waves." All the swimmers signed their names to the wall that day, making a pledge to come to practice and work on their skills to help the team make it all the way to the championship. It was a way to pull the team together on their goals of individual improvement and team success. "Swimming is a sport that makes it easy to feel part of something," Kaitlyn explained. "It has both an individual and a collective component. We could celebrate the success of individual swimmers after each meet and also point to the impact this had on the team's success. We made it a point to help them see that connection, to make them feel part of something bigger than their individual success or loss in each race."

As they worked to create a clear set of goals for the individual swimmers and for the team, Kevin and Kaitlyn took the time to understand each swimmer's strengths, challenges, and potential for contributing to the team's performance. With this knowledge, they could encourage each swimmer individually and celebrate his or her accomplishments with the rest of the team. "The first practice after each meet was always a fun game day," the coaches told us.

> We'd talk about the successes of the meet—there were always some, even if we lost the match—and then spend time just having fun in the water, being together and celebrating the hard work they'd all put in to get ready for the meet and the way they'd supported each other. It was enjoyable and pulled the team together.

Celebrations—from swim teams to work teams; across classrooms, homes, families, communities, and organizations; and around the globe—are an important part of what it takes to make extraordinary things happen. People take time off from classes or work to gather to mark special occasions. They march in elaborate parades down the city's main street to shower a championship team with cheers of appreciation. They set off fireworks to commemorate historical events or the beginning of a new year. They convene impromptu ceremonies to cheer the victories of their colleagues. They attend banquets to show their appreciation for individuals and groups who've accomplished an extraordinary feat. They sit down at elaborate feasts to give thanks for the bountiful harvest. They join with classmates at the end of a capstone project, give each other high-fives for a job well done, and make plans to get together and celebrate. And in tragic times, people come together with eulogy and song to honor those who showed courage, conviction, and sacrifice.

People take the time to come together, tell stories, and raise their spirits because celebrations are among the most significant ways people all over the world proclaim respect and gratitude, renew a sense of community, and remember shared values and traditions. Celebrations are as important in defining a group as the things that make up its day-to-day existence.

Performance improves when leaders on campus and in communities and corporations publicly honor those who have excelled and demonstrated to others that "we are all in this together." Leaders make the group a place where people want to both be and stay. That is why exemplary student leaders make a commitment to Celebrate the Values and Victories by mastering these essentials:

- **Create a spirit of community**
- **Be personally involved**

When leaders bring people together, rejoice in collective successes, and directly display their gratitude, they reinforce the essence of community and commitment. By being personally involved they make it clear that making extraordinary things happen requires everyone's commitment.

CREATE A SPIRIT OF COMMUNITY

Too often, organizations operate as if social gatherings were a nuisance. That's nonsense, because they aren't. Human beings are social animals—hardwired to connect with others.[1] This is evident all the time on campuses around the world. Students have a desire to connect with other students, so they form and join student governments, fraternities and sororities, honor and service societies, residential learning groups, intramural sports teams, and the like. People are meant to do things together and form communities, demonstrating a common bond. When social connections are strong and numerous, there's more trust, reciprocity, information flow, collective action, and happiness.

One of the rules Kevin and Kaitlyn lived by was that the Hurricanes team was about more than swimming. It was about a spirit of good health, fun, friendship, and support. They made it a point to create opportunities to do things together outside of practice and meets. "We did outside activities for the whole team, like a car wash fundraiser," they told us. "But we also did things to let the different age groups connect. We did movie night for the seniors and pizza supper for the little guys. It was fun for everyone to be together away from the pool."

Exemplary student leaders know that promoting a culture of celebration fuels a sense of unity. Whether celebrations, ceremonies, and similar events are to honor an individual or group achievement or to encourage team learning and relationship building, they offer leaders the perfect opportunity to explicitly communicate and reinforce the actions and behaviors that are important in realizing shared beliefs and shared goals. Sometimes celebrations can be elaborate, but more often they are about connecting everyday actions and events to the values of the organization and the accomplishments of the team. In the college environment, populated by students eager to have fun and "party down," celebrations can, however, lose their potential for these purposes.

Celebrations are not about having a great party. They often contain the same elements as a great party, but there's an additional ingredient that makes them so significant. True celebrations contain a clear articulation of the achievements of the members of the group and say in a loud, clear voice, "This is what we stand for, this is what we believe in, and this is what we are proud of." Exemplary leaders seldom let an opportunity pass to ensure that everyone knows why they're all together and how they should act in service of the celebration. Moreover, recognition and celebrations often are not just about what has already occurred and been accomplished; leaders also use these occasions to build the foundation for future contributions.

Celebrate Accomplishments in Public

Kaitlyn and Kevin took the opportunity to highlight the successes of individual team members after each meet. Swimmers who made personal-best times were recognized on a "Hurricane Heroes" bulletin board for all club members to see. The coaches also took time during the first practice after each meet to highlight the contributions of individual or relay wins and personal bests. "We'd let them know the points each win added to the team's score, and give a round of applause for a personal-best time," Kevin said. "That recognition makes a difference; whether it's for a six-year-old who just beat their very first time or a senior swimmer who hasn't set a personal-best time in a long while, the recognition reinforces that their accomplishment matters." Kevin and Kaitlyn understand that individual recognition increases the recipient's sense of worth and improves performance. Public celebrations have this effect as well, and they add other lasting contributions to the welfare of individuals and organizations that private, individual recognition can't accomplish. It's these added benefits that make celebrating *together* so powerful.

For one thing, public events are an opportunity to showcase real examples of what it means to "do what we say we will do." When the spotlight shines on certain people, and others tell stories about what they did, those spotlighted individuals become role models. These people visibly represent how the organization would like everyone to behave and concretely demonstrate that it is possible to do so. Public celebrations of accomplishment also build commitment, among both the individuals recognized and those in the audience. When you communicate to individuals, "Keep up the good work; it's appreciated," you are also speaking to the larger group. You are saying, "Here are people just like you who are examples of what we stand for and believe in. You can do this. You too can make a significant contribution to our success."

Exemplary leaders point out the accomplishment of the individual and effectively reinforce that the entire group wins when people excel in this way. They understand that celebrations are not about making people feel as though there are favorites in the group but about making them feel proud of what they have accomplished because of contributions of particular members. The secret is in the word *we*. Leaders might point to individual accomplishments, but they connect how one person's excellence contributes to a win for all, pulling the group together and reinforcing the sense of community. The process of creating community helps ensure that people feel that they belong to something greater than themselves and are working collectively toward a common cause. Public celebrations of accomplishment serve to strengthen the bonds of teamwork and trust.

Some people are reticent or reluctant to recognize others in public, fearing that it might cause jealousy or resentment. Forget these fears. All winning teams present Most Valuable Player (MVP) awards, with the recipients usually selected by their teammates. Public celebrations are meaningful occasions to reinforce shared values and to recognize individuals for their contributions. They provide opportunities to say thanks to specific individuals for their outstanding performance, and they also provide occasions to remind people of exactly what it is that the organization stands for.

Private recognition is a wonderful thing. It motivates and builds the relationships essential for leading others, but it doesn't have the same impact on the team as public acknowledgment. To generate community-wide energy and commitment for the common cause, you need to celebrate successes in public. Awards ceremonies or banquets are familiar to most people, but there are other ways to celebrate publicly, even when you can't get everyone together in the same room.

Kenzie Crane, for example, created an online "Brag Room." Responsible for overseeing recruitment for all the sororities on her campus, she worked with a team of twenty recruiters, and the Brag Room was the way she provided a mechanism for people to be recognized "publicly" by their peers. Setting it up on the web was easy enough, but the key was making sure that everyone understood the intention of the space and participated. The Brag Room's message was: "Here's where we want you to post and share the stories about someone you've seen doing something that made you proud to be associated with that person, and with recruiters in general." Heaps of stories and appreciations were posted. There was a posting about how someone dealt with a medical emergency in a special way; another acknowledged someone making a valuable introduction; and others gave examples of people going out of their way to stand up for the sorority system. All those stories, Kenzie said, "really made us all feel great and proud of the work we were doing."

Provide Social Support

Ceremonies and celebrations are opportunities to build healthier groups, to enable members of the organization to know and care about each other and offer social support. Research across a broad range of disciplines consistently demonstrates that social support enhances productivity, psychological well-being, and even physical health. Studies have shown that among undergraduate students, the best predictor of their happiness is social support; it is even more important than such factors as GPA, family income, SAT scores, age, gender, or race.[2] Social support not only enhances wellness but also buffers against disease, particularly during times of high stress. This latter finding is true regardless of an individual's age, gender, or ethnic group. In fact, George Vaillant, Harvard professor of psychiatry who directed the world's longest continuous study of physical and mental health, when asked what he had learned from his forty years of research, said, "The only thing that really matters in life are your relationships to other people."[3]

Take it from Angela Close, who started a school club called Letters to Soldiers when she was a high school sophomore. A teacher suggested that students write a letter to a US soldier to show appreciation for his or her service. When Angela wrote her letter, she included a few facts about herself plus "some cheesy jokes" and events that were happening around her town and condolences for the loss of friends in the line of duty. It took nearly five months for her to get a response, but the letter she received was filled with gratitude for her caring and sharing. The reply was from A. J. Pascuiti, a Marine gunnery sergeant who had graduated from her same high school. About the letter, he said, "It was the nicest thing anyone has ever done for me. Although the students may never physically get to see how they change lives, they are doing something that is helping soldiers who are out on the front lines; it validates what we do."

From that moment, Angela knew she had to continue sending letters to soldiers abroad. She started the letter-writing club, and it has been growing ever since. The club members receive very few letters back, but that is not the goal. Their purpose is to offer the support and connection they believe the soldiers who are serving the nation deserve. As one student explained, "I feel like it's a small way to change the world."

Social support is not just good for your physical and mental health. It's also essential to outstanding performance. You have probably heard a class valedictorian's presentation at graduation. You may not remember the exact message, but if you recall the spirit of the speech, it was most likely one of appreciation for the support received along the way, gratitude for the friendships and meaningful relationships that led to the speaker's success, and optimism for the future of his or her classmates. These sentiments are consistent with what researchers found when analyzing the speeches of baseball players when inducted into the National Baseball Hall of Fame.[4] As elite athletes, they had achieved the highest recognition in a field demanding top physical skills. Yet for almost two-thirds of them, their words of appreciation were not so much about technical or practical assistance as they were about emotional support and friendship.

What's true at home, in the community, and on the playing field is just as true for student organizations. People who have friends at work or on their team or in their classes are more productive, feel informed, and comfortable sharing ideas; they report not only being more creative but also having more fun in these activities and getting more done in less time.[5]

Think about how these findings translate to the activities you are involved in as a student leader. Isn't it more fun to work side by side on an event with people you know, trust, and can share and laugh with? Doesn't it feel as though you get more done when you are communicating with people you understand and appreciate? Leaders find every opportunity to strengthen the personal relationships in their groups, not only because it helps get the job done but also because in doing so, they boost the groups' spirits and well-being.

Our files are full of personal-best leadership cases in which robust human connections produced spectacular results. When people feel a strong sense of affiliation and attachment to the people in their group, they're much more likely to have a higher sense of personal well-being, to feel more committed to the organization, and to perform at higher levels. When people feel distant and detached, they're unlikely to accomplish much of anything.[6] When people are personally involved with the task and feel connected with their colleagues, they can perform extraordinary feats.

Student leaders understand that celebrations provide concrete evidence that individuals aren't alone in their efforts and struggles, that other people care about them, and that they can count on their support. Celebrations reinforce the fact that people need each other and that it takes a group of individuals with a common purpose working together in an atmosphere of trust and collaboration to get extraordinary things done. Kenzie told us that when sorority rush ended at her school, everyone met in a large open space on campus to welcome their new members. All the recruiters she had worked with came to this event, and had the chance to see the results of their hard work. "I looked around and saw all the recruiters, some in tears, some holding hands, all of them smiling," Kenzie told us. "We had done good work, and so many were benefiting. That event really helped them see that."

Have Fun Together

Every personal-best leadership experience was a combination of hard work *and* fun. In fact, students agreed that without the enjoyment and pleasure they experienced interacting with others on the project or team, they wouldn't have been able to sustain the intensity and diligence required to achieve their personal best. People just feel better about the work they are doing when they enjoy the people they're working with.[7]

Having fun sustains productivity because it lightens the load. And it's not all about parties, games, festivities, and laughter. Leaders who make addressing challenging issues fun are clearly passionate about their purpose, what they believe in, and how they pass this on to others. They understand that the work required to meet the dreams and goals of the group can be difficult and demanding and that people need a sense of personal well-being to go the distance. And leaders set the tone.

John Gray was a resident assistant (RA) in the Honors Program at his southwestern US college, where student-created events were held throughout the year to help bring members together as a community. John was responsible for creating and supervising one of these events, which was scheduled to take place late in the academic year. Because the school calendar was issued early in the year, when the details of many events were not finalized, his event was simply listed on the calendar as "John Gray Day."

As the date approached, John found himself wondering what kind of event to create. Many fun events took place at the beginning of the school year, but they tended to have a more educational focus to get everyone off on the right foot. "I felt like it was time to get together just to have fun," John told us. But he still wasn't clear on what he wanted to plan. Then John noticed that people were getting curious about what was on the calendar, asking one another, "What is John Gray Day?" He decided to build on the mystery and have fun with it.

The whole point of these campus events was to bring people together, so John began to hatch plans simply to call one "John Gray Day." Don't think this was a product of arrogance or self-absorption; it was John's way to play on people's curiosity and reward them with a lot of fun. "It didn't hurt that John already had a reputation as a warm, funny, engaging guy," Michelle Madsen, resident community director, told us. "People were drawn to him. They'd wait outside their rooms when they knew he was doing rounds just to talk with him and laugh. That's the kind of appeal he had, and it meant that people anticipated that John Gray Day would be like him—fun—and it was."

John Gray Day was a big hit, offering lots of entertaining ways for students to get involved in the festivities. John assembled a bunch of people's baby pictures, including some of himself, and held a contest to "find the real John Gray." He made copies of black-and-white pictures of himself that people could color in. There was a chocolate fountain and lots of food from a local restaurant. "Everyone had a good time," Michelle told us, "but what I remember the most is the laughter."

John created a space for people to come together and have fun being themselves and being part of a community. John Gray Day spoke to the spirit of the Honors Program: members work hard, but they want to have fun and enjoy each other's company too.

John Gray Day took on a life of its own and continued for the next three years that John was an RA. Each year, people got more excited about it, and the energy grew. Students even created a "flat John Gray" and took it to different locations, even over the summer, to capture their adventures with John Gray and then post them for their fellow Honors Program classmates to see. John has graduated and gone on to medical school, but as a student leader he has left a legacy: John Gray Day continues.

Leaders set the tone. When student leaders openly demonstrate the joy and passion they have for their organizations, team members, and challenges, as John did, they send a very powerful message to others that it's perfectly acceptable for people to make public displays of playfulness and gratitude. They know that on today's campuses, group assignments, in and outside the classroom, are demanding, and that consequently people need to have a sense of personal well-being to sustain their commitment. It works for everyone when leaders show enthusiasm and excitement about the work required.

BE PERSONALLY INVOLVED

Our discussion of exemplary student leadership started with Model the Way, and we've come full circle. If you want others to believe in something and behave according to those beliefs, you must set an example by being personally involved. You must practice what you preach. If you want to build and maintain a culture of excellence and distinction, then you must be personally involved in celebrating the actions that contribute to and sustain the culture.

While enrolled in college, Kyle Harvey was coaching a local high school basketball team. At the end of the first season, he got some feedback from the team and their families that he had been focusing more on the negatives than the positives during games and practices, and that it was affecting the players' enthusiasm and commitment. In his second year of coaching, Kyle was determined to be more upbeat and focus on developing his players, not only on the basketball court but also as individuals.

On the first day of practice, Kyle told the team that he intended to be positive and said that he hoped that the team would do the same, keeping an eye out for the things that their fellow players did that were helping the team. As a result, Kyle got much more personally involved with the athletes, and this helped him discover even more positive qualities in his players. He began recognizing them much more for what they were doing well rather than pointing out what they were doing wrong—and he did it out loud, for the whole team to hear.

Over time, Kyle observed the team working harder and holding *each other* to higher standards.

> I could tell that when I was celebrating positive contributions, whether or not the individual played in the game, it boosted that player's confidence and gave us extremely positive results.

One example was a kid who had really been struggling with the game. Kyle spent time getting to know this player better, made it a point to be patient, and concentrated on applauding the improvements in his game and the successes he was having. As a result, the young athlete's performance improved dramatically, and subsequently had a huge impact on the success of the team. This experience proved to Kyle that getting more engaged with his players and recognizing their individual contributions to the entire team resulted in stronger relationships with each player, greater individual development, and notable advancement for the entire team.

If you want to build and maintain a culture of excellence and distinction, then you need to do as Kyle did: recognize, reward, reinforce, and celebrate exceptional efforts and successes. And you need to get personally involved in celebrating the actions that contribute to and sustain the culture. If you want people to have the courage to push through the tough times, you need to encourage them yourself.

Getting personally involved puts the spotlight on connecting what you preach with what you celebrate. If they are not one and the same, your celebrations will come off as insincere and phony—and your credibility will suffer. Recognition events and celebrations must be honest expressions of commitment to key values and to the hard work and dedication of the people who have lived the values. Remember, it's not just another chance to party. Treat it that way and you lose one of the best opportunities you have as a leader to pull people together, help them feel great about being part of the group, and inspire them to keep going. Elaborate productions that lack sincerity or do not connect in some clear way to the values of the group are more entertainment than encouragement. Authenticity is what makes conscious celebrations work.

When it comes to sending a message throughout an organization, nothing communicates more clearly than what leaders do. By directly and visibly showing others that you're there to cheer them along, you're sending a positive signal. When you set an example that communicates the message that "around here we say thanks, show appreciation, and have fun," others will follow your lead. The group will develop a culture of celebration and recognition. Everyone becomes a leader, everyone adheres to the same values and norms, and everyone makes the time to be involved with celebrating the values and victories. As Kyle learned with his basketball team, when leaders are encouraging, others follow their example, and an organization develops a reputation that magnetically holds people together.

Show You Care

People don't care about how much you know until they know how much you care for them. In other words, they must believe that you want them to be safe and secure, to feel supported and valued; that you want them to be successful, learning and developing themselves; and that you wouldn't ask them to do something where they could intentionally be embarrassed, injured, or hurt. Demonstrating this isn't rocket science. Take it from David Braverman.

Iowa summers can be brutally hot, and before heading back to college, David found himself in an organic tomato field supervising an eclectic group of people. There were two other college students, a teacher interested in learning about organic farming firsthand, an "aging gentleman" who had dabbled at various careers and thought this one might be interesting, and a local health food store employee who had decided to stray from the air conditioning on this particular day to pick tomatoes. As the day wore on, however, the crew became demoralized, and David sensed that they were all about ready to quit. He realized that they needed someone to care about them; they needed encouragement if they were going to continue. With this epiphany, David said:

> First I ran from the tomato fields and got all my coworkers an ice-cold glass of lemonade. Next, I explained to them that I knew the work was tough and that the day was hot, but that we needed to finish the tomato harvest so as to eliminate any possibility of tomatoes rotting. I asked them to stay positive.
>
> I then pointed out their strong suits as farmworkers. I told them to look and see all of the tomatoes we had already harvested and how close we were to completing our task. We were in this together; we were all sweating as one. I thanked them for their help and explained that we were well capable of completing the task and that the faster we did so, the faster we could be by the nearest swimming pool.

They did finish the job that afternoon, and David says that the lesson from this experience was profound: "When people are down and demoralized, they need to be picked up and encouraged. Every person needs to be valued not just for themselves as a person but for their contribution to the team." As David realized, "Showing that you care about someone is a simple yet overlooked quality essential to the success of a leader."

What David says is spot-on. Also true is that one of the most significant ways in which student leaders show others that they care is to be there with them—as David was. Thank-you notes and emails expressing your appreciation are important, but being visible makes you more real, more genuine, more approachable, and more human. You show you care when you spend time sweating in the fields yourself, when you are there helping set up for an event and cleaning up afterward, and when you are attending meetings, work sessions, and organizational functions even when you're not directly responsible.

Being there also helps you stay in touch, quite literally, with what's really going on. And it shows you walk the talk about the values you and others share. Credibility goes up when leaders show they care.

Spread the Stories

Getting involved personally in showing that you care provides an opportunity to both find and convey stories that put a human face on values. The stories you tell give up-close-and-personal accounts of what it means to put into practice shared values and aspirations. In the process, you create organizational role models to whom everyone can relate. You put the behavior in a real context. Values become more than simply rules; they come alive. Through the stories you tell, you dramatically and memorably illustrate how people should act and make decisions.

Storytelling is how people pass along lessons from person to person, generation to generation, culture to culture. Stories aren't meant to be hush-hush; they're meant to be told. And because they're public, they're tailor-made for celebrations. The stories that leaders tell have much the same impact as the stories that parents tell their children, in the sense that the stories chosen provide a viewpoint about what is important and what matters, or not. The content of the stories underscores what values are important and the actions that matter. They help set both a moral and a practical compass.[8] In fact, you can think of stories as celebrations, and celebrations, in turn, are stories.

Being part of the action by showing that they care and getting personally involved in celebrating the group's achievements gives leaders the opportunity to both create and find stories to share. First-person examples always have more impact than third-party examples. It's that critical difference between "I saw for myself" and "someone told me about." Exemplary student leaders are constantly on the lookout for "catching people doing things right," and this is difficult to do if you are not out where the action is. Tell a story if you want to quickly translate information about how people are supposed to act and make decisions.[9]

By telling stories, you accomplish more effectively the objectives of teaching, mobilizing, and motivating people than you can through bullet points in a PowerPoint presentation or tweets on a mobile device. Listening to and understanding the stories leaders tell does more to inform people about the values and culture of a group than do its organizational policies or operational guidelines. Well-told stories are effective in reaching people's emotions and pulling them along. They make the message stick. They simulate the experience of actually being there and give people a compelling way of learning what is most important about the experience. Reinforcing stories through celebrations deepens the connections between people.

Make Celebrations Part of Organizational Life

One of the Hurricanes swim team's traditions was the awards banquet at the end of the season after the league championship. The swimmers all looked forward to the slide show featuring candid shots of the team taken throughout the summer. Coaches Kaitlyn and Kevin also saw the awards banquet as an opportunity to reinforce the values and messages shared throughout the season and a chance to celebrate individual and team excellence. "We made a 'paper plate' award for each swimmer," they told us.

> We handed the award plate out with the final stats for the season on it. It also had a name or title we assigned to each swimmer based on his or her unique personality and contribution to the team. For example, an eight-year-old boy who was always giggling and making people laugh might get the name "Lucas the Laugh Maker." A swimmer who had made

huge strides during the season might be called "Bonnie the Buzzsaw." Sometimes we think they looked forward to those plates more than the ribbons and trophies. It was fun for us to get ready for the event and really reinforced what summer swim league is all about.

You need to put celebrations on your calendar, just as the Hurricanes do with their awards banquet. These scheduled events serve as opportunities to get people together so that you can show them how they are part of the larger vision and have a shared destiny. Celebrations are highly visible ways for you to affirm shared values, mark meaningful progress, and create a sense of community.

You probably already put birthdays, holidays, and anniversaries on your calendar. You also should do it for the significant milestones in the life of your team and organization. Giving them a date, time, and place announces to everyone that these things matter. It also creates a sense of anticipation. Scheduling celebrations doesn't rule out spontaneous events; it just means that certain occasions are of such significance that everyone needs to pay attention to them and remember why they are special.

That's the message Lee LeBoeuf communicated when she started a new tradition to commemorate the accomplishments of her university's senior class before graduation. As class president, Lee led a team to create a celebration for the class that would continue through the years. She conferred with her classmates about experiences that had meant a lot to them as first-year students. One stood out: the Welcome Tunnel, an event welcoming new students to campus. "I thought it would be really cool to create an event for everyone to celebrate the end of our time together on campus, to kind of bookend the freshman experience," Lee said.

Lee and her colleagues decided to put on an event called "The Final Lap." It would be a symbolic final trip around campus, complete with a party at the end of the race open to everyone. Graduating seniors would jog or walk a lap around the campus as music played. Afterward, they would meet their friends and other students for a celebration with food and dance to mark the end of their collegiate career.

It was a bigger undertaking than anything the senior class had ever put together for a year-end celebration. It was difficult at times to keep everyone motivated over the course of the entire year, particularly with their time at the university wrapping up. "I struggled to keep my fellow seniors motivated and working toward the event, because their other responsibilities on campus were coming an end," Lee told us. "My entire team was made up of seniors, so it was difficult to motivate them to work during a time when they wanted to be celebrating all the work they had already put into their undergraduate careers."

Lee broke down each large task—for example, charting the course for The Final Lap—into smaller tasks, such as reaching out to the groundskeeping staff to figure out where they would have electricity to play music and put lights along the course. Completing each task served as a celebration point for the student council members who had worked on that task.

> We'd celebrate each smaller milestone so that we could see how each piece contributed to the entire experience—it wasn't so daunting when we could have small victories along the way. It also made the whole process more fun.

Also, having a strong narrative to tell about why the event was important helped keep Lee's team motivated, she said.

> We had a story to tell about how this was something we'd done as first-year students, and how much it would mean to our whole class to be able to recreate that experience in a

different context. I could also say to my team, "Look, this is going to be an experience we want to continue in the future; this is going to be the new tradition for graduating seniors, and you got to help start it. When we come back for our ten-year reunion, people will still be doing this run, and they'll have improved it and made it even better." That went a long way to keeping everyone involved and motivated.

Finally, Lee noted that it was important for her student council to know that The Final Lap and the celebration afterwards were as much for them as for their fellow graduates. "This was our last chance to have a hoorah as a group, to celebrate all of our hard work and see it embodied for our peers," Lee said. Part of the driving motivation was to have one last time to have fun and to celebrate together, both as a student council and as a student body.

In setting up celebrations, student leaders like Lee decide which organizational values, events of historical significance, or remarkable successes are of such importance that they warrant a special ritual, ceremony, or festivity. Perhaps you want to honor the group or team of people who started your organization or created an astounding event; maybe you want to praise those who reached amazing levels of community service or thank the parents and families of the members of your group. Whatever you wish to celebrate, formalize it, announce it, and tell people how they become eligible to participate.

The importance of celebrations is borne out by how students report feeling when their leaders "find ways for us to celebrate accomplishments." The data in Figure 10.1 shows that the more their leaders celebrated accomplishments, the more strongly students felt that they were making a difference. Similarly striking results are shown in Figure 10.2 about how finding ways to celebrate has a strong impact on student's feelings about the extent to which the leader values their work.

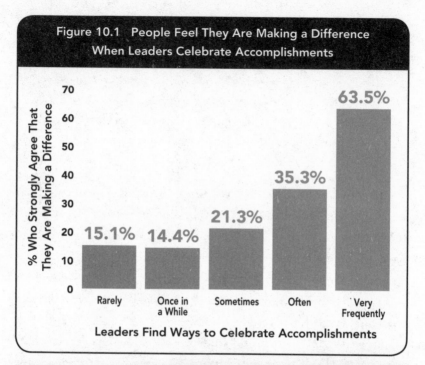

Figure 10.1 People Feel They Are Making a Difference When Leaders Celebrate Accomplishments

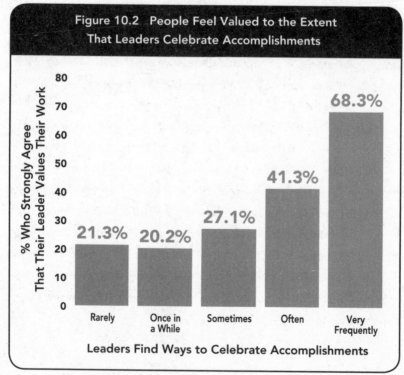

Figure 10.2 People Feel Valued to the Extent That Leaders Celebrate Accomplishments

There is no shortage of opportunities to bring people together to celebrate your group's values and victories. In good times or bad, gathering together to acknowledge those who've contributed and the actions that led to success signal to everyone that their work and determination is well worth the effort. Their energy, enthusiasm, and well-being—and yours—will be all the better for it.

REFLECT AND ACT: CELEBRATE THE VALUES AND VICTORIES

Celebrating together reinforces the fact that extraordinary performance is the result of many people's efforts. By visibly and publicly acknowledging the team's accomplishments, student leaders create and foster community and sustain team spirit. By basing celebrations on consistency with core values and achievement of small wins, student leaders reinforce and sustain people's focus.

Social interaction increases the commitment that individuals have to the standards of the group and has a profound effect on people's well-being. When people are asked to go beyond their comfort zones, the support and encouragement of others enhances their resiliency and resistance to stress.

By getting personally involved, student leaders demonstrate that recognition and celebration are the norm. Telling stories about individuals who have made exceptional efforts and achieved outstanding successes provides role models for others to emulate. Stories make people's experiences memorable, often even profound in ways they hadn't envisioned, and serve as a guide for future actions. Making personal connections with people in a culture of celebration also builds and sustains credibility for the cause, as well as for the people involved. Leaders make it a point to bring people together to bear testimony about what has been accomplished because of their collective efforts.

Reflect

The second commitment of Encouraging the Heart requires leaders to *celebrate the values and victories by creating a spirit of community.* Reflect on this commitment and answer these questions:

1. What is the most important idea or lesson about exemplary leadership that you learned from this chapter?

    _____

    _____

    _____

    _____

2. What changes do you need to make in your leadership to better Celebrate Values and Victories?

    _____

    _____

    _____

    _____

3. In the next section, there are some suggestions on what you can do to put Celebrate Values and Victories into practice. After you have reflected on what you learned and what you need to improve, select an action that you can take immediately to become a better leader.

    _____

    _____

_____

_____

_____

Take Action

Here are actions you can take to more effectively follow through on your commitment to **Celebrate the Values and Victories:**

- Plan to set aside time at a future group gathering to share a success with everyone.
- Make sure to relate the fundamental principles being honored when you bring people together to celebrate.
- Never pass up any opportunity to publicly relate true stories about how people in your group went above and beyond the call of duty. Make sure that everyone understands how they are "part of the whole" and that many others are working to achieve success for the group, even if they don't know those people personally.
- Repeat this phrase—"We are in this together"—at every celebration.
- Don't wait until the whole project is completed to celebrate. Plan a festive celebration for even the smaller milestones that your team reaches or the remarkable efforts people put forth.
- Whatever the celebration, experiment with ways to keep this ritual fresh, meaningful, genuine, and fun.

A Call to Action for Leaders

Throughout this book, we have shared stories and research that clearly demonstrate the ability of students to lead others, making extraordinary things happen for their classmates and colleagues, their schools, and their communities. We believe that everyone is capable of leadership and that you can do everything we've written about if you want to. The Five Practices of Exemplary Leadership gives you the framework to liberate the leader within. But exploring your leadership potential while you are a student is just the beginning. Let your time in school be the opportunity to learn about yourself, about how to work with others, and about how to put your heart into doing what you believe matters.

YOUR CONTINUING LEADERSHIP JOURNEY

The student leaders we have talked about are from campuses all over the globe and in different stages of their academic lives. Chances are you haven't read about them or heard them mentioned in the press.

They're not public figures, celebrities, or megastars. They're individuals who might sit next to you in a classroom or at another table in the student union, live in the room down the hall or in an apartment across the street. In short, they are people just like you.

We've focused on everyday exemplary leaders because leadership is not about position or title. It's not about power or authority. It's not about fame or fortune. It's not about the family you are born into or your cultural heritage. And it's definitely not about being a superhero. Leadership is about relationships, and about what you do.

Julie Guillaumin, a college junior, shared this epiphany after thinking about her leadership experiences:

> I can be a leader without taking on an official leadership role. I can be a leader in the classroom, at my internship, and in socializing with my peers. Leadership is a state of mind and a deliberate practice that I can act on in everyday life.
>
> It's an ongoing process of committing to take action, taking that action, and reflecting on the execution and results. It doesn't have so much to do with a position, but everything to do with the actions you take. I can be a leader every day, no matter how "busy" or tight my schedule is.

After reviewing their personal-best leadership experiences, many students came to a similar conclusion: "I learned that anyone can be a leader regardless of their years of experience and whether the words 'manager' or 'supervisor' are in their job title. This realization applies to my everyday life in and outside of school and the workplace."

You don't have to look up or out for leadership—you only have to look inward. You have the potential to lead others to places they have never been. But before you can lead others, you have to believe that you can have a positive impact on them. You have to believe that what you do counts. You have to believe that your words can inspire and that your actions can move others. And you have to be able to convince others that the same is true for them.[1]

We're confident that you want to become the best leader you can be, not just for your own sake, but also for the sake of others and for the success of the endeavors you are pursuing. After all, it's unlikely that you'd be reading this book if you didn't. But how can you learn to lead better than you do now? In addition to understanding and utilizing The Five Practices of Exemplary Leadership as an *operating system for leadership,* here are a few more essential lessons we've learned from our research that you need to keep in mind as you continue your leadership development journey.

Leadership Development Requires Deliberate Practice

Nearly every time we give a speech or conduct a workshop, someone asks, "Are leaders born or made?" Whenever we're asked this question, our answer, always offered with a smile, is this: "We've never met a leader who wasn't born. We've also never met an accountant, artist, athlete, engineer, lawyer, physician, writer, or zoologist who wasn't born. We're all born. That's a given. It's what you do with what you have before you die that makes the difference."

Let's get something straight. Leadership is not preordained. It is not a gene, and it is not a trait. There is no hard evidence to support the assertion that leadership is imprinted in the DNA of only some individuals, and that everyone else missed out and is doomed to be clueless. There was no way that anyone would have picked out from some university bulletin or catalog the student leaders we shared with you in this book. None of them got to where they were by winning any leadership competition.

Exemplary student leaders like those profiled in this book know that making extraordinary things happen requires learning. They understand that their learning never stops; learning from experience is the fuel that keeps them inspired and enables them to keep going when things don't work out the first time.

Leadership can be learned. It's an *observable pattern of practices and behaviors* and a *definable set of skills and abilities.* And any skill can be learned, strengthened, honed, and enhanced, given the motivation and desire, along with practice, feedback, role models, and coaching. When we track the progress of students who participate in leadership development programs, for example, the research demonstrates that they improve over time.[2] They learn to be better leaders.

But here's the thing. Although leadership can be learned, not everyone wants to learn it, and not all those who learn about leadership master it. Why? Because becoming the very best requires having a deep desire to excel, a strong belief that new skills and abilities can be learned, a willing devotion to deliberate practice, and continuous reflection and experimentation. No matter how good you are, you must always want to be better. The truth is that the best leaders are the best learners.

What truly differentiates any expert performer from the merely good ones is hours of practice developing his or her skills. It doesn't matter whether it's in sports, music, medicine, computer programming, mathematics, leadership, or any other field, you've got to work at becoming the best, and it sure doesn't happen over a weekend or by taking a single class. Dancers dance better by dancing. Runners run faster by running. Writers write better by writing.

The point is that to sharpen any skill, you need to put in the time and effort. Leadership is no different. To be a good leader, you'll have to practice. As Julie went on to tell us:

> What fascinates me is that while there are ladders in corporations for climbing to the top, leadership remains a level playing field. Many people blindly trudge through a mediocre work and school life because so many "busy" tasks prevent

significant reflection and taking initiative. We overlook how
school and work can actually be our greatest opportunity for
discovery and growth of our leadership capabilities.

You must have a passion for learning to become the best leader
you can be. You must be open to new experiences and open to honestly examining how you and others perform, especially when the going gets tough or the future is uncertain. You must be willing to learn
quickly from your failures as well as your successes and find ways to
try out new behaviors without hesitation. You won't always be right or
do things perfectly, but you will get the chance to develop and grow.

Leadership Is a Relationship

Leaders never get extraordinary things done all by themselves. As we
say in the beginning of this book, *leaders mobilize others to want to
struggle for shared aspirations,* and this means that, fundamentally,
leadership is a relationship. Leadership is a relationship between those
who want to lead and those who choose to follow. It's the quality of
this relationship that matters most when trying to make extraordinary
things happen. A leader-follower relationship that's characterized by
fear, mistrust, or hurt feelings will never stand the test of time.

When Tarek Aly and a classmate began working on the idea of
how to assist survivors of a major hurricane, they were less than two
weeks into their first college semester. Still, in just about a month's
time, they recruited a small core of first-year students to help them
get started, then enlisted more classmates to join them in producing
a series of small events leading up to a finale called the Emergency
Mardi Gras. They enlisted local business support, attracted other students and community guests to participate in the daylong event, and
raised over $28,000. Their fundraising success proved that Tarek had
come to grips with a fundamental leadership fact: leadership is not

possible without a strong relationship with others who will be part of the change effort.

Trust is at the center of both building and fostering relationships. People trust a leader who promotes shared values, consults and involves team members in important decisions, and has the best interest of others at heard. We heard loud and clear from students that what goes around comes around: "When the leader trusted me, I trusted that individual in return, and together we worked hard to make something extraordinary happen."

Leadership Development Is Self-Development

Engineers have computers; painters, canvas and brushes; musicians, instruments. Leaders have only themselves and their experiences. The instrument of leadership is the self, and mastery of the art of leadership comes from mastery of the self. Leadership development is self-development, and self-development is not about stuffing in a whole bunch of new information or trying the latest technique. It's about leading from what is already in your soul. It's about liberating the leader within you. And it starts with taking a look inside. You can't lead others until you've first led yourself on a journey of self-discovery. If you are to become the leader you aspire to be, then you will have to take the time to step back and reflect deeply on your past, your present, and your future.

"As someone who's struggled with self-doubt in the past," Adam Schellenberg told us just before his college graduation,

> I did not believe I had the capacity to be a leader. I believed that leaders were born with many qualities that I simply did not possess. But having the opportunity to think more deeply about my personal values and clarify my aspirations, I now have a path forward and believe I can make a difference.

Like Adam, you need to have confidence in yourself; and your ability to excel as a leader begins with how well you know yourself. The better you know yourself, the better you can make sense of the often confusing and conflicting messages you receive daily as a student: "Do this, do that; support this, support that; decide this, decide that; change this, change that." You need internal guidance to navigate the turmoil in today's highly uncertain environment.

There is no shortcut when it comes to knowing yourself and discovering who you are, what drives you, what's important to you, whom or what you want to serve, and the like. What it takes is self-reflection, and the more you engage in such reflection the better you come to know who you are. When you know who you are, you will find it easier to connect with other people and communicate more effectively about what matters to you. Your leadership becomes authentic—because it is an expression of who you are and not some means to an end. Other students joined Tarek's Emergency Mardi Gras because it gave them an opportunity to express their best selves, to learn, and to develop.

To grow as a leader, you need to push yourself out of your comfort zone and have the desire to build and hone your skills. You need to embrace discomfort and challenge and do what it takes to know that at the end of the day, you are a better version of yourself than the person who woke up that morning.

Leadership Development Is an Ongoing Process

Many of his peers over the years have echoed what Zachary Chien told us he took away from reflecting on his personal-best leadership experience: "I learned that the more I think I know about leadership, the less I actually know. There's always room for growth and improvement, and it's a never-ending process."

Learning to be an exemplary student leader requires that you build a pattern of practice into your life. You commit to taking action, you act, you reflect on that action, and you start again. This iterative process is available to everyone, and the only requirement for making it work is a full heart. It won't always be pretty, but nothing in the research hints that leaders should be perfect. Leaders aren't saints. They're human beings, full of flaws and failings, and like everyone else, they make mistakes.

Perhaps the very best advice for all aspiring leaders is to remain humble and unassuming—always to remain open and full of wonder. As you move into the next phases of your life, there will be ongoing leadership opportunities that are very different from those you are having as a student. You will be able to embrace leadership roles in your professional life, your partnerships, your parenting, and your communities. All the leaders whose stories we have told built the foundation of their leadership capacity during their collegiate experiences, which informed their decisions to seize the leadership opportunities they continued to find long after graduation. The same will be true for you.

Your Leadership Makes a Difference

Here's one final lesson. You may or may not be aware of it, but people are watching you. Right now, whether or not you hold a leadership position in some student organization, classroom project, or community service group, you are having an impact on the other members of whatever group, project, or team you are involved with, intentionally or not.

After Kayla Richard tore her ACL in her first year playing on her university's basketball team and while having to sit out the rest of the season, she believed she still had a role on the team. For example, before each away game, when Kayla couldn't travel because of her injury, she would write a note to each teammate, cheering her on, listing specific individual strengths, and offering personalized words of encouragement. "To me," Kayla said, "it was just a way of letting the girls know that I was there with them in spirit and I believed in them. My teammates loved it! They were really touched and told me that it motivated them to play harder."

Leadership comes in many different forms and formats. What you say and do affects peoples' choice to stay or leave, to be involved or not, to follow through with commitments, to support and celebrate each other, and to share the group's values and vision, or not. As you continue your journey, if you become a parent, teacher, coach, or community or corporate leader, *you* will be the person who's setting the leadership example for a new group of people who will look to you for inspiration. Give up the myth once and for all that leadership is about position and power. It simply is not. Leadership is about the actions you take.

Wherever you now are in your leadership journey, regardless of whether you hold some official position now or in the future, and no matter what role you embrace, we believe in you and all you offer the world. Your chances to lead will never stop appearing. They are only limited by your ability to recognize them as opportunities and your willingness to accept them. If you can commit to this ongoing developmental adventure, if you can keep learning as you lead, and if you can always lead with your heart, you will make a difference. Of that, we have no doubt.

Notes

Introduction   When People Are at Their Best As Leaders

1. Unless otherwise noted, all stories and quotations are from student leaders around the world who shared with us, in their own words, their personal-best leadership experiences, their most admired leaders, and the lessons they have learned about leadership. Most will have moved on, and the organizations in which some of their personal-best leadership experiences occurred may no longer exist by the time you read this, but the details on their roles, organizations, and experiences were accurate at the time of this writing.

2. When we use the term *group,* we mean any collective organization that a student is a member of or is leading: an athletic team, a club or common-interest group, any specialized activity or project, an academic team, or even a class project group or group of house mates. We also use the word *leaders* to refer to students we have studied, not just students in formal leadership positions but students who have taken the challenge and worked with others to make extraordinary things happen in groups to which they belong. For example, in many classroom situations, no one is officially designated as "the" leader for the group.

3. Visit http://www.studentleadershipchallenge.com for continuing updates on personal-best leadership stories from young leaders around the world. For detailed information on our research methodology, the theory and evidence behind The Five Practices of Exemplary Leadership, Personal-Best Leadership Experience questionnaire, the psychometric properties of the *Student Leadership Practices Inventory* (S-LPI), and abstracts of studies which have used The Five Practices framework and S-LPI, take a look at the research section of our website: www.leadershipchallenge.com/WileyCDA/Section/id-131060.html.

4. J. M. Kouzes and B. Z. Posner, *The Truth about Leadership: The No-Fads, Heart-of-the-Matter Facts You Need to Know* (San Francisco: Jossey-Bass, 2010).

5. We use *cooperate* and *collaborate* synonymously. Their dictionary definitions are very similar. In the Merriam-Webster Unabridged online dictionary, the first definition of *cooperate* is, "To act or work with another or others to a common end: operate jointly" (http://unabridged.merriam-webster.com/unabridged/cooperate). The first definition of *collaborate* is, "To work jointly with others or together especially in an intellectual endeavor" (http://unabridged.merriam-webster.com/unabridged/collaborate).

6. The research described here and throughout this book uses the normative database from online responses to the *Student Leadership Practices Inventory* (S-LPI). The S-LPI contains thirty behavior-based statements constructed from the personal-best leadership experiences of students and will be familiar to you if you complete it as part of reading this book. Each statement is measured on a 5-point Likert scale in terms of the frequency with which the individual completing the instrument engages in the particular behavior, with the following response categories: (1) rarely, (2) once in a while, (3) sometimes, (4) often, and (5) very frequently. There are six statements which make up the scale of each of The Five Practices: Model the Way, Inspire a Shared Vision, Challenge the Process, Enable Others to Act, and Encourage the Heart. The sample used for this edition included 91,561 self-reports and 365,747 observer reports.

The analysis of the impact of the leader's behavior uses data *only* from observers. In addition to indicating how frequently they observe the leader engaging in the various leadership behaviors, these respondents also provide information about how they feel working with this leader. For example:

- Overall, I am satisfied with the leadership exhibited by this person;
- When working with this leader, I'm highly productive in what I do;
- I'm proud to tell others that I am working with this leader;
- I feel like this leader values my work; and,
- When working with this leader, I feel like I am making a difference around here.

Responses to these statement are on a 5-point scale: (1) strongly disagree, (2) disagree, (3) neither disagree nor agree, (4) agree, and (5) strongly agree.

Combining the responses to all five questions produced an "engagement" scale, with scores ranging between 5 and 25, and the internal reliability coefficient for this scale was quite strong (Cronbach's alpha = .894). In addition, observers are asked if they believe "that the leadership skills of the person I just reported about compared to their peers" are (1) not well developed, (2) somewhat underdeveloped, (3) similar with their peer group, (4) somewhat developed, and (5) well developed. A similar question is asked of the leaders themselves.

7. B. Z. Posner, "The Impact of Gender, Ethnicity, School Setting, and Experience on Student Leadership: Does It Really Matter?" *Management and Organizational Studies* 1, no. 1 (2014): 21–31. See also B. Z. Posner, "Effectively Measuring Student Leadership," *Administrative Sciences* 2, no. 4 (2012): 221–234, doi:10.3390/

admsci2040221; and B. Z. Posner, "What Does the Research Show about Student Leadership?" paper presented at The Leadership Challenge Forum, San Diego, CA, August 2010.

1 Commitment #1: Clarify Values

1. C. Daniels, "Developing Organizational Values in Others," in D. Crandall (ed.), *Leadership Lessons from West Point* (San Francisco: Jossey-Bass, 2007), 62–87.
2. R. A. Stevenson, *Clarifying Behavioral Expectations Associated with Espoused Organizational Values,* PhD dissertation, Fielding Institute, 1995.

2 Commitment #2: Set the Example

1. F. A. Blanchard, T. Lilly, and L. A. Vaughn, "Reducing the Expression of Racial Prejudice," *Psychological Science* 2, no. 2 (1991): 101–105.
2. B. D. Rosso, K. H. Dekas, and A. Wrzeniewski, "On the Meaning of Work: A Theoretical Integration and Review," *Research in Organizational Behavior* 30 (2010): 91–127.

3 Commitment #3: Envision the Future

1. D. Gilbert, *Stumbling on Happiness* (New York: Knopf, 2006), 5–6.
2. For an in-depth discussion of what people look for in their leaders, see J. M. Kouzes and B. Z. Posner, *Credibility: How Leaders Gain It and Lose It, Why People Demand It,* 2nd ed. (San Francisco: Jossey-Bass, 2011). See also J. M. Kouzes and B. Z. Posner, *The Leadership Challenge: How to Make Extraordinary Things Happen in Organizations,* 6th ed. (Hoboken, NJ: Wiley, 2017). What's also true is that the importance placed on "forward looking" increases both with years of work experience and level in the organization.
3. J. P. Schuster, *The Power of Your Past: The Art of Recalling, Recasting, and Reclaiming* (San Francisco: Berrett-Koehler, 2011); J. T. Seaman Jr. and G. D. Smith, "Your Company's History as a Leadership Tool," *Harvard Business Review,* December 2012, 44–52. For an example of learning from the past, see E. Florian, "The Best Advice I Ever Got," *Fortune,* February 6, 2012, 14.
4. See E. L. Deci with R. Fiaste, *Why We Do What We Do: Understanding Self-Motivation* (New York: Penguin, 1995). For another excellent treatment of this subject, see K. W. Thomas, *Intrinsic Motivation at Work: Building Energy and Commitment* (San Francisco: Berrett-Koehler, 2000); and for an extensive academic treatment, see C. Sansone and J. M. Harackiewicz (eds.), *Intrinsic and Extrinsic Motivation: The Search for Optimal Motivation and Performance* (New York: Academic Press, 2000).
5. D. Pink, *Drive: The Surprising Truth about What Motivates Us* (New York: Penguin Group, 2009); and L. Freifeld, "Why Cash Doesn't Motivate," *Training* 48, no. 4 (July/August 2011): 17–22.

6. Deci with Fiaste, *Why We Do What We Do,* 25.

7. J. M. Kouzes and B. Z. Posner, "To Lead, Create a Shared Vision," *Harvard Business Review,* January 2009.

8. B. L. Kaye and S. Jordon-Evans, *Love 'Em or Lose 'Em: Getting Good People to Stay,* 5th ed. (San Francisco: Berrett-Koehler, 2014).

4 Commitment #4: Enlist Others

1. "'I Have a Dream' Leads Top 100 Speeches of the Century," press release from the University of Wisconsin, December 15, 1999, http://news.wisc.edu/i-have-a-dream-leads-top-100-speeches-of-the-century/. The full list is available online at http://news.wisc.edu/archive/misc/speeches/ and http://www.americanrhetoric.com/top100speechesall.html. See also S. E. Lucas and M. J. Medhurst, *Words of a Century: The Top 100 American Speeches, 1900–1999* (New York: Oxford University Press, 2008). Other leaders often seen on international lists of great speakers from recent history are Winston Churchill, Charles de Gaulle, Mahatma Gandhi, Vaclav Havel, Robert Kennedy, Nelson Mandela, Jawaharlal Nehru, Barack Obama, Ronald Reagan, Eleanor Roosevelt, Gloria Steinem, Mother Teresa, Margaret Thatcher, and Lech Walesa.

2. The audio version of the "I Have a Dream" speech that we have found to be most instructive is the version running 6 minutes and 11 seconds that contains the most famous passages. It is in the collection *Greatest Speeches of All Time* (Vol. 1) available from Amazon.com: https://www.amazon.com/Greatest-Speeches-All-Time-Various-Artists/dp/1885959435/ref=tmm_abk_swatch_0?_encoding=UTF8&qid=1499268211&sr=8-1-spell. A printed version of this portion of the speech is in C. S. King (ed.), *The Words of Martin Luther King, Jr.* (New York: Newmarket Press, 1983), 95–98. A video can be viewed on YouTube at http://www.youtube.com/watch?v=smEqnnklfYs.

3. D. Goleman, *Social Intelligence: The New Science of Human Relationships* (New York: Bantam, 2006).

4. H. S. Friedman, L. M. Prince, R. E. Riggio, and M. R. DiMatteo, "Understanding and Assessing Nonverbal Expressiveness: The Affective Communication Test," *Journal of Personality and Social Psychology* 39, no. 2 (1980): 333–351; D. Goleman, R. Boyatzis, and A. McKee, *Primal Leadership: Realizing the Power of Emotional Intelligence* (Boston: Harvard Business School Press, 2002); J. Conger, *Winning 'Em Over: A New Model for Management in the Age of Persuasion* (New York: Simon & Schuster, 1998); and M. Greer, "The Science of Savoir Faire," *APA Monitor* 36, no. 1 (2005): 28.

5. J. L. McGaugh, *Memory and Emotion* (New York: Columbia University Press, 2003), 90. See also R. Maxwell and R. Dickman, *The Elements of Persuasion: Use Storytelling to Pitch Better Ideas, Sell Faster, & Win More Business* (New York: HarperCollins, 2007), especially "Sticky Stories: Memory, Emotions and Markets," 122–150.

6. McGaugh, *Memory and Emotion*, 92.

7. McGaugh, *Memory and Emotion*, 92.

8. D. A. Small, G. Loewenstein, and P. Slovic, "Sympathy and Callousness: The Impact of Deliberative Thought on Donations to Identifiable and Statistical Victims," *Organizational Behavior and Human Decision Processes* 102 (2007): 143–153.

5   Commitment #5: Search for Opportunities

1. T. S. Bateman and J. M. Crant, "Proactive Behavior: Meaning, Impact, Recommendations," *Business Horizons* 42, no. 3 (May-June 1999): 63–70; J. M. Crant, "Proactive Behavior in Organizations," *Journal of Management* 26, no. 3 (2000): 435–463; J. A. Thompson, "Proactive Personality and Job Performance: A Social Capital Perspective," *Journal of Applied Psychology* 90, no. 5 (2005): 1011–1017; S. E. Seibert and M. L. Braimer, "What Do Proactive People Do? A Longitudinal Model Linking Proactive Personality and Career Success," *Personnel Psychology* 54 (2001): 845–875; and D. J. Brown, R. T. Cober, K. Kane, P. E. Levy, and J. Shalhoop, "Proactive Personality and the Successful Job Search: A Field Investigation of College Graduates," *Journal of Applied Psychology* 91, no. 3 (2006): 717–726.

2. E. L. Deci with R. Fiaste, *Why We Do What We Do: Understanding Self-Motivation* (New York: Penguin, 1995). See also D. Pink, *Drive: The Surprising Truth about What Motivates You* (New York: Riverhead Press, 2011); and K. W. Thomas, *Intrinsic Motivation at Work: What Really Drives Employee Engagement* (San Francisco: Berrett-Koehler, 2009).

3. See, for example, J. Ettlie, *Managing Innovation*, 2nd ed. (Abingdon, UK: Taylor & Francis, 2006); S. Johnson, *Where Good Ideas Come From: The Natural History of Innovation* (New York: Riverhead Press, 2010); E. Ries, *The Lean Startup: How Constant Innovation Creates Radically Successful Businesses* (New York: Penguin Group, 2011); T. Davila, M. J. Epstein, and R. Shelton, *Making Innovation Work: How to Manage It, Measure It, and Profit from It*, updated ed. (Upper Saddle River, NJ: FT Press, 2012); and I. Asimov, "How Do People Get New Ideas?" *MIT Technology Review,* October 20, 2014, https://www.technologyreview.com/s/531911/isaac-asimov-asks-how-do-people-get-new-ideas/.

4. G. Berns, *Iconoclast: A Neuroscientist Reveals How to Think Differently* (Cambridge, MA: Harvard Business School Press, 2008); and B. Andreatta, *Wired to Resist: The Brain Science of Why Change Fails and a New Model for Driving Success* (Santa Barbara, CA: 7th Mind Printing, 2017).

5. M. M. Capozzi, R. Dye, and A. Howe, "Sparking Creativity in Teams: An Executive's Guide," *McKinsey Quarterly,* April 2011.

6. A. W. Brooks, F. Gino, and M. E. Schweitzer, "Smart People Ask for (My) Advice: Seeking Advice Boosts Perceptions of Competence," *Management Science* 61, no. 6 (June 2015): 1421–1435.

7. Z. Achi and J. G. Berger, "Delighting in the Possible," *McKinsey Quarterly,* March 2016, 5.

NOTES

6 Commitment #6: Experiment and Take Risks

1. For a history of the research, see S. R. Salvatore, "The Story of Hardiness: Twenty Years of Theorizing, Research, and Practice," *Consulting Psychology Journal: Practices and Research* 54, no. 3 (2002): 175–185. See also S. R. Maddi and S. C. Kobasa, *The Hardy Executive: Health under Stress* (Chicago: Dorsey Press, 1984); S. R. Maddi and D. M. Khoshaba, "Hardiness and Mental Health," *Journal of Personality Assessment* 67 (1994): 265–274; and S. R. Maddi and D. M. Khoshaba, *Resilience at Work: How to Succeed No Matter What Life Throws at You* (New York: AMACOM, 2005).

2. R. A. Bruce and R. F. Sinclair, "Exploring the Psychological Hardiness of Entrepreneurs," *Frontiers of Entrepreneurship Research* 29, no. 6 (2009): 5; P. T. Bartone, R. R. Roland, J. J. Picaño, and T. J. Williams, "Psychological Hardiness Predicts Success in US Army Special Forces Candidates," *International Journal of Selection and Assessment* 16, no. 1 (2008): 78–81; and P. T. Bartone, "Resilience under Military Operational Stress: Can Leaders Influence Hardiness?" *Military Psychology* 18 (2006): S141–S148.

3. K. E. Weick, "Small Wins: Redefining the Scale of Social Problems," *American Psychologist* 39, no. 1 (1984): 43. For a related treatment of this topic, see P. Sims, *Little Bets: How Breakthrough Ideas Emerge from Small Discoveries* (New York: Free Press, 2011), 141–152.

4. D. Bayles and T. Orland, *Art and Fear: Observations on the Perils (and Rewards) of Artmaking* (Eugene, OR: Image Continuum Press, 2001).

5. R. W. Eichinger, M. M. Lombardo, and D. Ulrich, *100 Things You Need to Know: Best Practices for Managers & HR* (Minneapolis, MN: Lominger, 2004), 492.

6. L. M. Brown and B. Z. Posner, "Exploring the Relationship between Learning and Leadership," *Leadership & Organization Development Journal,* May 2001, 274–280. See also J. M. Kouzes and B. Z. Posner, *The Truth about Leadership: The No-Fads, Heart-of-the-Matter Facts You Need to Know* (San Francisco: Jossey-Bass, 2010), 119–135.

7. C. Dweck, *Mindset: The New Psychology of Success* (New York: Random House, 2006), 6–7. See also C. Dweck, "Carol Dweck Revisits the 'Growth Mindset,'" *Education Week,* September 22, 2016, http://www.edweek.org/ew/articles/2015/09/23/carol-dweck-revisits-the-growth-mindset.html.

8. J. Barash, M. Capozzi, and L. Mendonca, "How Companies Approach Innovation: A McKinsey Global Survey," *McKinsey Quarterly,* October 2007.

9. A. Bandura and R. E. Wood, "Effects of Perceived Controllability and Performance Standards on Self-Regulation of Complex Decision Making," *Journal of Personality and Social Psychology* 56 (1989): 805–814. See also Dweck, *Mindset,* for a discussion of numerous research studies in these and other domains.

10. A. Carmeli, D. Brueller, and J. E. Dutton, "Learning Behaviours in the Workplace: The Role of High-Quality Interpersonal Relationships and Psychological

Safety," *Systems Research and Behavioral Science Systems Research* 26 (2009): 81–98.

11. A. L. Duckworth, *Grit: The Power of Passion and Perseverance* (New York: Simon & Schuster, 2016).

12. M.E.P. Seligman, "Building Resilience," *Harvard Business Review,* April 2011, 101–106. For a more complete treatment of this subject, see M.E.P. Seligman, *Flourish: A Visionary New Understanding of Happiness and Well-Being* (New York: Free Press, 2011).

13. It may be difficult to overcome a habitual pattern of avoidance, but it is possible to learn to cope assertively with stressful events. For example, see Maddi and Kobasa, *The Hardy Executive*; D. M. Khoshaba and S. R. Maddi, "Early Experiences in Hardiness Development," *Consulting Psychology Journal* 51 (1999): 106–116; S. R. Maddi, S. Kahn, and K. L. Maddi, "The Effectiveness of Hardiness Training," *Consulting Psychology Journal* 50 (1998): 78–86; Maddi and Khoshaba, *Resilience at Work*; K. Reivish and A. Shatte, *The Resilience Factor: 7 Keys to Finding Your Inner Strength and Overcoming Life's Hurdles* (New York: Broadway Books, 2003); and J. D. Margolis and P. G. Stoltz, "How to Bounce Back from Adversity," *Harvard Business Review* 88, no. 1 (January-February, 2010): 86–92.

7   Commitment #7: Foster Collaboration

1. P. S. Shockley-Zalabak, S. Morreale, and M. Hackman, *Building the High-Trust Organization: Strategies for Supporting Five Key Dimensions of Trust* (San Francisco: Jossey-Bass, 2010).

2. P. Lee, N. Gillespie, L. Mann, and A. Wearing, "Leadership and Trust: Their Effect on Knowledge Sharing and Team Performance," *Management Learning* 41, no. 4 (2010): 473–491.

3. R. Axelrod, *The Evolution of Cooperation,* rev. ed. (New York: Basic Books, 2006). See also W. Poundstone, *Prisoner's Dilemma: John Von Neumann, Game Theory, and the Puzzle of the Bomb* (New York: Anchor, 1993). These findings were replicated in an extensive probability analysis, which used high-powered computing to run hundreds of "games" and found that cooperativeness, rather than selfishness, won in the end. For more information, see C. Adami and A. Hintze, "Evolutionary Instability of Zero-Determinant Strategies Demonstrates That Winning Is Not Everything," *Nature Communications* 4, no. 2193 (2013), available online at http://dx.doi.org/ 10.1038/ncomms3193.

4. Axelrod, *Evolution of Cooperation,* 20, 190.

5. H. Ibarra and M. T. Hansen, "Are You a Collaborative Leader?" *Harvard Business Review,* July-August 2011, 69–74; "Secrets of Greatness: Teamwork!" *Fortune,* June 12, 2006, 64–152; A. M. Brandenburger and B. J. Nalebuff, *Co-Opetition: A Revolution Mindset That Combines Competition and Cooperation: The Game Theory Strategy That's Changing the Game of Business* (New York: Currency, 1997); P. Hallinger and R. H. Heck, "Leadership for Learning: Does Collaborative

Leadership Make a Difference in School Improvement?" *Educational Management Administration & Leadership* 38, no. 6 (2010): 654–678; W. C. Kim and R. Mauborgne, *Blue Ocean Strategy: How to Create Uncontested Market Space and Make the Competition Irrelevant,* expanded ed. (Boston: Harvard Business School Publishing, 2015); and D. Tjosvold and M. M. Tjosvold, *Building the Team Organization: How to Open Minds, Resolve Conflict, and Ensure Cooperation* (New York: Palgrave Macmillan, 2015).

6. M. Moriesen and T. B. Neeley, "Reflected Knowledge and Trust in Global Collaboration," *Management* Science 58, no. 12 (2012), 2207–2224. See also D. Cohen and L. Prusak, *In Good Company: How Social Capital Makes Organizations Work* (Boston: Harvard Business School Press, 2001), 20.

7. D. Brooks, *The Social Animal: Hidden Sources of Love, Character, and Achievement* (New York: Random House, 2011).

8   Commitment #8: Strengthen Others

1. L. Wiseman, *Multipliers: How the Best Leaders Make Everyone Smarter* (New York: HarperCollins, 2010).

2. A. Bandura, *Self-Efficacy: The Exercise of Control* (New York: Freeman, 1997); M. J. McCormick, J. Tanguma, and A. S. Lopez-Forment, "Extending Self-Efficacy Theory to Leadership: A Review and Empirical Test," *Journal of Leadership Education* 1, no. 2 (2002): 34–49; D. L. Feltz, S. F. Short, and P. J. Sullivan, *Self-Efficacy in Sport* (Champaign, IL: Human Kinetics, 2007); F. C. Lunenburg, "Self-Efficacy in the Workplace: Implications for Motivation and Performance," *International Journal of Management, Business, and Administration* 14, no. 1 (2011): 1–6; and J. E. Maddux, "Self-Efficacy: The Power of Believing You Can," in S. J. Lopez and C. R. Snyder (eds.), *The Oxford Handbook of Positive Psychology,* 2nd ed. (New York: Oxford University Press, 2011), 335–344.

3. A. Wrzeniewski and J. Dutton, "Crafting a Job: Revising Employees as Active Crafters of Their Work," *Academy of Management Review* 26, no. 2 (2001): 179–201; and M. S. Christian, A. S. Garza, and J. E. Slaugher, "Work Engagement: A Quantitative Review and Test of Its Relations with Task and Conceptual Performance," *Personnel Psychology* 64 (2011): 89–136.

4. Evolutionary psychology demonstrates that in ecosystems, collaboration is what assists species to survive rather than become extinct; the group ends up eradicating bad or inefficient behavior. See R. Wright, *The Moral Animal: Why We Are the Way We Are: The New Science of Evolutionary Psychology* (New York: Vintage, 1995). For another interesting look at the origins of social cooperation, see A. Fields, *Altruistically Inclined? The Behavioral Sciences, Evolutionary Theory, and the Origins of Reciprocity* (Ann Arbor: University of Michigan Press, 2004).

5. Psychologists often refer to this as self-efficacy. See, for example, Bandura, *Self-Efficacy;* and E. Chester, *On Fire at Work: How Great Companies Ignite Passion in Their People Without Burning Them Out* (Shippensburg, PA: Sound Wisdom, 2015).

6. P. Sweeny, V. Thomson, and H. Blanton, "Trust and Influence in Combat: An Interdependence Model," *Journal of Applied Social Psychology* 39, no. 1 (2009): 235–264.

9 Commitment #9: Recognize Contributions

1. Hundreds of research studies have since been conducted to test this notion, and they all clearly demonstrate that people tend to act in ways that are consistent with the expectations they perceive. See, for example, D. Eden, *Pygmalion in Management: Productivity as a Self-Fulfilling Prophecy* (Lexington, MA: Lexington Books, 1990); D. Eden, "Leadership and Expectations: Pygmalion Effects and Other Self-Fulfilling Prophecies in Organizations," *Leadership Quarterly* 3, no. 4 (1992): 271–305; S. Maddon, J. Willard, M. Guyll, and K. C. Scherr, "Self-Fulfilling Prophecies: Mechanisms, Power, and Links to Social Problems," *Social and Personality Psychology Compass* 5/8 (2011: 578–590; and A. Smith, L. Jussim, J. Eccles, M. Van Noy, S. Madon, and P. Palumbo, "Self-Fulfilling Prophecies, Perceptual Biases, and Accuracy at the Individual and Group Levels," *Journal of Experimental Social Psychology* 34, no. 6 (1998): 530–561.

2. K. S. Cameron, *Positive Leadership: Strategies for Extraordinary Performance* (San Francisco: Berrett-Koehler, 2008). Fostering virtuousness, according to Cameron, is about facilitating the best of the human condition. He argues that an inclination exists in all human systems toward goodness for its own intrinsic value.

3. J. E. Dutton, R. E. Quinn, and K. S. Cameron, *Positive Organizational Scholarship: Foundations of a New Discipline* (San Francisco: Berrett-Koehler, 2003); Cameron, *Positive Leadership: Strategies for Extraordinary Performance;* D. Whitney and A. Trosten-Bloom, *The Power of Appreciative Inquiry: A Practical Guide to Positive Change,* 2nd ed. (San Francisco: Berrett-Koehler, 2010); and M.E.P. Seligman, *Flourish: A Visionary New Understanding of Happiness and Well-Being* (New York: Free Press, 2011).

4. J. E. Sawyer, W. R. Latham, R. D. Pritchard, and W. R. Bennett Jr., "Analysis of Work Group Productivity in an Applied Setting: Application of a Time Series Panel Design," *Personnel Psychology* 52 (1999): 927–967; and A. Gostick and C. Elton, *Managing with Carrots: Using Recognition to Attract and Retain the Best People* (Layton, UT: Gibbs Smith, 2001).

5. K. A. Ericsson, M. J. Prietula, and E. T. Cokely, "The Making of an Expert," *Harvard Business Review* 85, no. 7/8 (2007): 114–121, 193.

6. For more on this topic, see Truth 9 in J. M. Kouzes and B. Z. Posner, *The Truth about Leadership: The No-Fads, Heart-of-the-Matter Facts You Need to Know* (San Francisco: Jossey-Bass, 2010).

7. J. A. Ross, "Does Friendship Improve Job Performance?" *Harvard Business Review* 54, no. 2 (March–April 1977): 8–9. See also K. A. Jehn and P. P. Shah, "Interpersonal Relationships and Task Performance: An Examination of Mediating Processes in Friendship and Acquaintance Groups," *Journal of Personality and Social*

Psychology 72, no. 4 (1997): 775–790. There is an important caveat, however. Friends have to be strongly committed to the group's goals. If not, then friends may not do better. This is precisely why we said earlier that it is absolutely necessary for leaders to be clear about standards and to create a condition of shared goals and values. When it comes to performance, commitment to standards and good relations between people go together.

8. E. Harvey, *180 Ways to Walk the Recognition Talk* (Dallas, TX: Walk the Talk, 2000); J. W. Umias, *The Power of Acknowledgment* (New York: International Institute for Learning, 2006); L. Yerkes, *Fun Works: Creative Places Where People Love to Work,* 2nd ed. (San Francisco: Berrett-Koehler, 2007); B. Nelson, *1501 Ways to Reward Employees* (New York: Workman, 2012); and B. Kaye and S. Jordan-Evans, *Love 'Em or Lose 'Em: Getting Good People to Stay,* 5th ed. (San Francisco: Berrett-Koehler, 2014).

9. B. Fredrickson, *Positivity: Top-Notch Research Reveals the 3-to-1 Ratio That Will Change Your Life* (New York: Random House, 2009).

10 Commitment #10: Celebrate the Values and Victories

1. D. Brooks, *The Social Animal: The Hidden Sources of Love, Character, and Achievement* (New York: Random House, 2011); and E. Aronson, *The Social Animal,* 11th ed. (New York: Worth Publishers, 2012).

2. S. Achor, *The Happiness Advantage: The Seven Principles of Positive Psychology That Fuel Success and Performance at Work* (New York: Crown Books, 2010), 176.

3. J. W. Shenk, "What Makes Us Happy?" *Atlantic,* June 2009. Available from http://www.theatlantic.com/magazine/print/2009/06/what-makes-us-happy/7439/.

4. R. D. Cotton, Y. Shen, and R. Livne-Tarandach, "On Becoming Extraordinary: The Content and Structure of the Developmental Networks of Major League Baseball Hall of Famers," *Academy of Management Journal* 54, no. 1 (2011): 15–46.

5. T. Rath, *Vital Friends: The People You Can't Afford to Live Without* (New York: Gallup Press, 2006), 52; and T. Rath and J. Harter, *Wellbeing: The Five Essential Elements* (New York: Gallup Press, 2010), 40–43.

6. R. E. Baumeister and M. R. Leary, "The Need to Belong: Desire for Interpersonal Attachment as a Fundamental Human Motivation," *Psychological Bulletin* 117 (1995): 497–529; H. W. Perkins, "Religious Commitment, Yuppie Values, and Well-Being in a Post-Collegiate Life," *Review of Religious Research* 32 (1991): 244–251; D. G. Myers, "The Funds, Friends, and Faith of Happy People," *American Psychologist* 55, no. 1 (2000): 56–67; and S. Crabtree, "Getting Personal in the Workplace: Are Negative Relationships Squelching Productivity in Your Company?" *Gallup Management Journal,* June 10, 2004. Available from www.govleaders.org/gallup_article_getting_personal.htm.

7. Myers, "The Funds, Friends, and Faith of Happy People"; M. Csikszentmihalyi, "If We Are So Rich, Why Aren't We Happy?" *American Psychologist* 54 (1999): 821–827; D. G. Myers and E. Diener, "The Pursuit of Happiness," *Scientific*

American 274 (1996): 54–56; and D. Gilbert, *Stumbling on Happiness* (New York: Knopf, 2006).

8. D. Westen, *The Political Brain: The Role of Emotion in Deciding the Fate of the Nation* (New York: Public Affairs, 2008), 28.

9. G. Klein, *The Power of Intuition: How to Use Your Gut Feelings to Make Better Decisions at Work* (New York: Crown Business, 2004). After studying professionals in life-and-death situations, Klein concludes that "the method we found most powerful for eliciting knowledge is to use stories."

Afterword   A Call to Action for Leaders

1. J. M. Kouzes and B. Z. Posner, *The Truth about Leadership: The No-Fads, Heart-of-the-Matter Facts You Need to Know* (San Francisco: Jossey-Bass, 2010).

2. B. Z. Posner, "A Longitudinal Study Examining Changes in Students' Leadership Behavior," *Journal of College Student Development* 50, no. 5 (2009): 551–563; and B. Z. Posner, R. G. Crawford, and R. Denniston-Stewart, "A Longitudinal Study of Canadian Student Leadership Practices," *Journal of Leadership Education* 14, no. 2 (2015): 161–181. See also, B. Z. Posner, "Effectively Measuring Student Leadership," *Administrative Sciences* 2, no. 4 (2012): 221–234; and, B. Z. Posner, "The Impact of Gender, Ethnicity, School Year and Experience on Student Leadership: Does It Really Matter?" *Management and Organizational Studies* 1, no. 1 (2014): 21–31.

Acknowledgments

One of the truths about leading is that you can't do it alone. This is equally true about writing. One of the great joys of writing a book is the opportunity to work with scores of talented, dedicated, and inspiring people. We are profoundly grateful to them, and we cherish the opportunity to say thank you to all who have joined us on this journey.

Foremost, a shout-out of appreciation to the thousands of students we've worked with over the years. You inspire us and bring us hope. You give us immense confidence that the future is held in capable hands and generous hearts. And a special round of applause for all those students whose stories, experiences, lessons, and wisdom make up the centerpiece of this edition of *The Student Leadership Challenge*. Thank you for what you've accomplished and for who you are. And many thanks to scores of other students who have shared their experiences with us, even if we couldn't put everyone's stories into this book. We know that people will become better leaders as a result of reading about the lessons of your experiences.

We had a behind-the-scenes partner in this endeavor, Leslie Stephen, to whom we continue to be indebted. We've worked with

ACKNOWLEDGMENTS

Leslie for many years, and we are always overjoyed whenever she signs on for a new project. She's our developmental editor, our collaborator, our cheerleader, and our *dream weaver*. Leslie generously and graciously shared her remarkable talents throughout the project by pulling together our voices, keeping us focused, and endlessly offering encouragement and a calm presence. We want to acknowledge her substantial and significant role in this book and make public our deepest gratitude.

Our colleagues at John Wiley & Sons have been our constant companions on our journey of developing emerging leaders since before publication of the first edition of this book. Kate Gagnon, executive editor, was the champion of this third edition. Her focus on crafting high-quality resources in the education field has enabled us to produce a book that builds on the solid foundation of the past while creating a unique and distinctive volume that includes the most up-to-date research and integrates new resources into its pages. Joining Kate on *The Student Leadership Challenge* team were Alyssa Benigno, marketing manager; Michael Freeland, cover designer; Susan Geraghty, project manager; Paula Goldstein, interior layout designer; Roger Hunt, administrative support; Andrew Hallam, production editor; Michele Jones, copyeditor; Kathy Nebenhaus, publisher; Connor O'Brien, project editor; and Halley Sutton, development editor. We are blessed to be working with such a passionate team of professionals who make us better every day.

We also give a shout-out to Marisa Kelley, our brand manager from Wiley's Workplace Learning Solutions side of the house. Marisa has been with us every step of the way. She is dedicated to creating one brand and one community in support of developing exemplary leaders of all ages around the globe, and her passion inspires all of us who have the privilege of working with her.

As always, we cannot say enough how appreciative we are of our immediate loved ones—to Tae and Nick, and to Jackie, Amanda and

Darryl. You bring great joy into our lives. We have witnessed—and experienced—your extraordinary feats of leadership; you have taught us more than we can ever share.

We wrote this book, as we have each of our books, in order to liberate the leader that lies within each person and to increase the quality and quantity of leaders for the world. That's our mission and our passion. Each and every individual matters. Each and every one makes a difference. The real challenge is to make sure that we're leaving the places we are, and will be in the future, better because we were there. Let's be sure to live life forward.

About the Authors

Jim Kouzes and Barry Posner have been working together for more than thirty years, studying leaders, researching leadership, conducting leadership development seminars, and serving as leaders themselves in various capacities. *The Student Leadership Challenge* has been adopted and used by faculty and student personnel staff in more than one hundred collegiate institutions, for both academic classes and cocurricular student programs, around the world. *The Leadership Challenge,* now in its sixth edition, has sold more than 2.5 million copies worldwide and is available in twenty-two languages. It has won numerous awards, including the Critics' Choice Award from the nation's book review editors and the James A. Hamilton Hospital Administrators' Book of the Year Award. It has been named a Best Business Book of the Year by *Fast Company* and continues to be included in *The 100 Best Business Books of All Time.*

Jim and Barry have coauthored many other best-selling and award-winning leadership books, including:

- *Learning Leadership: The Five Fundamentals of Becoming an Exemplary Leader*

- *The Truth about Leadership: The No-Fads, Heart-of-the-Matter Facts You Need to Know*
- *Credibility: How Leaders Gain and Lose It, Why People Demand It*
- *Encouraging the Heart: A Leader's Guide to Rewarding and Recognizing Others*
- *A Leader's Legacy*
- *Extraordinary Leadership in Australia and New Zealand: The Five Practices That Create Great Workplaces* (with Michael Bunting)
- *Making Extraordinary Things Happen in Asia: Applying The Five Practices of Exemplary Leadership*

They also developed the highly acclaimed *Leadership Practices Inventory* (LPI), a 360-degree questionnaire for assessing leadership behavior, which is one of the most widely used leadership assessment instruments in the world, along with the *Student LPI*. More than seven hundred empirical studies, doctoral dissertations, and academic papers have used The Five Practices of Exemplary Leadership framework in their research.

The Association for Talent Development's (ATD) highest award for Distinguished Contribution to Workplace Learning and Performance is among the honors that Jim and Barry have received. In addition, they have been named Management/Leadership Educators of the Year by the International Management Council; ranked by *Leadership Excellence* magazine in the top twenty on its list of the Top 100 Thought Leaders; named among the 50 Top Coaches in the United States (according to *Coaching for Leadership*); ranked as Top 100 Thought Leaders in Trustworthy Business Behavior by Trust Across America; listed among *HR* magazine's Most Influential International Thinkers; *Inc.* magazine's Today's Top 50 Leadership Innovators Changing How We Lead, and Global Guru's Top 30 Leadership Gurus.

Both Jim and Barry are frequent keynote speakers, and each has conducted numerous leadership development programs for corporate and for-purpose organizations around the globe. These include Alberta Health Services, Apple, Applied Materials, Australia Institute of Management, Australia Post, Bain Capital, Bank of America, Bose, Charles Schwab, Chevron, Cisco Systems, Clorox, Conference Board of Canada, Consumers Energy, Dow Chemical, Electronic Arts, FedEx, Genentech, Google, Gymboree, HP, IBM, Johnson & Johnson, Kaiser Foundation Health Plans and Hospitals, Korean Management Association, Intel, L.L. Bean, Lawrence Livermore National Labs, Lockheed Martin, Lucile Packard Children's Hospital, Merck, Monsanto, NetApp, Nationwide Insurance, Northrop Grumman, Novartis, Nvidia, Oracle, PayPal, Petronas, Pixar, Roche Bioscience, Telstra, Siemens, Smithsonian Institution, St. Jude Children's Research Hospital, Texas Medical Center, 3M, TIAA-CREF, Toyota, United Way, Universal Orlando, USAA, Verizon, VISA, Vodafone, Walt Disney Company, Western Mining Corporation, and Westpac. They have lectured at over seventy college and university campuses.

Jim Kouzes is the Dean's Executive Fellow of Leadership, Leavey School of Business at Santa Clara University, and lectures on leadership around the world. He is a highly regarded leadership scholar and an experienced executive; the *Wall Street Journal* cited him as one of the twelve best executive educators in the United States. In 2010, Jim received the Thought Leadership Award from the Instructional Systems Association, the most prestigious award given by the trade association of training and development industry providers. He received a Lifetime Achievement in 2015 from Trust Across America. In 2006, Jim was presented with the Golden Gavel, the highest honor awarded by Toastmasters International. Jim served as president, CEO, and chairman of the Tom Peters Company from 1988 through 2000, and prior to that led the Executive Development Center at Santa Clara University (1981–1988). He founded the Joint Center for Human Services Development at San Jose State University (1972–1980) and was on the staff of the School of Social Work, University of Texas. Jim's career in training and development began in 1969 when he conducted seminars for Community Action Agency staff and volunteers in the War on Poverty. Following graduation from Michigan State University (BA degree with honors in political science), he served as a Peace Corps volunteer (1967–1969). Jim can be reached at jim@kouzes.com.

Barry Posner holds the Michael J. Accolti S.J. Chair and is professor of leadership at the Leavey School of Business, Santa Clara University. In addition to serving as dean of the school for twelve years, he also led the Executive Development Center and was associate dean for graduate programs. He has been a distinguished visiting professor at the Hong Kong University of Science and Technology, Sabanci University (Istanbul), and the University of Western Australia. At Santa Clara, Barry has received the President's Distinguished Faculty Award, the Business School's Extraordinary Faculty Award, and many other teaching and academic honors. An internationally renowned scholar and educator, Barry has authored or coauthored more than one hundred research and practitioner-focused articles. He currently serves on the editorial advisory board for the *Leadership & Organizational Development Journal* and the *International Journal of Servant-Leadership* and received the Outstanding Scholar Award for Career Achievement from the *Journal of Management Inquiry.*

Barry received his BA with honors in political science from the University of California, Santa Barbara; his MA in public administration from The Ohio State University; and his PhD in organizational behavior and administrative theory from the University of Massachusetts, Amherst. Having consulted with a wide variety of public and private sector organizations worldwide, Barry also works at a strategic level with a number of community-based and professional organizations. He has served on the board of directors of Uplift Family Services, Global Women's Leadership Network, American Institute of Architects (AIA), SVCreates, Big Brothers/Big Sisters of Santa Clara County, Center for Excellence in Nonprofits, Junior Achievement of Silicon Valley and Monterey Bay, Public Allies, San Jose Repertory Theater, and Sigma Phi Epsilon Fraternity, as well as several publicly traded and start-up companies. Barry can be reached at bposner@scu.edu.

Index

Page references followed by *fig* indicate an illustrated figure.

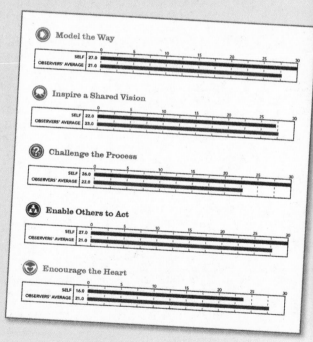